New Testament Theology
An Introduction

New Testament Theology
An Introduction

Paul Haffner

GRACEWING

HAFFNER, Paul
New Testament Theology : An Introduction
Leominster (UK): Gracewing, 2008
272 pages ; 14x21.6 cm

ISBN 978–88–90226–80–9

Cover design: photo from the church of the Multiplication of the Loaves and the Fishes, Tabgha, Israel.

Contents

Contents

Preface

This work started life as a class manual for my students at Duquesne University Roman campus, but it is now addressed to others who wish to deepen their understanding of and love for the New Testament. It is of course no substitute for reading the Biblical text itself, which is the first and foremost task of the student. This book is simply a companion to guide the reader of the New Testament on his or her pilgrimage. It furnishes a few key signposts in terms of the basic ideas of how the biblical text came about, its objective value and special character and inspiration, the Synoptic Problem and the Canon of the New Testament. Some tools for interpretation are offered, and then some basic themes are treated, in particular the Church, the Holy Eucharist, Mary, the Mother of God, the role of the Apostles Peter and Paul, and the interplay between faith and reason in the New Testament.

I should like to thank the following people who have helped in the preparation of this volume. First, Dr. Roberta Aronson, Executive Director of Duquesne University Office of International Programs, and Mr. Michael Wright, Director of the Italian campus, who supported the project on behalf of the university. Then, gratitude is due to Dr. and Mrs. Frank and Philomena Whitesell who have helped me with their support. I dedicate this work to the students of Duquesne University, past and present.

To one and all I commend the words of St Jerome, in his letter to the maiden Demetrias: "Love the Bible and wisdom will love you; love it and it will preserve you; honour it and it will embrace you; these are the jewels which you should wear on your breast and in your ears."

Rome, 25 January 2006
Feast of the Conversion of St Paul

Abbreviations

AAS =   *Acta Apostolicae Sedis. Commentarium offi-ciale.*
Rome: Vatican Polyglot Press, 1909– .

CCC =   *Catechism of the Catholic Church.*
Dublin: Veritas, 1994.

CCL =   *Corpus Christianorum series latina.*
Tournai: Brepols, 1954– .

CSEL =   *Corpus Scriptorum Ecclesiasticorum Latinorum.*
Wien: 1866–   .

DS =   H. Denzinger. *Enchiridion Symbolorum, Definitionum et Declarationum de rebus fidei et morum.* Bilingual edition edited by P. Hünermann. Bologna: EDB, 1995.

ED =   Pontifical Council for Christian Unity, *Ecumenical Directory.* Vatican City: Vatican Polyglot Press, 1993.

EV =   *Enchiridion Vaticanum.* Documenti ufficiali della Chiesa. Bologna: Edizioni Dehoniane.

IG =   *Insegnamenti di Giovanni Paolo II.* Vatican City: Vatican Polyglot Press, 1978–2005.

IP =   *Insegnamenti di Paolo VI.* Vatican City: Vatican Polyglot Press, 1963–1978.

OR =   *L'Osservatore Romano,* daily Italian edition.

ORE =   *L'Osservatore Romano,* weekly English edition.

ND =   J. Neuner and J. Dupuis, *The Christian Faith in the Doctrinal Documents of the Catholic Church.* Sixth edition. New York: Alba House, 1996.

PG =   J.P. Migne. *Patrologiae cursus completus, series graeca.* 161 vols. Paris: 1857–1866.

PL =   J.P. Migne. *Patrologiae cursus completus, series latina.* 221 vols. Paris: 1844–1864.

SC =   *Sources Chrétiennes.* Paris: Cerf, 1942– .

Acknowledgments

In Chapter 6 of this work, use is made of Chapter 3 of my work *The Mystery of Mary* (Leominster: Gracewing: 2004).

In Chapter 7 of this work, use is made of Chapter 2 of my work *The Mystery of Reason* (Leominster: Gracewing: 2002).

1

The New Testament phenomenon

*All Sacred Scripture is but one book, and that one book is Christ,
because all divine Scripture speaks of Christ, and all divine
Scripture is fulfilled in Christ.*

Hugh of St Victor, *De arca Noe*

1.1 The Old Testament and the New Testament

The word 'New Testament' suggests an 'Old Testament'. In
the Old Testament, *berith*, a Hebrew word, signified a binding agreement between two persons or between a person
and God. In the divine Covenants, God takes the initiative.
There are five covenants in Old Testament — with Adam,
Noah, Abraham, Israel, David. Specifically, the Old
Covenant is the covenant with Moses or Israel. In the Letter
to the Hebrews it is called the 'first covenant'(Heb 8:7).

For the New Testament, the Greek expression *diatheke*
translates the Hebrew *berith*. A Testament or Covenant
implies a relationship between God and His people, before
any written document, which simply expresses the relationship. This is rather like the case of a married couple,
where we see what they are from their life, rather from than
their marriage certificate. Thus, the New Testament is not
just a legal document, but a living relationship between
God and His people, instituted by Jesus Christ: 'This cup is
the new testament (covenant) in My blood, which is shed

for you' (Lk 22:20, King James Version). Christ is the Mediator of the New Testament (Heb 9:15), and the Letter to the Hebrews chapter nine fully develops the similarities and contrasts between the two covenants. The expression 'covenant' is preferable as a translation of the Greek word *diatheke*.

The unity between the Old and New Testaments is expressed through *prophecy* and *prefiguration*. In the Old Testament, God's economy of salvation gradually unfolds towards the coming of Christ the Saviour, born of the Virgin Mary. The Old Covenant is a preparation, prefiguration, and prophetic foretelling of the coming of Christ. Prefiguration involves the foreshadowing of the New Testament in the Old Testament through persons, events and things. The Old Testament as a whole prefigures the New Testament. In particular, *typology* in an Old Testament story serves as a prelude for an event in the New Testament. An obvious example of typology is how the crossing of the waters of the Red Sea from slavery in Egypt to the Promised Land prefigures the waters of Baptism transforming a person from the captivity of original sin to new life in Christ. The life of Jesus Christ was foreshadowed in the Old Testament, as also were His apostles, His Church, His sacraments and above all His Mother. Mary is prefigured by some of the prominent women of the Old Testament, in a similar way that Adam, Moses and David prefigure Christ in some fashion. This idea is related to the typical sense of Bible texts which is the deeper meaning that some elements (persons, places, things and events) of the Bible have, because God, the divine author of the Bible, intended that these elements foreshadow or prefigure further things. The Church, as early as Apostolic times, (see 1 Co 10:6, 11; Heb 10:1; 1 Pt 3:20-21), and then constantly in her Tradition, has illustrated the unity of the divine plan (or economy of salvation) in the two Testaments through typology, which discerns in God's works of the Old Covenant prefigurations of what He accomplished in the fullness of time in the Person of His incarnate Son. Christians therefore read the Old Testament in the light of Christ crucified and risen. This typological reading discloses the inexhaustible content of the Old Testament; but it must not make us forget that the Old Testament retains its own intrinsic value as Revelation reaffirmed by our Lord Himself (see Mk 12:29-31). Besides, the New Testament has to be read in the light of the Old. Early Christian catechesis made constant use of the Old Testament (see 1 Co 5:6–8; 10:1–11). As an ancient saying put it, 'The New is in the Old contained; the Old is in the New explained.'[1] Typology indicates the dynamic movement toward the fulfilment of the divine plan when 'God [will] be everything to everyone' (1 Co 15:28). Of course, the calling of the patriarchs and the exodus from Egypt, for example, do not lose their own value in God's plan from the fact that they were intermediate stages.

On the other hand, biblical prophecy involves the use of words rather than deeds. This prophecy is a teaching relating to the Covenant relationship between God and His people going back to the beginning of their history as a nation. The prophets of the Old Testament communicated God's love for His people. The prophets often indicated future events that God would bring about, sometimes in their lifetime and sometimes in the far distant future. Above all, these future events were connected with the coming of Jesus the Messiah, and His Passion, Death and Resurrection: 'Then Jesus said to them, "You foolish men! So slow to believe all that the prophets have said! Was it not necessary that the Christ should suffer before entering into His glory?" Then, starting with Moses and going through all the prophets, He explained to them the passages throughout the scriptures that were about Himself' (Lk 24:25–27). The New Testament has thus left its mark on the Old Testament.

1.2 Some basic characteristics

The length of the New Testament is 27 books while the Old Testament has 46 books; in fact, the New Testament represents approximately 25% of the Holy Bible. The timescale of the New Testament is the first century. The events span the period 5 BC to AD 95; the writing process spanned the years around 49 to 95 AD, while some argue that the New Testament was effectively written before 70 AD. The language of the New Testament is Greek with Aramaic, Hebrew and Latin words present in the text.

Why was the New Testament written in Greek? In the 330's BC, Alexander the Great conquered most of the Mediterranean. Alexander was a Macedonian, and, by this time, Macedonia was culturally Greek. When he died, his kingdom was divided among his generals, who were called the *diadochi*. They were Greeks as well. Because Greek was the official language of Alexander's administration, it became the *lingua Franca* for much of the Mediterranean. Even in Italy, where Latin was the primary language, Greek came to exert stronger and stronger influence. Roman schoolchildren had to learn Greek in school, whereas students in Greek schools didn't have to learn Latin. The predominance of Greek was very helpful for someone like Paul, who could write in Greek to the churches in Corinth, Philippi, Thessalonica, and Rome. Wherever Paul went, for the most part, he could speak Greek. Had he actually made it to Spain, however, his Greek wouldn't have been as useful.

It only makes sense, then, that when Christians started writing down their accounts of Jesus' life, or when they started recording His sayings or writing letters to one another, they would write in Greek. The kind of Greek that we find in the New Testament is called *Koine*. It was the sort of Greek that most people used in letters, conversations, and everyday life.

1.2.1 The context of the Roman Empire

By the dawn of the Christian era, Rome ruled a vast propor-
tion of the known world. From our point of view, (looking
at early Christianity), it is important to note that the eastern
Mediterranean had been Hellenised since the fourth
century BC when it was conquered by Alexander the Great
and subsequently ruled by his heirs until the Romans
assumed over–riding power by the first century BC. Asia
Minor was covered with Greek City states, prosperous, well
organised and run by their local councils. The Romans
encouraged them to continue that pattern under the
over–lordship of Rome, gradually turning them into Roman
provinces as opportunity arose. In 133 BC, Pergamum was
given to Rome by its last king on his death and became the
Province of Asia. Pisidia was added in 103 and Cilicia in
101. These city states were highly sophisticated Greek
constructions and Paul, who came from Tarsus, chief city
of Cilicia, was a Roman citizen, as well as being a Jew. The
city was a major port as well as a capital city, exporting the
cloth of the area, and its citizens were cosmopolitan. Paul
had already travelled before he started his Christian
missionary activities. In the west, Julius Caesar conquered
Gaul in the 50's BC and prepared for the take–over of
Britain. All over its new territories, the process of Roman-
ization gently took over and transformed settlements and
villages, bringing with it its forms of local government, its
baths and games, its culinary tastes and wines, pottery and
glass. We find the evidence everywhere, from the plentiful
and beautiful examples of Roman glass in Amiens in northern France to artefacts up on the Rhine and along the
Danube. Roman temples, baths and amphitheatres abound
from Britain to Syria. This taking on of a Roman persona
was not enforced so much as enticed. New members of the
empire wanted the things and the styles that copied their
conquerors in Rome itself. Policies like those of Claudius
(41–54 AD) allowed Gallic men to become senators and

serve in Rome, and were all part of a policy of ensuring and rewarding loyalty to the mother city.

Of course, it was not all plain sailing and progress. In the late first century BC, there were horrendous civil wars in Italy as powerful generals like Caesar and Augustus bludgeoned their way to the top and slaughtered their opponents, who equally powerful generals and their followers. The Augustan peace was however no fiction, and the Romans recognised its benefits. The Italian peninsula was largely pacified once more after the terrifying depredations of the civil war and was to remain free of war for most of the next 200 years; the exception being the civil war of 68–9. Augustus poured money and employment into the reconstruction of the public buildings and spaces in Rome and elsewhere, all stressing the concord and peace of his reign, from temples, theatres, to the Ara Pacis, his magnificent altar of peace near the Tiber, described as 'an enduring symbol of Roman identity.'

Since Pompey had rid the Mediterranean of pirates in a brilliant lightning campaign against them in 67 BC, sea travel was much safer and commerce thrived. Augustus was an old fashioned moralist and attempted (with limited success), to clean up the habits of the aristocracy and to get them to produce heirs, future governing classes for the city and empire. Under his leadership Rome became strong and secure. There was a plentiful cheap slave labour supply for all the building work as a result of their conquests, and work and grain for the poor of the cities. The general ethos was one of success and security. It was into this world that Jesus was born.[2]

St Luke made a conscious decision to present his Gospel of Jesus within imperial time and peace, emphasising the advantages it brought in terms of a cessation of the rampant violence of the civil war and the petty rebellions that it had sparked. As a consequence of renewed order and easier travel, movement around the empire was considerably improved, and the roads built to facilitate the army also aided other travellers, in trade and also the spreading of the Gospel. Frequently, Luke would write from within the social norms of the empire, respecting them and appealing to them for the help they gave in spreading the gospel. He addressed his literary works to the 'Most Excellent Theophilus', a senator, and most likely someone big in the provincial administration, since senators required imperial permission to be out of Rome and their presence in the east was usually on imperial business, in the administration. The first missionaries used the roads and open sea lanes to spread the word; the patronage system facilitated their mission and the establishment of house churches and they met and converted men and women from the highest and lowest social orders. Early in his gospel, Luke appeals to that sense of Roman order and security as he speaks of the birth of Christ and the mission of John the Baptist. Much more than mere historical dating is going on here:

> In those days a decree went out from Caesar Augustus that all the world should be enrolled This was the first enrolment, when Quirinius was governor of Syria. And all went to be enrolled, each to his own city. And Joseph also went up from Galilee, from the city of Nazareth, to Judea, to the city of David, which is called Bethlehem, because he was of the house and lineage of David, to be enrolled with Mary, his betrothed, who was with child. And while they were there, the time came for her to be delivered. (Lk 2:1–6) (RSV)

Although the New Testament covers a relatively short time period, compared to the Old Testament, coinage was complex because Hebrews used coins issued by many different countries. This mirrors the varied cultural mix of the time, which we have just described. The table below is an attempt to assemble some approximate equivalents, including an idea of the current values of the various articles of coinage.

Figure 1: Money in the New Testament (* A sum of money, not an actual coin)

Greek	Roman	Hebrew	Dollar value/ Reference
Talent *	6000 Denarii; 240 aurei		$960
Argurion[3]=120 drachmas	120 Denarii	30 Shekels	$19.2 Compensation for accidentally slain servant, Judas' bribe for betraying Jesus. Ex 21:32, Mt 26:15
Mina[4] *	100 Denarii		$16 Ez 45:12 (60 shekels); Lk 19:12f.
25 drachmas	1 Roman aureus		$4.00
Tetradrachma[5] 17.5 g silver. 4 Greek Drachmas	Stater: 4 Roman denarii	Shekel[9]	$0.64; See Mt 17:27
Two Drachmas	2 Denarii	half-shekel	$0.32 Temple Tax (Ex 30:13,16, Mt 17:24)
Drachma[6]	Denarius		$0.16 Labourer's Day's Wages in Mt 20:9-10. Civil tribute to Caesar in Mt 22:21. Drachma in Lk 15:8
Assarius[7]	1/4 Denarius		Cost of two sparrows. About 1 cent. See Mt 10:29
Dilepton 1.5-3 g bronze	Quadrans 1/16 Denarius	2 "mites"	$0.0024 or 1/4 cent
Lepton[8] 0.5-1 g bronze		"Mite"	1/32 Denarius; 1/8 cent. Widow's offering in Mk 12:42

1.2.2 New Testament statistics

The order of the books in the New Testament is based on traditional and canonical criteria and is not chronological. As regards its authorship, the New Testament has nine authors, St Paul, responsible for thirteen books, St John, for five books, St Luke and St Peter for two books each, and St Matthew, St Mark, St James, St Jude, and the author of Hebrews responsible for one book each. Among these various authors, St Luke is considered to be the only Gentile. It is fascinating to explore the range of places or origin and of destination for the various books of the New Testament. This again indicates, considering the limited resources and transport facilities of New Testament times, that this whole enterprise cannot have been merely human in order to succeed. Not only do we say that the New Testament is inspired, but also the whole process of composition and distribution of these books was guided by God. The provenance and destination of the various books of the New Testament is indicated in the table (Figure 2) below.

We also indicate below the statistics of the New Testament, in another table (Figure 3), which offers an overview of the number of verses in each chapter, the number of chapters in each book, and the total number of verses in each book. This may seem a dry analysis of the New Testament, but it simply meant to give the reader a quick summary of the various books and their respective lengths and sizes, in order to familiarize him or her with the great variety and yet great unity involved in the Scriptures. The table should be seen in the context of the further detailed description offered in section 1.2.3 below.

Figure 2: Provenance and destination of the various books of the New Testament

Book	Provenance	Destination
Matthew	Antioch	Antioch
Mark	Rome	Rome
Luke	Rome	
John	Ephesus	Asia
Acts	Rome	
Romans	Corinth	Rome
1 Corinthians	Ephesus	Corinth
2 Corinthians	Macedonia	Corinth
Galatians	Antioch	Galatia
Ephesians	Rome	Asia
Philippians	Rome	Philippi
Colossians	Rome	Colossae
1 Thessalonians	Corinth	Thessalonica
2 Thessalonians	Corinth	Thessalonica
1 Timothy	Macedonia	Ephesus
2 Timothy	Rome	Ephesus
Titus	Macedonia	Crete
Philemon	Rome	Colossae
Hebrews	Rome	
James	Jerusalem	Diaspora Jews
1 Peter	Rome	Pontus, Galatia, Cappodocia, Asia, Bithynia
2 Peter	Rome	Pontus, Galatia, Cappodocia, Asia, Bithynia
1 John	Ephesus	Asia
2 John	Ephesus	Asia
3 John	Ephesus	Asia
Jude		
Revelation	Patmos	7 Asian Churches

Figure 3: Number of Chapters and Number of Verses per Chapter in each New Testament Book[10]

Chapter	1	2	3	4	5	6	7	8	9	10	11	12	13	14	15	16	17	18	19	20	21	22	23	24	25	26	27	28	Total
Matthew	25	23	17	25	48	34	29	34	38	42	30	50	58	36	39	28	27	35	30	34	46	46	39	51	46	75	66	20	1071
Mark	45	28	35	41	43	56	37	38	50	52	33	44	37	72	47	20													678
Luke	80	52	38	44	39	49	50	56	62	42	54	59	35	35	32	31	37	43	48	47	38	71	56	53					1151
John	51	25	36	54	47	71	52	59	41	42	57	50	38	31	27	33	26	40	42	31	25								878
Acts	26	47	26	37	42	16	60	40	43	48	30	25	52	28	41	40	34	28	41	38	40	30	35	27	27	32	44	31	1008
Rom	32	29	31	25	21	23	25	39	33	21	36	21	14	23	33	27													433
1 Co	31	16	23	21	13	20	40	13	27	33	34	31	13	40	58	24													437
2 Co	24	17	18	18	21	18	16	24	15	18	33	21	14																257
Galatians	24	21	29	31	26	18																							149
Ephesians	23	22	21	32	33	24																							155
Phil	30	30	21	23																									104
Col	29	23	25	18																									95
1 Th	10	20	13	18	28																								89
2 Th	12	17	18																										47
1 Tm	20	15	16	16	25	21																							113
2 Tm	18	26	17	22																									83
Titus	16	15	15																										46
Philemon	25																												25
Hebrews	14	18	19	16	14	20	28	13	28	39	40	29	25																303
James	27	26	18	17	20																								108
1 Peter	25	25	22	9	14																								105
2 Peter	21	22	18																										61
1 John	10	29	24	21	21																								105
2 John	13																												13
3 John	14																												14
Jude	25																												25
Rev	20	29	22	11	14	17	17	13	21	11	19	17	18	20	8		21	18	24	21	15	27	21						404

1.2.3 A Brief Overview of each Book and Letter[11]

The Gospels

The *Gospel of St Matthew* was written by Matthew the tax collector and apostle (Mark 3:18; Matt 9:9; 10:3; Luke 6:15; Acts 1:13), who was a multi–lingual (Aramaic and Greek) Jewish Christian. His Gospel was addressed to better educated Jews who already believed in Jesus, as a book of 'heritage' (Mt 1:1) and much 'teaching' (Mt 28:20). St Matthew reproduces some sixty or seventy passages from the Old Testament; the other Evangelists together quote the Old Testament about fifty times. Again, St Mark and St Luke as a rule adduce only those quotations which occur in our Lord's discourses; St Matthew, on the other hand, argues from the pages of the sacred text. While proving that Jesus is the fulfilment of the ancient prophecies, St Matthew at the same time explains how the Jews, always resisting the inspirations of divine grace, rejected Him Who came upon earth in the first place to save the Jews. Although St Matthew wrote chiefly for Jewish converts, his Gospel is not restricted to them. The adoration of the Magi, who represent the first fruits of the conversion of the Gentiles to Christ, should more naturally find a place in the Luke's Gospel, the Gospel of universal salvation; yet the account of it is found in the first Gospel. Again, St Matthew narrates parables in which special preference is given to the Gentiles, such as, for example, the parables of the two sons, of the wicked husbandmen, and of the marriage of the king's son. He quotes prophecies concerning the Gentiles (8:11; 12:18, 21; 21:42 to 22:14; 25:32) and narrates miracles worked by our Lord for them (8:5–13; 15:21–28). He declares the universality of the Messiah's kingdom in narrating Christ's commission to His Apostles to go and teach all nations (28–19). On the other hand, Matthew's Gospel leaves to Luke the narration of such specifically Jewish incidents as the mission of the Precursor, the Circumcision, the finding of Jesus in the Temple, and the Presentation of the Lord. While the opening chapters of St Luke's Gospel are composed from the viewpoint of the Mother of Jesus, those of St Matthew are composed from the viewpoint of St Joseph. In St Luke's Gospel all events seem to converge toward Mary, in St Matthew's Gospel all events gravitate around St Joseph.

St Matthew's Gospel was probably written from in or near Antioch in Syria, in the late 70's or 80's, based on a core text of earlier sources, to teach a community that has internal divisions and external enemies. The Greek style betrays Semitic influence. There are numerous testimonies, starting from Papias and Irenaeus, that Matthew originally wrote in Hebrew letters, which is thought to refer to Aramaic. The 16th–century scholar Erasmus was the first to express doubts on the subject of an original Aramaic or Hebrew version of the Gospel of Matthew. Here Erasmus distinguishes between a Gospel of Matthew in Hebrew letters and the partly lost Gospel of the Hebrews and Gospel of the Nazoraeans, from which patristic writers do quote, and which appear to have some relationship to Matthew, but are not identical to it.

The geographical focus of this Gospel concerns Galilee, especially the mountains in mostly Jewish areas. The principal literary features are five major discourses; well–organized sections of collected pericopes. The literary introduction is the 'Book of Genealogy' (1:1). At the beginning of this gospel lies the declaration of Jesus as Emmanuel (1:2–2:23); there is also the contrast between the 'King of Jews' and King Herod. The inaugural event is the Sermon on the Mount; and the concept of the fulfilment of the Law (chapters 5–7). In St Matthew's Gospel, Jesus' chief opponents are the scribes and Pharisees, who are referred to as 'hypocrites and blind guides'. As in St Mark's Gospel, Jesus' last words on the Cross are: 'My God, my God, why have you forsaken me?' (Mt 27:46). The focus of the Passion is seen in terms of plots and treachery in chapters 26 and 27.

The last major event is the Great Commission, on the mountain in Galilee (28:16–20), where, in the final literary ending, Jesus tells the disciples, 'I am with you always' (28:20). The major Christological titles adopted by St Matthew are Son of David, Son of Abraham; Great Lawgiver and Teacher (like Moses). The major Christological actions of Jesus consist in teaching His disciples and decrying religious hypocrisy. For Matthew, discipleship involves the call to righteousness, to continual forgiveness, to living the Golden Rule; to fulfilling God's laws, especially the law of charitable deeds. The eschatological expectations of St Matthew are that false prophets will arise, that many will fall away and that the Gospel must first be preached to all (24:10–14). The basis for final judgement is whatever you do for 'the least' people, you do for Christ as portrayed in the Sheep and Goats parable (25:31–46). Other major themes in St Matthew's Gospel are the idea of the fulfilment of Scripture; divisions within the community; and the final separation of good from the bad. The aim of Matthew's Gospel is thus to show that Jesus of Nazareth is the Messiah, the Christ or the 'Anointed One', promised in the Old Testament, and that His Kingdom is the Church which He founded. This book is full of allusions to passages of the Old Testament which the book interprets as predicting and foreshadowing Jesus's life and mission. This Gospel contains no fewer than sixty–five references to the Old Testament, forty–three of these being direct verbal citations, thus greatly outnumbering those found in the other Gospels. St Matthew constantly refers to prophecies fulfilled in Our Lord in words such as these: 'As it is written.' St Matthew is represented by a human being or by an angel in religious art (see Rev 4:7), and his liturgical feast day is 21st September.

The *Gospel of St Mark* was written by 'John Mark of Jerusalem' (Acts 12:12; 15:37; Col 4:10; Phlm 1:24; 1 Pt 5:13) who was a Greek–speaker of second Christian generation. Some conjecture that the youth who fled naked from Gethsemane (14:51) was the Evangelist himself. St Mark was baptized and instructed by St Peter. In about the year 42 AD he came to Rome with the Prince of the Apostles. His Gospel is a record of the substance of St Peter's preaching concerning our Lord. St Peter's discourse in the house of the Roman centurion Cornelius (Acts 10:34–43) has been justly considered as an outline of St Mark's Gospel, as St Mark's Gospel in miniature. The Gospel of St Mark gives special attention to St Peter. The vivid descriptions, the swift movement of thought, the frequent use of such words as 'straight away,' 'immediately,' 'quickly,' 'forthwith,' 'at once,' strongly recall the quick and impulsive fisherman of Galilee. The Gospel suppresses incidents indicative of his position and dignity among the Apostles, such as, for example, the walking upon the water (Mt 14:29), the finding of the coin in the fish's mouth (Mt 17:26), the promise of the Primacy (Mt 16:16–19), and the commission to confirm the brethren (Lk 22:31–32). On the other hand, events which are derogatory to St Peter are deliberately emphasized, even when they are minimized or passed over by the other Evangelists. Nowhere, for example, is the depth of St Peter's fall more fully indicated than in Mark's Gospel. One can well imagine St Peter supervising 'over St Mark's shoulder' the composition of the Gospel so that the Apostle's defects rather than his merits are emphasized. Papias and Irenaeus confirmed this tradition, as did Origen and Tertullian. Clement of Alexandria, writing at the end of the second century, reported this ancient tradition that Mark was urged by those who had heard Peter's speeches in Rome to write what the apostle had said; as a result, scholars have generally thought that this Gospel was written at Rome. There is an impending sense of persecution in the Gospel, and this could indicate it being written to sustain the faith of a community under such a threat. As the main Christian persecution at that time was in Rome under Nero, this has also been used to place the writing of the Gospel in Rome. Furthermore, it has been argued that the Latinized vocabulary employed in Mark (and in neither Matthew nor Luke) shows that the Gospel was written in Rome. He uses Latin terms which no other Evangelist employs; for example, 'spiculator,' soldier of the guard (6:27), 'sextarius,' a pitcher (7:4), 'quadrans' a farthing (12:42), 'centurio,' a Roman officer in charge of 100 soldiers (15:39).[12] Also cited in support of a Roman origin for this Gospel is a passage in First Peter: 'The chosen one at Babylon sends you greeting, as does Mark, my son'(1 Peter 5:13); Babylon is here interpreted as a derogatory or code name for Rome, as the famous ancient city of Babylon ceased to exist in 275 BC.

St Mark's Gospel was addressed to Gentile Christians who are fairly new in their faith, and narrated 'good news' about Jesus and his actions (Mk 1:1). Internal evidence shows that the Gospel was written for Gentiles, especially for Roman Gentile converts. The Gospel quotes but seldom from the Old Testament (cf. 1:2, 3; 15:28), since an appeal to the prophets would have been meaningless to the Romans. So, too, the title 'Son of David' is rarely applied to our Lord. Comparisons between the Old and the New Law, which form so striking a feature in the Sermon on the Mount, are also missing. On the other hand, St Mark is careful to explain Jewish rites and customs which might prove unintelligible to a pagan reader, as, for example, the purifications (7:3), the passover (14:12), the day of preparation (15:42). He explains words and expressions which Gentile converts would not be likely to understand; for example: 'Boanerges' (3:17), 'Talitha cumi' (5:41), 'Ephpheta' (7:34), 'Corban' (7:11), 'Bartimaeus' (10:46), 'Two mites' (12:42). St Mark's Gospel was thus most probably written from Rome; maybe other possibilities would be from Galilee, Syria or Decapolis.

The time of writing is estimated by biblical scholars to be very late 60's or early 70's, to encourage a community undergoing difficult trials and persecutions. Many contemporary scholars regard Mark as the earliest of the canonical gospels, and a source for material in the other synoptic gospels, Matthew and Luke. The Greek style is grammatically simple. The geographical focus of this Gospel concerns Galilean towns and villages and some Gentile territory. The literary introduction involves 'Beginning of Good News' (1:1). The literary features, as we have said, involve quick action ('and then'; 'immediately') in a series of loosely connected episodes. At the beginning of this gospel we find John the Baptist's preaching and then Jesus' ministry begins (1:2–15). The inaugural event is the Exorcism in Synagogue of Capernaum (1:21–28). In this Gospel, Jesus' chief opponents are the Pharisees and Herodians, and the chief priests, scribes and elders. Jesus' last words on the Cross are: 'My God, my God, why have You forsaken me?' (15:34), and the focus of the Passion is seen in terms of death as tragedy. The last major event is the Empty Tomb, outside of Jerusalem (16:1–8). The final literary event is when the women leave tomb in fear and silence (16:8), and the appearances of the Risen Christ (16:9–20). The major Christological titles adopted by St Mark are Christ or Messiah and Son of God; Suffering Son of Man; eschatological Judge. The major Christological actions of Jesus are miracles, overcoming evil powers, and arguing with Jewish religious authorities.

The aim of St Mark's Gospel is to show, especially from our Lord's miracles, that Christ is true God, that He alone verifies in Himself the Roman title of 'Lord of All.' The very first verse of the Gospel contains the triumphant assertion of Christ's Divinity: 'The beginning of the Gospel of Jesus Christ, the Son of God.' The Evangelist not only affirms the fact of our Lord's Divinity but also indicates its consequences. He shows that all things in heaven and upon earth are subject to Christ. It is for this reason that Mark insists so much on miracles and dwells upon them with a fullness of detail not found in St Matthew's and St Luke's Gospels. Writing for the pagans who peopled nature with divinities and admitted the existence of 'many gods,' St Mark describes especially Christ's miracles over nature and shows that even evil spirits must be subject to Him. In St Mark's account, Christ never uses explicitly the title 'Son of

God' but always refers to Himself as 'Son of Man.' Our Lord's humble ways thus stand in sharp contrast with those of the Roman Emperors who boldly and proudly styled themselves the gods, lords and saviours of the world. Thus for Mark, discipleship involves perseverance in faith despite suffering, following Jesus 'on the way' to the cross, being ready for His return. The eschatological expectations of St Mark involve Christ coming as imminent and happening suddenly, but no one knows when, so one must 'Keep awake' (13:1–37). The basis for final judgement is whether you persevere in faith despite persecutions (13:13). Another major theme in St Mark's Gospel is that of the Messianic secret where main disciples don't understand, but minor characters do believe. St Mark is represented by a lion in religious art (see Rev 4:7), and his liturgical feast day is 25th April.

The *Gospel of St Luke* was written by Luke the physician and companion of Paul (Col 4:14; 2 Tm 4:11; Phm 1:24 only), a well–educated Greek convert to Christianity. The earliest surviving witnesses that place Luke as the author are the Muratorian Canon (c. 170), the writings of Irenaeus (c. 180), Clement of Alexandria (c. 150–215). The evidence in favour of Lucan authorship is based on two main things: first, the use of 'we' in Acts 16, 20, 21 and 27 suggests the writer travelled with Paul; second, the 'medical language' employed by the writer is identical with those employed by such medical writers as Hippocrates, Arctæus, Galen, and Dioscorides. According to this view, Paul's 'dear friend Luke the Doctor' (Col 4:14) and 'fellow worker' (Phlm 24) remains the most likely candidate for authorship out of all the companions mentioned in Paul's writings.

St Luke's Gospel is a record of Christ's life and teaching as preached by St Paul. It stresses those facts which illustrate, in the spirit of the Apostle of the Gentiles, the universality of salvation for both Jew and Greek. It sets Christ forth as the Saviour of mankind. In exquisitely tender colours, it depicts our Lord as the merciful and pitying Divine Physician, as the Friend of sinners and Consoler of afflicted. It describes those incidents which would touch the hearts of the heathen and awaken their confidence in God. The love of Christ for sinners is illustrated in the accounts of Zacchaeus (19:2), the sinful woman (7:37), and the penitent thief (23:42–43). It is St Luke's Gospel alone that narrates the beautiful parables of the Good Samaritan (10:25), the Prodigal Son (15:11), the Unjust Steward (16:1), Dives and Lazarus (16:19), the Pharisee and the Publican (18:10). The doctrine of universal salvation appears even in the genealogy of Christ, which is brought down from Adam, the father of all mankind (3:23–38), and not, as in St Matthew's Gospel, from Abraham, the father of the chosen people.

St Luke's Gospel has in a special manner been designated as the 'Gospel of women.' It places before us and describes the following feminine characters: Elizabeth, the Mother of John the Baptist; Anna, the aged prophetess; the 'sinful woman' who anointed the Lord's feet in the house of the Pharisee (7:36–50); the women 'who ministered unto Jesus of their substance,' among whom was Mary Magdalen (8:2); Martha, the sister of Lazarus, and Mary, Martha's sister (10:38–42); 'the woman in the crowd' who lifted up her voice and said to Jesus: 'Blessed is the womb that bore You' (11:27); the widow of Nain (7:11–17); the woman whom our Lord delivered from her infirmity (13:10–17); the women of Jerusalem who met Jesus on the way to Calvary (23:27–31). Pre–eminent among all these is Mary, the Mother of God, who occupies a prominent place especially in the first two chapters of the Gospel.[13]

St Luke's Gospel was addressed to wealthier Gentile Christians in urban settings, and represented an 'orderly account' for 'secure knowledge' (Lk 1:1–4). It was probably written from Greece or possibly Syria (in connection with the Pauline missions), in the late 70's or 80's, but based on many earlier sources, to challenge believers to put their faith into practice more fully. The Greek style is good, elegant, and literary. The geographical focus of this Gospel concerns one long journey to the goal which is Jerusalem. The principal literary features are stories often in pairs (especially with male and female characters), as well as many extra parables, with respect to the other Gospels. The literary introduction lies in the concept of an 'Orderly Account' (1:1–4), in the scientific manner of Luke. At the beginning of this gospel we find the account concerning the parallel birth stories of John the Baptist and Jesus from Elizabeth and Mary respectively (1:5–2:52). The inaugural event is the Jubilee reading from Isaiah 61 and Jesus' rejection at Nazareth (4:14–30). In St Luke's Gospel, Jesus' chief opponents are unjust authorities (civil and religious) as well as rich and corrupt people. In this Gospel, Jesus' last words on the Cross are to the good thief 'You will be with me in Paradise' (23:43); and to His Father 'Father, into your hands I commend my Spirit' (23:46). The focus of St Luke's Passion is seen in terms of the innocence of Jesus in chapters 22 and 23. The last major event is the Ascension, from Bethany just East of Jerusalem (24:50–53). In the final literary ending, the disciples return to the Jerusalem temple with joy praising God (24:53). The major Christological titles adopted by St Luke are Great Prophet; Lord (of all nations); Saviour (especially of the poor). The major Christological actions of Jesus consist in healing sick and impaired people, and forgiving sinners and debtors. For Luke, discipleship involves the call to leave everything to follow Jesus; to share with poor; to accept everyone, especially outcasts, women, and enemies. The eschatological expectations of St Luke include the time after Jerusalem is destroyed and the fulfilment of the time of the Gentiles' time. The eschatological times will not be so soon, the command is to pray (21:20–24, 28, 36). The basis for final judgement is how you use wealth and possessions, as seen in the parables of Rich and Poor (16:1–31). Other major themes in St Luke's Gospel are the fulfilment of God's plan; the theme of eschatological reversal; the fact that tax collectors and sinners are favoured. St Luke is represented by an ox in religious art (see Rev 4:7), and his liturgical feast day is 18th October.

The *Gospel of St John* was written by John, son of Zebedee, one of the twelve apostles (Mark 1:19; 3:17; cf. John 21:2), the 'beloved disciple.' A decisive testimony in regard to the Johannine authorship of the fourth Gospel comes to us from St Irenaeus, a disciple of St Polycarp who in turn was a disciple of St John himself. St Irenaeus wrote: 'John, the disciple of the Lord, who also leaned on His breast, himself also published a Gospel while he was at Ephesus in Asia.'[14] From Egypt comes the testimony of Clement of Alexandria who in his works quotes the fourth Gospel more than one hundred times and refers to it as the work of the Apostle John. Clement says: 'John, perceiving that the other Evangelists had set forth the human side of the Person of Jesus, at the instance of his disciples composed a spiritual Gospel.'[15]

The particular scope of the author and the time of composition have given the fourth Gospel a character quite different from that of the Synoptics. In the first place, St John's Gospel has little of the Synoptic material. This absence is not due to St John's ignorance of the first three Gospels, for he knows the Synoptics and makes a clear allusion to their contents (1:26–33; 6:68; 12–27). St John's aim is not to rewrite the Synoptics but to give the Church another Gospel, a more profound presentation of the Person and teaching of Christ. St John goes beyond the Synoptics, and presents a number of incidents and discourses which prove the special object which he set for himself. He is not a mere chronicler, and consequently passes over what the Synoptics had already told and what everyone already knew. He says nothing of the institution of the Eucharist and of Baptism, not because he did not know of these two sacraments, but because his Gospel is primarily doctrinal and not narrative. Instead of relating the institution of these two sacraments, he gives us two dogmatic discourses in which Christ foretells and explains the nature of each. That, on the other hand, so little of the Johannine material is found in the Synoptics likewise presents no serious difficulty. The Synoptics do not purport to be a complete history of Christ. No one Gospel pretends to be an exhaustive account of His life and teaching. The synoptic writers addressed the newly converted pagans and Jews who had to be taught the elements of Christianity; St John wrote for the third generation of Christians, who already knew the Synoptics and whose deeper theological learning enabled them to understand the more profound aspect of our Lord's teaching, as well as to detect the errors of heresy and false speculation. The Synoptics deal largely with our Lord's life and teaching in Galilee; St John concentrates on the happenings in Judea.

Technically, the Gospel of John does not contain any parables. It does, however, contain metaphoric stories, such as The Shepherd and The Vine. Synoptic parables are poetic stories, each of which illustrates a single message or idea. John's metaphoric stories are allegories, in which each individual element corresponds to a specific group or thing. John 10:1–5 is potentially a stand–alone parable of Jesus, which is sometimes termed the 'Parable of the Sheepfold'; John 10:6 calls it a 'figure of speech'. In John 10:7, Jesus states 'I am the gate', which makes the passage a metaphor.

St John's Gospel was addressed to a mixed audience of mostly Jews, but some Gentiles and Samaritans. He stresses 'testimony' and 'signs' for belief (Jn 20:30f; 21:24f). Traditionally, the received view was that it was probably written from Ephesus, but maybe originally Galilee. While an early edition may have been ready in the 50's, the final edition was ready in the 90's, to strengthen the identity of a group ostracized by other Jews for their faith. The Greek style is simple, but highly symbolic. The geographical focus of this Gospel concerns multiple visits back and forth to Jerusalem. The principal literary features are the expression 'Amen, Amen, I say to you'; the use of irony and of paradox; and multiple levels of meaning. The literary introduction is the Prologue, a Cosmic Hymn (1:1–18). At the beginning of this gospel, John the Baptist points to Jesus, the 'Lamb of God'; also, the first disciples are called (1:19–51). The inaugural event is the Wedding Feast at Cana the first of Jesus' 'signs' (2:1–11). In St John's Gospel, Jesus' chief opponents are the Jewish leaders especially the Pharisees. In this Gospel, Jesus' last words on the Cross are addressed to His Mother, and to His beloved disciple: 'Behold your son; behold you mother' (19:26f); then He said 'I am thirsty' (19:28); and finally 'It is finished' (19:30). The focus of St John's Passion is seen in terms of Jesus' exaltation in chapters 18–19. The last major events are the Resurrection episodes with the disciples and Thomas (20:19–29), and with Peter and the beloved disciple (21:1–23). The final literary ending speaks of many more signs (20:30f) and many other books that would need to have been written to contain them (21:24f). The major Christological titles adopted by St John are the Divine Word made Flesh; the Son, sent from the Father; the Passover Lamb; the expression 'I Am...' denoting the equality of Jesus to God. The major Christological actions of Jesus consist in speaking God's words; doing God's works; revealing God and Himself. For John, discipleship involves seeing, believing, knowing, remaining in Jesus and God, despite hostility; loving one another; being in unity; serving humbly. In John, we find a realized eschatology, whereby all who hear and believe have eternal life already now and are not judged (5:21–25). The basis for final judgement is whether or not you believe in Jesus (3:16–18; 5:19–24; 12:44–50). Other major themes in St John's Gospel are those of 'eternal life' meaning 'life in His name'; the Paraclete who is the Holy Spirit; Christian unity; and the mutual indwelling of God and Jesus. St John is represented by an eagle in religious art (see Rev 4:7), and his liturgical feast day is 27th December.

The Other Books of the New Testament

The *Acts of the Apostles* are traditionally ascribed to 'Luke', a physician and companion of Paul (Col 4:4; 2 Tm 4:11;

Phlm 24); definitely a well–educated Greek writer, probably
of Gentile heritage. The word 'Acts' (Greek *praxeis*) denoted
a recognized genre in the ancient world, 'characterizing
books that described great deeds of people or of cities.'[16]
There is substantial evidence to indicate that the author of
the Gospel of Luke also wrote the Book of Acts. The most
direct evidence comes from the prefaces of each book. Both
prefaces are addressed to Theophilus, the author's patron—
and perhaps a label for a Christian community as a whole
as the name means 'Lover of God'. Furthermore, the pref-
ace of Acts explicitly references 'my former book' about the
life of Jesus—almost certainly the work we know as The
Gospel of Luke. Furthermore, there are linguistic and theological similarities between the Luke and Acts.

The named recipient is 'Theophilus' (1:1), a
well–educated Greek–speaking person, or a group familiar
with Paul's teaching. Some scholars date the book of Acts
between 60–62 AD, noting that the absence of any mention
of the destruction of Jerusalem in AD 70 would be unlikely
if the book were written afterwards. Since the book does not
mention the death of Paul, a central character in the final
chapters, it was probably penned before his death. Other
scholars propose the date of redaction is the late 80's,
shortly after St Luke's Gospel. It is not exactly known from
where Acts was written: possibly Antioch in Syria. It is definitely a single work, but compiled from multiple older
sources (see Luke 1:1–4). Its literary genre is an 'Acts', or a
partial account of the growth of early Christianity, focusing
only on certain Apostles. It is composed in good literary
Greek, and quoted speeches use various Greek styles. The
purpose of Acts is to continue the 'orderly account' begun
in the Gospel of Luke, showing the growth of Christianity.

The *Letter of St Paul to the Romans* was written by 'Paul, a
slave of Jesus Christ, called to be an apostle' (1:1–6). Its
authenticity is not disputed and it was definitely written by
Paul, although taken down by the scribe Tertius (16:22). It
was written in Greek. The named recipients are all God's

beloved in Rome, who are called to be saints (1:7), or mixed groups of Jewish Christians and Gentile Christians in Rome, the capital of the Roman Empire, whom Paul has never visited before. The date of writing is probably late 50's (winter of 57/58?), as Paul is concluding his mission around the Aegean Sea (early in the fourth period of Paul's missionary work – see Rm 15:19, 22–29). The Letter was definitely written from Corinth (see 16:23; also 15:25–26; 16:1). As regards its unity, it is probably a single letter; although some scholars suggest chapter 16 was originally separate. Its literary genre is a personal letter of introduction; in parts more formal, like a sermon or exhortation. In the doctrinal section (1:16 to 11:26), St Paul explains the necessity of justification for both Gentiles and Jews, the method of justification, the effects and fruits of justification, and the special problem of the justification of the Jewish people. In the moral section (12:1 to 15:13), he explains our duties to God, to our neighbour and to ourselves.

The *First Letter of Paul to the Corinthians* was written by 'Paul, called to be an apostle of Christ Jesus by the will of God, and our brother Sosthenes' (1:1). The letter, originally composed in Greek, is addressed to 'the church of God that is in Corinth, to those who are sanctified in Christ Jesus, called to be saints, together with all those who in every place call on the name of our Lord Jesus Christ, both their Lord and ours' (1:2). This was a mixed community with some Jewish Christians but mostly Gentile converts in Corinth, a very prosperous Greek city which was the capital of the Roman province of Achaia. The date of writing was about 54 AD, early in the third period of Paul's missionary activity. It was definitely written from Ephesus (16:8). It is an authentic writing of Paul himself; but not Paul's 'first' letter to this church (see 5:9). It consists of a literary unity, most likely a single letter, although possibly written in stages over a few weeks. Its literary genre is that of a personal letter of exhortation and instruction. This letter is a solution of pastoral problems which arose in his mission at Corinth and which were referred to the Apostle for solution. After the customary greetings (1:1–9), the Apostle proceeds to deal with the abuses in the Corinthian church (1 :10 to 6:20): He condemns their dissensions, orders the ejection of the incestuous man, and commands the Christians not to bring their difficulties before pagan judges. He then answers the questions which had been submitted to him (7:1 to 15:58) and which dealt with marriage, virginity, meats sacrificed to idols, the proper decorum in worship, the Eucharist and the love feasts, charismatic gifts and the resurrection of the dead. In the epilogue (16:1–24), the Apostle lays down the rules for collecting alms and promises to visit the Corinthians shortly.

The *Second Letter of Paul to the Corinthians* was written in Greek by 'Paul, an apostle of Christ Jesus by the will of God, and Timothy our brother' (1:1a). It was addressed 'to the church of God that is in Corinth, including all the saints throughout Achaia' (1:1b), a larger group based around the same people as in the First Letter of Paul to the Corinthians. It is dated around the mid–50's AD, later in the third period of Paul's missionary activity. It was probably written from Ephesus; later portions possibly from Macedonia, as Paul is travelling back to visit Corinth. It is definitely a work of St Paul, but some scholars propose that it is mostly likely a composite of between 2 and 5 originally separate letters written over a period of several years. Its literary genre is that of a personal letter of exhortation and instruction. The Judaizers, who had invaded Corinth, were making various insinuations about St Paul's character and his work. Paul, they said, was dishonest, inconstant, ambitious, weak, compromising in his attitude, contemptible in his appearance and in his speech. This Second Letter is St Paul's defence of his apostolic authority and of the purity of his Gospel. In the first part of the Letter (1:12 to 7:16) he explains to the faithful the character of his apostolic office; in the second (8:1 to 9:15), he urges the faithful to give alms; and in the third (10:1 to 13:10), answers his adversaries.

The *Letter of Paul to the Galatians* was written in Greek by 'Paul an apostle–sent neither by human commission nor from human authorities, but through Jesus Christ and God the Father, who raised him from the dead–and all the members of God's family who are with me' (1:1–2a). This letter was written 'To the churches of Galatia' (1:2b – plural churches in the Province of Galatia); probably Northern Galatia, a region around Ancyra in what is now central Turkey; or possibly Southern Galatia: the area around Pisidian Antioch, Lystra, and Derbe, where Barnabas and Paul preached in Acts 13–14. The dating of this work is not certain, but is likely to be already the early 50's AD in the second period of Paul's missionary activity, or possibly 54–55 AD in the third period of Paul's missionary activity. It may well have been written from Ephesus. Its authenticity is not disputed, and it constitutes a single literary unit. Its literary genre is that of a personal letter of exhortation and admonishment. The Judaizers – certain Christian Pharisees of Judea – followed closely upon St Paul's heels, invaded the Apostle's Galatian mission and maintained that if the Gentiles wished to be saved they must, in addition to embracing Christianity, 'be circumcised, and be commanded to observe the law of Moses' (Acts 15:5). The Epistle to the Galatians was written to refute these zealots of the Mosaic Law. After the customary salutation (1:1–5), St Paul at once states the central theme of his Epistle: His Gospel is of divine origin, it is immutable, and therefore cannot be supplemented or perfected by man (1:6–10). He defends this thesis by a historical argument (1:11 to 2:21) and by a Biblical argument (3:1 to 4:31). First, he shows that his Gospel was received directly from God, approved by the Apostles, and applied in practice. Second, he proves that the Galatians received the Holy Spirit not because of their observance of the Law but because of faith; that Abraham was justified by faith before circumcision or the giving of the Law; that the Law was a pedagogue unto Christ and abrogated at His coming. In the parenetic part of the Letter

(5:1 to 6:10), he exhorts the Galatians to abide in that freedom with which Christ made them free, and in the concluding section (6:11–18) affirms that he himself will glory in Christ alone.

The *Letter of Paul to the Ephesians* was written in complex Greek by 'Paul, an apostle of Christ Jesus by the will of God' (1:1a). It was addressed to 'the saints who are in Ephesus and are faithful in Christ Jesus' (1:1b); these were mostly Gentile converts to Christianity in Ephesus, the capital of the Roman province of Asia, a major Pauline centre. It was dated to be most likely from the late first–century AD, very likely near the end of Paul's life in the mid–60's AD. It could have been written from Caesarea or Rome. Some scholars think it is clearly 'deutero–Pauline', namely not written by Paul himself, but by a later follower, and written from Ephesus itself in that case. Its literary genre is that of a general letter of exhortation, possibly a cover–letter for a collection of Paul's letters. In the doctrinal section of the Epistle (1:1 to 3:29) the Apostle explains our redemption by Christ and the incorporation of all men, Jews and Gentiles, into the one Church of which Christ is the Head. Of this mystery or Gospel, St Paul proclaims himself the privileged preacher. In the moral section (4:1 to 6:9) the Apostle explains our individual as well as social duties.

The *Letter of Paul to the Philippians* is a letter of gratitude and joy addressed by the Apostle to his beloved converts at Philippi, who had befriended him and helped him on more than one occasion. It is attributed to 'Paul and Timothy, servants of Christ Jesus' (1:1a). It was addressed in Greek to 'all the saints of Christ Jesus who are in Philippi, with the bishops and deacons' (1:1b); these were mostly Gentile converts to Christianity in Philippi, a prosperous Roman colony (Acts 17:12) within Greek Macedonia on the highly travelled Via Egnatia. It is dated to around 56–57 AD (if from Ephesus), in the third period of Paul's missionary activity; it could possibly even be from the fourth period of his missionary activity. It was very likely written from prison, probably in Ephesus or possibly later from Caesarea or Rome. Its authenticity is not disputed, and the letter is definitely by Paul. Many scholars see it as a combination of what were originally three different letters (called Philippians A – 4:10–12; Philippians B – 1:1–3:1 and 4:2–9, 21–23; Philippians C – 3:1–4:1). Interestingly, Philippians 2:6–11 may have been an earlier Christian hymn adapted by Paul. Its literary genre is that of a personal letter of friendship and encouragement. Each part of the Letter has a different purpose. Part A thanks the recipients for their support; Part B encourages their faith; Part C warns them against errors.

The *Letter of Paul to the Colossians* was written by 'Paul, an apostle of Christ Jesus by the will of God, Timothy our brother' (1:1). Its language is more difficult Greek with long complex sentences. It was addressed to 'the saints and faithful brothers and sisters in Christ in Colossae' (1:2a); mostly Gentile Christians in Colossae (in Asia, about 100 miles East of Ephesus), a church founded by Epaphras (1:7; 4:12). It is generally dated around 60–64, from the fourth phase of his life. If it is a genuine Pauline letter by Paul, then it is considered to have been written by him possibly from Caesarea, or probably from Rome. Those who consider the Letter as deutero–Pauline propose that it may have been written from Ephesus. Many scholars believe that Colossians 1:15–20 is an earlier hymn adapted by the author of this letter. Its literary genre is that of a letter of exhortation. This Letter was written in defence of Christ's divinity and the dignity of our life in Christ against certain false teachers, who had invaded Colossae, and advocated the cult of angels as necessary for salvation, in this way minimizing the dignity of Christ, the one sole Mediator. They also inculcated a rigid abstinence from certain foods and strove to impose upon the faithful various Mosaic observances. In the dogmatic and doctrinal section of the Epistle (1:1 to 3:20), St Paul defends the unique dignity of Christ and refutes the false doctors. In the moral section (3:1 to 4:6) he urges the Christians to live up to their dignity as members of Christ's body, explains the moral obligations of various groups, and recommends prayer, vigilance and prudence.

The *First Letter of Paul to the Thessalonians* is attributed to 'Paul, Silvanus, and Timothy' (1:1a). It was addressed to 'the church of the Thessalonians in God our Father and the Lord Jesus Christ' (1:1b), made up of some Jewish Christians but mostly Gentile converts in Thessalonica, a culturally Greek city, which in the first century was the capital of the Roman province of Macedonia. Its language is Koine Greek, which is common everyday language, not a sophisticated literary style. It is dated around 50 or 51 AD, in the second period of Paul's missionary activity. It is considered to have been written by Paul from Corinth (3:1–7; cf. Acts 18:1–5). Its authenticity is undisputed and is Paul's oldest surviving letter. Its literary genre is that of a personal letter of encouragement and instruction.

Paul was concerned because of the infancy of the church. He had only spent a few weeks with them before leaving for Athens. In his concern, he sent his delegate, Timothy, to visit the Thessalonians and to return with a report. While, on the whole, the news was encouraging, it also showed that important misunderstandings existed concerning Paul's teaching of Christianity. Paul devotes part of the letter to correcting these errors, and exhorts the Thessalonians to purity of life, reminding them that their sanctification is God's will for their lives. Some of the Thessalonian Christians, whom St Paul converted about 50 AD, had not wholly emerged from the Gentile way of living, were given to leisure and laziness thinking that Christ's return was at hand, and were extremely anxious about the lot of the dead at the second coming of Christ. St Paul wrote his first Letter to explain certain doctrinal truths to them and especially whatever pertained to Our Lord's second coming. He assures them that the dead would share equally with the living in the blessings of Christ's return. In the historical section of the Epistle (chapters 1–3) the Apostle rejoices over the happy condition of the Thessalonians, recalls his ministry and labours among them, and expresses the desire of visiting them. In the parenetic part (chapters 4–5) he urges the Thessalonians to avoid luxury, avarice and laziness, instructs them about the second coming of Christ and the resurrection of the dead, and recommends obedience, peace, love, patience and prayer.

The *Second Letter of Paul to the Thessalonians* is attributed to 'Paul, Silvanus, and Timothy' (1:1a). It was addressed to 'the church of the Thessalonians in God our Father and the Lord Jesus Christ'(1:1b), exactly the same as in 1 Thessalonians. It is dated shortly after 1 Thessalonians, around 51 AD. It has the same common Greek style as 1 Thessalonians. It is considered to have been written by Paul also from Corinth, and its literary genre is that of a personal letter of instruction. The Christians persevered constant in their faith but were still too anxious about the day of Our Lord's coming which they thought was at hand. After thanking God in the opening chapter (chapter 1) for their faith and constancy, St Paul in the doctrinal part of the Epistle (chapter 2) instructs them about Our Lord's coming. The day of Our Lord's coming, though uncertain, is not yet at hand; it will be preceded by certain signs, such as the man of sin, the apostasy of many, the destruction of the adversary. In the parenetic part of the Letter (chapter 3), he urges the Thessalonians to pray and to avoid laziness.

The *First Letter of Paul to Timothy* is attributed to 'Paul, an apostle of Christ Jesus by the command of God our Saviour and of Christ Jesus our hope' (1:1). Its recipient is 'Timothy, my loyal child in the faith' (1:2a). Its language is good, philosophical Greek. If the Letter is truly Pauline, it is dated in the mid–60's AD, near the time of his death. It is uncertain where this letter was written from, maybe Ephesus, the major Pauline centre. Its literary genre is that of a 'Church Order', and is one of the three 'Pastoral Epistles'. Regardless of whether this epistle is seen as a fourth missionary journey not recorded in Acts or as being written at some other point of Paul's life, its intent seems clear that Paul is writing to encourage Timothy on his own ministry. Timothy is now pastor in the Ephesus Church and Paul writes him to tell him to stay there and continue his good work there. Paul had planted the Ephesus church himself putting three years of his blood and tears in to the effort (Acts 19:10; 20:31) and he is well pleased his former student is currently taking the post there. This is most likely a letter written in Paul's late life and can be seen as being among his departing advice to his former student who has risen up in the ranks of church leadership himself. As Paul becomes more aware of his impending end, soon to be at the hands of Nero, he is setting things in order for the next generation. It consists mainly of counsels to Saint Timothy regarding the forms of worship and organization of the Church, and the responsibilities resting on its several members, including *episcopi* ('bishops') and *diaconi* ('deacons'); and secondly of exhortation to faithfulness in maintaining the truth amid surrounding errors, presented as a prophecy of erring teachers to come.

The *Second Letter of Paul to Timothy* is attributed to 'Paul, an apostle of Christ Jesus by the will of God, for the sake of the promise of life that is in Christ Jesus' (1:1). Its recipient is 'Timothy, my beloved child' (1:2a). If the Letter is truly Pauline, it is dated in the late 60's AD just before his death. It is considered to have been written in Greek from Paul's final imprisonment in Rome. It is definitely a single letter, with the literary genre of a 'Testament'; it is one of the three 'Pastoral Epistles'. Its purpose is a personal exhortation to persevere in enduring suffering for the faith.

The *Letter of Paul to Titus* is attributed to 'Paul, a servant (slave) of God and an apostle of Jesus Christ' (part of the long theological introduction – 1:1–3). Its named recipient is 'Titus, my loyal child in the faith we share' (1:4a). Like 1 Timothy, if the Letter is truly Pauline, it is dated in the late 60's AD just before his death. Its composition is dated from the circumstance that it was written after Paul's visit to Crete (Titus 1:5). That visit could not be the one referred to in Acts 27:7, when Paul was on his voyage to Rome as a prisoner, and where he continued a prisoner for two years. Thus traditional exegesis supposes that after his release Paul sailed from Rome into Asia, passing Crete by the way, and that there he left Titus 'to organise everything that still had to be done' (Titus 1:5). Thence he would have gone to Ephesus, where he left Timothy, and from Ephesus to Macedonia, where he wrote the First Epistle to Timothy, and thence, according to the superscription of this epistle, to Nicopolis in Epirus, from which place he wrote to Titus, about A.D. 66 or 67. It is also considered to have been written in Greek from Paul's final imprisonment in Rome. Its literary genre is that of a 'Church Order', and is one of the three 'Pastoral Epistles'. Its purpose is to provide rules for ethical living and guidelines for church leadership.

The *Letter of Paul to Philemon* is attributed to 'Paul, a prisoner of Christ Jesus, and Timothy our brother' (v. 1a). It is addressed to 'Philemon our dear friend and co–worker, to Apphia our sister, to Archippus our fellow soldier, and to the church in your house' (1b–2), who are Paul's friends in Colossae, about 100 miles east of Ephesus. It is dated most likely in the mid–50's AD, in the third period of Paul's missionary activity. It was written in Greek from prison, probably in Ephesus (but possibly in Caesarea or in Rome). Its authenticity is not disputed: it is definitely by Paul. Its literary genre is that of a real personal letter attempting to influence someone. Its purpose is to influence Philemon to free his slave Onesimus, so the latter can work as a missionary with Paul.

The *Letter to the Hebrews* is not explicitly attributed to a specific author; however the mention of 'our brother Timothy' (13:23) has led some people to assume that it was written by Paul. However, even in antiquity doubts were raised about Paul's alleged authorship. The reasons for this controversy are fairly plain. For example, his letters always contain an introduction stating authorship, yet Hebrews includes none such. Also, while much of its theology and

33

teachings may be considered Pauline, it contains many
other ideas which seem to have no such root or influence.
Moreover, the writing style is substantially different from
that of Paul's authentic epistles. In particular, Hebrews
claims to have been written by a person who received the
Christian message from others (Heb 2:3–4) while in his
letter to the Galatians Paul forcefully defends his claim that
he received his gospel directly from Jesus himself. Nevertheless, in the fourth century, the Church largely agreed to
include Hebrews as the fourteenth letter of Paul. Jerome
and Augustine of Hippo were influential in affirming Paul's
authorship. In response to the doubts raised about Paul's
involvement, other possible authors were suggested as
early as the third century AD. Origen (c. 240) suggested that
either Luke the Evangelist or Clement of Rome might be the
author. Tertullian proposed Paul's companion Barnabas, to
whom some non–canonical works are attributed (such as
the *Epistle of Barnabas*). In favour of this hypothesis was the
fact that Barnabas was close to Paul in his ministry, and
exhibited skill with *midrash* of Hebrew Scripture; the other
works attributed to him reinforce the case for his authorship of Hebrews with similar style, voice, and skill.

The recipients named are definitely people familiar with
Jewish rituals. This New Testament book is dated around
the 60's AD. Its language is fairly sophisticated Greek. It is
not certain where this book was written from, it could possibly have been Rome (see a mention of greetings from 'those
from Italy' – 13:24b). It consists of a single writing literary
genre: not really a letter, but an exegetical sermon of exhortation (with an epistolary conclusion only). The purpose of
this Letter was to point out how the New Testament transcends and fulfils the Old. In this way, it tried to convince
the Christian Jews, under the stress of persecution, from
falling back into Judaism, which at the time had taken on a
new vigor and splendor. St Paul describes the dignity of
Christ, of Christ's priesthood and of his office (chapter 1 to
10:27) and warns the Christians not to return to the abro-

gated institutions of the Old Law. In order to encourage his readers he places before them examples of heroic faith in the Old Testament (chapter 11).

The *Letter of James* is attributed to 'James, a servant of God and of the Lord Jesus Christ' (1:1a); this is 'James of Jerusalem,' also called the 'brother of the Lord' (see Mark 6:3; Galatians 1:19). Not numbered among the Twelve Apostles, unless he is identified as James the Less, James was nonetheless a very important figure: Paul described him as 'the brother of the Lord' in Galatians 1:19 and as one of the three pillars of the Church in 2:9. He is traditionally considered the first of the Seventy Disciples. The language of the Letter is fairly elegant Greek. The named recipients are 'the Twelve tribes in the Dispersion' (1:1b), who are Jewish–Christians in the 'Diaspora'. It is dated at the 50's or early 60's AD, before James' death in 62 AD. It was probably written from Jerusalem or elsewhere in Palestine, due to its strong connections with Judaism. The literary genre starts as an encyclical or 'circular letter', but actually it is more like a homily or Jewish 'wisdom literature'. Its purpose is to stress the ethics of Christian living; also it corrects a misunderstanding of Paul's teaching (2:14–26)

The *First Letter of Peter* is attributed to 'Peter, an apostle of Jesus Christ' (1:1a). It is addressed to 'the exiles of the dispersion' in several Roman provinces of northern Asia Minor (1:1b–2). It was definitely written from Rome, since 'Babylon' (5:13) is a code name for Rome. It is dated at the early 60's AD. St Peter wrote this in Greek with the help of a scribe. Some scholars see 4:12–5:11 as a later addition, after some persecution has started. It constitutes a single writing, but possibly incorporating older hymns or statements of faith. The literary genre is an encyclical letter, intended for several different churches at the same time. Its purpose is to argue that Christians are not a threat to Roman social order, since they live ethically.

The *Second Letter of Peter* is attributed to 'Simon Peter, a servant and apostle of Jesus Christ' (1:1a). It is addressed in

Greek 'to those who have received a faith as precious as ours through the righteousness of our God and Saviour Jesus Christ' (1:1b), and is intended for a group of Gentile Christians, possibly in Asia. Some say that this was the last New Testament work written, as late as after 100 AD, but this would compromise the fact of its having been written by Peter. Clearly if Peter the Apostle wrote this epistle, then it must have been written prior to his death around 65–67 AD. Although 2 Peter internally proports to be a work of the Apostle, some biblical scholars have concluded that Peter is not the author, and instead consider the epistle *pseudepigraphical*. Reasons for this judgment include its linguistic differences from 1 Peter, its apparent use of Jude, possible allusions to second–century gnosticism, encouragement in the wake of a delayed parousia, and weak external support. In addition, specific passages offer further clues in support of pseudepigraphy, namely the author's assumption that his audience is familiar with multiple Pauline epistles (2 Peter 3:15–16), his implication that the Apostolic generation has passed (2 Peter 3:4), and his differentiation between himself and 'the apostles of the Lord and Saviour' (2 Peter 3:2).

A number of scholars, however, have disagreed with this position and forwarded reasons in support of genuine Petrine authorship. The text's claim to have been written by 'Simeon Peter' is unique. 'Simeon' is an archaic Hebrew form of the standard 'Simon', and appears only in Acts 15:14, and then just as 'Simeon' (not 'Simeon Peter'). 'Simeon' is not used in any other place in the New Testament, in any of the Apostolic Fathers, or in any pseudepigraphic literature. 1 Peter uses simply 'Peter', and it has been argued that it would be unlikely for a later writer attempting to feign an original letter to use a different name than one used in the genuine text, especially an archaic and obscure naming convention like 'Simeon Peter.' Concerning the relation between 2 Peter and Jude, three observations have been made. First, it could be that, conversely, Jude used 2 Peter, extracting information from it and adding a doxology, perhaps motivated by the prophetic statements of 2 Peter having been fulfilled. Second, even if 2 Peter used Jude, that does not exclude Petrine authorship. If the letter were pseudepigraphy, in many respects it would be unparalleled with other such literature. The common convention in pseudepigraphy, when attempting to further the verisimilitude of their claims to authorship, was to adopt a first–person narrative style; however, 2 Peter's claims do not do so, even in the passage concerning the Transfiguration, where it would be most expected. Furthermore, the account of the Transfiguration differs in certain details from the accounts in the synoptic gospels, unexpected of a forger, and the passage shows a complete lack of embellishment that sets it apart from the trend in apocryphal books. Also unusual is the description of Paul, 'our beloved brother' (2 Pt 3:15). Later literature referred to Paul as 'the blessed Paul', 'the blessed and glorious Paul', and 'the sanctified Paul right blessed', and thus the subdued usage in the letter is more fitting of genuine Petrine use than of a later forgery. Lastly, the statement that the author finds Paul's letters difficult to understand (2 Pt 3:15–16) runs counter to the tendency in pseudoepigraphy, which is to enhance the heroic alleged author. The Letter was probably written from Rome. The literary genre is a 'Testament,' but in the form of a letter. Its purpose is to emphasize apostolic teaching, ethical teachings, Christian hope.

The *First Letter of John* is attributed to no particular author and no specific recipients are named. It is clearly intended for one part of the Johannine community after it was divided. It is dated around 100 AD some time after the Gospel according to John was written. The language is a Greek with similar vocabulary but a somewhat different style from the Fourth Gospel. It was probably written from Ephesus, as traditionally maintained. Tradition holds that it was composed by St John the Apostle and Evangelist. One part may have been a later addition (5:6–8). The literary genre is not really a 'letter'; more like a homily or a treatise. Its purpose is to exhort readers to 'remain' with traditional Christian teachings about Jesus and to love one another; it warns them against errors associated with false interpretations of the Fourth Gospel. St John warns the Christians against certain heretics who denied Christ's divinity (Ebionites) or who denied that Christ came in the flesh (later called Docetists). The Apostle briefly explains the doctrines of the Incarnation and the Redemption and urges all to practice charity.

The *Second Letter of John* is attributed to 'the elder' (v. 1a), traditionally the same author as the Fourth Gospel. It is addressed 'to the elect lady and her children whom I love in the truth' (v. 1b–2), some part of the Johannine church after it has undergone a division. It is dated around 100 AD some time after the Gospel according to John was written. The language is a Greek with similar vocabulary but a somewhat different style from the Fourth Gospel. It was probably written from Ephesus, as traditionally maintained. Tradition holds that it was composed by St John the Apostle and Evangelist. The literary genre is a real letter. St John urges the Christians to preserve the faith, practice charity, and avoid heretics who were teaching that Christ did not come in the flesh (v.7).

The *Third Letter of John* is attributed to is attributed to 'the elder' (v. 1a), traditionally the same author as the Fourth Gospel. It is addressed 'to the beloved Gaius, whom I love in truth' (v. 1b), a leader of some Johannine church. It is dated around 100 AD some time after the Gospel according to John was written. The language is a Greek with similar vocabulary but a somewhat different style from the Fourth Gospel. It was probably written from Ephesus, as traditionally maintained. Tradition holds that it was composed by St John the Apostle and Evangelist. It may actually have been sent together at the same time as 1 John and 2 John. The literary genre is a real, personal letter. Its purpose is to praise Gaius for his hospitality, and to attack a rival Christian leader named Diotrephes.

The *Letter of Jude* is attributed to 'Jude, a servant of Jesus Christ and brother of James' (v. 1a; see Mark 6:3). Its named recipients are 'those who are called, who are beloved in God the Father and kept safe for Jesus Christ' (v. 1b), Jewish–Christians in some unknown area, possibly in or near Palestine. It was written in Greek, but the time is uncertain, maybe as early as the 50's AD. It was probably written from Jerusalem or nearby in Palestine, or even possibly Alexandria. The literary genre is a letter of exhortation and encouragement, incorporating some apocalyptic ideas. Its purpose is to warn the readers against false teachings which denied Christ's Divinity, His teachings and His second coming, blasphemed the angels, and inculcated pagan vices. St Jude bids the Christians to stand firm in the faith delivered to the saints, and exhorts them to live moral lives.

The *Book of Revelation* (or the *Book of the Apocalypse*) is attributed to 'John' (1:1, 4, 9), traditionally held to be the brother of James, son of Zebedee, named in the Gospels, the author of the 'Fourth Gospel' and the 'Johannine Epistles'. The traditional view holds that John the Apostle — considered to have written the Gospel and epistles by the same name — was exiled on Patmos in the Aegean archipelago during the reign of Emperor Domitian, and wrote the Revelation there. Those in favour of a single common author point to similarities between the Gospel and Revelation. For example, both works are soteriological (e.g. referring to Jesus as a lamb) and possess a high Christology, stressing Jesus' divine nature. In the Gospel of John and in Revelation, Jesus is referred to as 'the Word of God' (Ὅ λογος του θεου). Explanations of the differences among John's works by proponents of the single–author view include the presence of underlying motifs and purposes, authorial target audience, the author's collaboration with or utilization of different scribes and the advanced age of John the Apostle when he wrote Revelation. The named recipients are the 'seven churches' in Asia Minor (1:4; 2:1–22). It is dated around the mid–90's AD, near the end of the reign of Emperor Domitian (who died in 96 AD). It was written in highly symbolic Greek, including some Semitic influences, from the Roman Province of Asia (possibly the city of Ephesus itself). It constitutes a single work, but possible composed in stages, incorporating some older apocalyptic materials. The literary genre is an 'apocalypse' (1:1; 4:1), in an epistolary frame, with a letter–like introduction and conclusion (1:4; 22:21). Its purpose is to encourage Christians to preserve faith in the midst of trials and tribulations (cf. 13:10b; 14:12).

Notes

1. See St Augustine, *Quaest. in Hept.* 2, 73 in *PL* 34, 623: '*Novum Testamentum in Vetere latet, Vetus in Novo patet.*' The expression can also be translated as follows: 'The New is in the Old concealed, the Old is in the New revealed.' Or else: 'The New is in the Old enfolded; the Old is in the New unfolded.' See also Vatican II, *Dei Verbum*, 16.

2. See F. Flatman, *The New Testament and the Roman World* (2004), as yet unpublished.

3. See Matthew 27:3–10: 'When Judas, who had betrayed him, saw that Jesus was condemned, he was seized with remorse and returned the thirty silver coins (argurion) to the chief priests and the elders. "I have sinned," he said, "for I have betrayed innocent blood." "What is that to us"' they replied. "That's your responsibility." So Judas threw the money into the temple and left. Then he went away and hanged himself. The chief priests picked up the coins (argurion) and said, "It is against the law to put this into the treasury, since it is blood money." So they decided to use the money to buy the potter's field as a burial place for foreigners. That is why it has been called the Field of Blood to this day. Then what was spoken by Jeremiah the prophet was fulfilled: "They took the thirty silver coins (argurion), the price set on him by the people of Israel, and they used them to buy the potter's field, as the

Lord commanded me."' See also Zechariah 11:12–13: 'I told them, "If you think it best, give me my pay; but if not, keep it." So they paid me thirty pieces of silver. And the Lord said to me, "Throw it to the potter" — the handsome price at which they priced me! So I took the thirty pieces of silver and threw them into the house of the Lord to the potter.'

4. See Luke 19:12–24. Therefore Jesus said: 'A certain nobleman went into a far country to receive for himself a kingdom and to return. So he called ten of his servants, delivered to them ten minas, and said to them, "Do business till I come." But his citizens hated him, and sent a delegation after him, saying, "We will not have this man to reign over us." And so it was that when he returned, having received the kingdom, he then commanded these servants, to whom he had given the money, to be called to him, that he might know how much every man had gained by trading. Then came the first, saying, "Master, your mina has earned ten minas." And he said to him, "Well done, good servant; because you were faithful in a very little, have authority over ten cities." And the second came, saying, "Master, your mina has earned five minas." Likewise he said to him, "You also be over five cities." Then another came, saying, "Master, here is your mina, which I have kept put away in a handkerchief. For I feared you, because you are an austere man. You collect what you did not deposit, and reap what you did not sow." And he said to him, "Out of your own mouth I will judge you, you wicked servant. You knew that I was an austere man, collecting what I did not deposit and reaping what I did not sow. Why then did you not put my money in the bank, that at my coming I might have collected it with interest?" And he said to those who stood by, "Take the mina from him, and give it to him who has ten minas."'

5. See Matthew 17:24. After Jesus and his disciples arrived in Capernaum, the collectors of the two–drachma tax came to Peter and asked, 'Doesn't your teacher pay the temple tax?' 'Yes, he does,' he replied. When Peter came into the house, Jesus was the first to speak. 'What do you think, Simon?' He asked. 'From whom do the kings of the earth collect duty and taxes— from their own sons or from others?' 'From others,' Peter answered. 'Then the sons are exempt,' Jesus said to him.

'But so that we may not offend them, go to the lake and throw out your line. Take the first fish you catch; open its mouth and you will find a four–drachma coin (Stater). Take it and give it to them for my tax and yours.'

6. See Luke 15:8–10: 'Or suppose a woman has ten silver coins (Drachma) and loses one. Does she not light a lamp, sweep the house and search carefully until she finds it? And when she finds it, she calls her friends and neighbours together and says, "Rejoice with me; I have found my lost coin." In the same way, I tell you, there is rejoicing in the presence of the angels of God over one sinner who repents.'

7. See Matthew 10:29: 'Are not two sparrows sold for a penny (Assarius)? Yet not one of them will fall to the ground apart from the will of your Father.'

8. See Mark 12:42: 'But a poor widow came and put in two very small copper coins (Lepton), worth only a fraction of a penny.'

9. In the Old Testament book of the prophet Ezekiel (Ez 45:12), the shekel is said to consist of twenty gerahs.

10. Based on a compilation by Prof. Felix Just, S.J..

11. These summaries include material from Prof. Felix Just, S.J..

12. In Greek we see σπεκουλατορα ('soldier of the guard', Mk 6:27), ξεστων a Greek corruption of sextarius ('pitcher', Mk 7:4), κοδραντης ('penny', Mk 12:42), κεντυριων ('centurion', Mk 15:39, 44–45).

13. For more on St Luke's treatment of the Mother of God, see chapter 6, subsection 6.2.3–6.2.7 below.

14. St Irenaeus, *Against the heresies*, 3,1.

15. Cited by Eusebius, *Ecclesiastical History*, 6,14.

16. D. A. Carson, D. J. Moo, L. Morris, *An Introduction to the New Testament* (Leicester: Apollos, 1999), p. 181.

2

New Testament evidence

We account the Scriptures of God to be the most sublime philosophy. I find more sure marks of authenticity in the Bible than in any profane history whatsoever.
Sir Isaac Newton, Optics

Since it is from the New Testament that we gain our primary knowledge of Jesus, it is fitting to ask whether this literature is sound and historically accurate. Critics often falsely describe the Gospels as pious legend, having no historical competence, and designed only for propaganda purposes. It is acknowledged that the following facts give immense weight to the historical accuracy of the New Testament. One scholar has remarked in this regard: 'The excessive skepticism shown toward the Bible [by certain schools of thought] has been progressively discredited. Discovery after discovery has established the accuracy of numerous details.'[1]

2.1 The Bible is Unique

The New Testament is unique in several ways. First, it is unique in its continuity. Despite its various authors, languages, locations, there is one main message. This is the proof from convergence. Second, the New Testament is unique in its circulation. It was the first major book ever printed, in 1450 as the Latin vulgate on the Gutenberg press. It has been read by more people than any other book ever written. Third, the New Testament is unique in its translation: by the year 2000, the Bible had been translated into nearly 4000 languages. The New Testament is unique in its survival. While in 303 Diocletian issued an edict that every Bible be destroyed, it survived and indeed thrived. The Bible flourished in adversity. The New Testament is unique in its influence claims; two thousand years on, the New Testament proclaims 'this is what the Lord says' and continues to influence and inspire. Such impact is seen, for example, in the fact that it inspired many movies including *The Passion of the Christ* by Mel Gibson.

2.2 *The Manuscript Evidence*

We do not, of course, possess the 'originals' or 'autographs', as they are called. These have perished. However, we know what they looked like. It was common practice in the Greco–Roman world for people to write on wax tablets, which were made of a piece of wood that had been coated with wax. Whatever was inscribed on the tablets could be easily erased by simply rubbing it out. People also wrote on pottery shards and other such materials. However, when people wanted to write something for more official purposes or for preservation, they might write on papyrus. That is what happened with the New Testament. All were papyrus rolls. The papyrus (from which comes our word 'paper') is a plant of the sedge family which grows abundantly in marshy spots like the Nile Delta. When the old paper–makers set to work, their first task was to extract the pith from the papyrus reeds and cut it into fine strips. These strips they laid side by side vertically before crossing them with others horizontally, to form a page, generally about ten inches long and five broad. The rough sheets were then soaked in water and treated with gum, and after drying in the sun and polishing with an ivory roller were ready for use. All you needed now was a reed pen (*kalamos*) cut with a pen–knife into proper shape and some ink made from soot, gum and water. (In 2 John 12 and 3 John 13 you will find mention of such pen and ink.) If you had skill at it, you would do your own writing; but if you were a busy man, you might dictate to a scribe (cf. Rm 16.22: 'I Tertius, who took this letter down, add my Christian greetings').

A single papyrus sheet would suffice for a short letter like Paul's to Philemon. For longer works like Luke's Gospel you had to join many sheets together to form a roll, perhaps thirty feet long. If the roll was meant to be read often, it would be equipped with a stick at each end, for winding and unwinding. Such was the format of the New Testament autographs. But if these have perished, can we be confident that we know what was originally written on them? After all, for about 1400 years (roughly from AD 100 to 1450, the years between the writing of the books and the invention of printing) the New Testament was copied by hand. To err is human, and copying by hand perforce produces a crop of errors. No scribe, however expert, can avoid occasional mistakes. No later copyist finding such mistakes is likely to resist the temptation to correct his predecessors' slips. Thus errors arise and are perpetuated. Since the New Testament ran these risks for so many centuries, can we be sure that the best text we have today is close to what the original writers wrote? The answer is : We can, thanks to the discovery of thousands of New Testament manuscripts and the study done on them by experts called 'textual critics'.

Since we don't have the original Biblical writings (autographs), the question is, 'How accurate are the copies?' The confidence that we actually have reliable copies of the originals comes from four main areas:

(1) There are a massive number of copies of the original manuscripts, 5,000 complete New Testaments, far greater than those of other ancient books, religious and secular. These copies, upon comparison to one another, show by their uniformity how carefully and accurately they must have been copied from the originals.

(2) The time period from the writing of the original and their copying is extremely small. The shorter this period is,

the smaller the possibility of any tampering. The New Testament books were massively and rapidly copied and distributed throughout the quickly–expanding Christian world. The earliest manuscript known is a papyrus fragment containing portions of the verses of John 18:31–33,37–38. It is dated with certainty to at least as early as AD 125. It is housed at the John Rylands Library in Manchester. There are also two Greek fragments from the Dead Sea Scrolls that may very well be from the Gospel according to Mark and 1 Timothy. Both of these fragments date to before AD 70. The earliest complete copy of the New Testament is the Codex Sinaiticus which dates to the AD 300's. It is on public display in the British Museum in London.

Figure 4: Rylands Library Papyrus P52 recto, also known as the St John's fragment

(3) The New Testament documents were translated into several other languages at an early date; translation was rare in the ancient world, so this is an added plus for the New Testament. The translators held that the message was vital. The Greek New Testament was translated into Syrian, Egyptian, Coptic, Latin and other languages before 100 AD. Again, translation into a new language ensures the originals from being tampered with. There is thus a principle of mutual corroboration between translation and reliability.

(4) Apart from these manuscripts, including translations, we can reconstruct 98% of the New Testament through writings (secondary sources) from the first century that quote it. Indeed these citations are so extensive that if all other sources of our knowledge of the text of the New Testament were destroyed, they would be sufficient alone for the reconstruction of practically the entire New Testament.[2] Thus we can extrapolate and converge to an inspired New Testament. Therefore, to tamper with the New Testament, one would have to make an addition or deletion to the original before any copies were made, originals which the Church Fathers would have guarded with their lives. Alternatively, one would need to obtain all the copies, and correct them, plus any copies translated into new languages, as well as to get hold of any letter quoting a New Testament book. The conclusion is that the Bible has far stronger manuscript support than any other work of ancient literature, including the works of Plato, Aristotle, Caesar and Tacitus and so forth.

So what does this mean, that the works of Plato are of questionable accuracy? Of course not. However, if you choose to discount the Bible because of the time lag between the writing of its original manuscripts and its copies, you should, on the same basis, discount the accuracy and truthfulness of every other literary work of the ancient world. In all of the ancient Greek and Latin literature, the Iliad by Homer ranks next to the New Testament in the greatest number of manuscripts in existence.

Figure 5: Timescale comparison between New Testament and other ancient books

Work	Accuracy of copies	When written	Earliest copy	Time span between original and copy	N° of copies
Lucretius		died 55 or 53 BC		1100 years	2
Pliny		61-113 AD	850 AD	750 years	7
Plato		427-347 BC	900 AD	1200 years	7
Demos-thenes		4th Cent. BC	1100 AD	800 years	8
Herodotus		480-425 BC	900 AD	1300 years	8
Suetonius		75-160 AD	950 AD	800 years	8
Thucydides		460-400 BC	900 AD	1300 years	8
Euripides		480-406 BC	1100 AD	1300 years	9
Aristo-phanes		450-385 BC	900 AD	1200 years	10
Caesar		100-44 BC	900 AD	1000 years	10
Livy		59 BC-AD 17		???	20
Tacitus		circa 100 AD	1100 AD	1000 years	20
Aristotle		384-322 BC	1100 AD	1400 years	49
Sophocles		496-406 BC	1000 AD	1400 years	193
Homer (Iliad)	95%	900 BC	400 BC	500 years	643
New Testament	99+%	50-100 AD	125 AD	25 years	5000

There are in existence over 5,000 complete or partial Greek manuscripts of the New Testament (the original language in which it was written). In total, there are over 24,000 extant manuscripts of the complete New Testament or portions of it, if copies in different languages are included. Notice in the following table some of the distinctive features of the New Testament when compared to one of the most reliable writings in ancient literature, the Iliad.

Bruce Metzger, a textual scholar, has compared the accuracy of the New Testament to that of other works of antiquity using various textual tests. He has determined that of the 15,600 lines in the Iliad, 764 of them are in question while of the 20,000 lines of the New Testament, 40 are in doubt (about 400 words). These are the accuracy figures in the table. Furthermore, none of the questionable words profoundly affects the message of the New Testament text.

2.2.1 English Translations of the Bible

Why are there so many different English translations of the Bible? And why can't churches or scholars agree on just one translation? The answer consists of several points. First, no original manuscript of any biblical book has survived. All of the texts written by the biblical authors themselves have been lost or destroyed over the centuries. All we have are copies of copies of copies, most of them copied hundreds of years after the original texts were written. Second, *the extant manuscripts contain numerous textual variations.* There are literally thousands of differences in the surviving biblical manuscripts, many of them minor (spelling variations, synonyms, different word orders), but some of them major (whole sections missing or added). Third, important old manuscripts were found in the last 200 years. Recent discoveries of older manuscripts (especially the Dead Sea Scrolls and the *Codex Sinaiticus*) have helped scholars get *closer* to the original text of the Bible, so that modern translations can be more accurate than medieval ones. Fourth, the meanings of some biblical texts are unknown or uncertain. Some Hebrew or Greek words occur only once in the Bible, but nowhere else in ancient literature, so their exact meanings are unknown; and some biblical phrases are ambiguous, with more than one possible meaning. Fifth, ancient languages are very different from modern languages. Not only do Ancient Hebrew and Greek use completely different alphabets and vocabularies, but their grammatical rules and structures (word order, prepositions, conjugations of verbs, and so forth) are very different from modern English. Sixth, every 'translation' is already inevitably an 'interpretation'. Anyone who knows more than one modern language realizes that 'translations' often have meanings that are slightly different from the original, and that different people inevitably translate the same texts in slightly different ways. Finally, all living languages continually change and develop over time. Not only is 'Modern English' very different from sixteenth century English, but the linguistic expressions adopted in America, Britain, Australia, and other countries are slightly different from each other (in spelling, grammar, idioms, word meanings, and so forth).

There are two basic philosophies or styles of *translation*, 'formal correspondence' and 'dynamic equivalence.' Other popular versions of the Bible in English are *not* really 'translations' but are 'paraphrases' instead. 'Formal Correspondence Translations' try to stick as closely as possible to the original wording and word–order of the Hebrew and Greek texts. Thus they may seem more accurate or 'literal,' but often require detailed explanations in footnotes to avoid being misinterpreted by modern readers. They are good for in–depth academic study of the Bible, but may be less suited for public proclamation, since they can be difficult to understand when heard or read aloud. Among Formal Correspondence translations can be found the Douay–Rheims Bible, the King James Version and New King James Version, the Revised Standard Version, New Revised Standard Version, the New American Bible, and the New International Version.

Figure 6: English translations of the Bible

Older Translations	Updated Translations
Douay-Rheims (1582 NT; 1609-1610 OT)	(some revisions 1749 and 1941, but no recent revision)
King James Version (KJV - 1611)	New King James Version (NKJV - 1979-1982)
Revised Standard Version (RSV - 1946 NT; 1952 OT)	New Revised Standard Version (NRSV - 1989)
Amplified Bible (AB - 1958 NT; 1964-65 OT)	(combined edition reprinted in 1987, but not revised)
New English Bible (NEB - 1961)	Revised English Bible (REB - 1992)
Today's English Version (TEV - 1966)	Contemporary English Version (CEV - 1996)
Jerusalem Bible (JB - 1966)	New Jerusalem Bible (NJB - 1985)
New American Bible (NAB - 1970)	(only the NT and Psalms revised as of 1987)
New International Version (NIV - 1973 NT; 1978 OT)	(not yet revised)

'Dynamic Equivalence Translations' try to put the sense of the original text into the best modern English, remaining close to the ideas expressed but not always following the exact wording or word–order of the Hebrew or Greek originals. Thus they may seem less 'literal' than the formal correspondence translations, but can be just as 'faithful' to the original text, and are therefore generally better suited for public proclamation or liturgical use. Among Dynamic Equivalence translations are to be found the New English

Bible and the Revised English Bible, Today's English Version and the Contemporary English Version, the Jerusalem Bible and the New Jerusalem Bible.

'Biblical Paraphrases' are *not* (and do not even claim to be) accurate translations, although they are usually still called 'Bibles.' These popular books (especially those intended for children or teenagers, and the 'Living Bible' of 1971) not only condense and omit much of the material, but they freely change the wording of the original texts to make the stories easier to understand and/or more 'relevant' for their intended readers.

For example, the system of measuring time in ancient Israel was very different from our own. They counted twelve hours from sunrise to sundown, and subdivided the night into three (or sometimes four) 'watches.' Thus the same time that is called 'the eleventh hour' in a formal correspondence translation would be translated 'five o'clock in the afternoon' in a dynamic equivalence version (and might simply say 'in the late afternoon' in a biblical paraphrase).

Since there are over 500 different English translations of the Bible, the above chart lists only a few of the most popular or important ones. The Authorized Version (AV) is another name for the KJV; the Good News Bible (GNB) is exactly the same as TEV. Many other *editions* of the Bible are based on the above *translations*; the *Oxford Annotated Bible* uses the RSV, the *Catholic Study Bible* uses the NAB, and the *HarperCollins Study Bible* uses the NRSV; so these are *not* separate translations. For academic study of the Bible by anyone who does not know Hebrew or Greek, it is good to *compare at least three or four different modern translations*; it is wise to use at least one 'dynamic equivalence' and one 'formal correspondence' translation. If one adopts other translations, it is helpful to try and find out *when* they were translated, by whom, and what translation philosophy was used.

Among Catholic translations of the bible are to be found

the Douay–Rheims Bible, the Jerusalem Bible and the New Jerusalem Bible, and the New American Bible. Among Protestant translations are the King James Version and New King James Version, Today's English Version and the Contemporary English Version, the New International Version. Ecumenical translations, approved and used by *both* Catholics and Protestants, include the New English Bible and the Revised English Bible, the Revised Standard Version, and the New Revised Standard Version.

2.3 Eyewitness Credential

The reliability of Scripture is also confirmed through the eyewitness credentials of the authors. Moses, for example, participated in and was an eyewitness to some remarkable events: Israel's captivity in Egypt, the Exodus, the Forty Years in the Desert, and Israel's final encampment before entering the Promised Land, all of which are accurately chronicled in the Old Testament. Even sceptical authorities grudgingly agree that the Old Testament is a remarkably accurate historical document. The New Testament has an even more penetrating eyewitness authenticity. Matthew and John were with Jesus during His ministry, being two of the original twelve apostles called by Jesus. Mark, according to early Church fathers wrote his gospel, as delivered to him by another eyewitness, the Apostle Peter. Luke, though not an eyewitness of Christ, gathered the testimonies of numerous eyewitnesses and all available records, then sifted through the data, 'carefully investigating everything' regarding the life of Jesus (Luke 1:1–3). The epistles too, were written by eyewitnesses–Paul, Peter, John, James. The eyewitness testimony provided bedrock confidence to the hearers and writers that their teaching was reliable. Peter, for example, reminded his readers that the disciples 'did not follow cleverly invented stories' but were 'eyewitnesses of His majesty' (2 Peter 1:16). Many New Testament authors later died for refusing to deny their testimonies, illustrating their certainty that what they wrote was the Truth.

2.3.1 The notion of Apostle[3]

For the idea of who were the Twelve, see Matthew 10:2–4: 'Now the names of the twelve apostles are these: The first, Simon, who is called Peter, and Andrew his brother; and James the son of Zebedee, and John his brother; Philip and Bartholomew; Thomas and Matthew the tax–gatherer; James the son of Alphaeus, and Thaddaeus; Simon the Zealot, and Judas Iscariot, the one who betrayed Him.'

The title of apostle was gradually extended beyond those who constituted the group of the Twelve. Matthias was elected to fill the place left by Judas, and so was listed as one of the twelve Apostles (Ac 1:15–26). James, mentioned in the Letter to the Galatians, is no longer considered to be James the son of Alphaeus, but rather one who had known Jesus and who had a certain prominence in the primitive Church. He is regarded as enjoying apostolic power (Gal 1:19; 2:9). The title of apostle was also assigned to Paul and Barnabas (Ac 14:4, 14). The progression in the use of this title is seen in St Paul's description of the appearances of the risen Christ: 'First He appeared to Cephas and secondly to the Twelve. Next He appeared to more than five hundred of the brothers at the same time, most of whom are still alive, though some have died; then He appeared to James, and then to all the apostles; and last of all He appeared to me too' (1 Co 15:5–8). The office of being an apostle involved an investiture which consisted of the laying–on of hands and a prayer, as can be seen in the case of Paul and Barnabas (Ac 13:3). Those who were apostles, but not numbered among the Twelve shared in common with the Twelve an episcopal power and also the privilege of having seen the risen Christ, and sharing the foundational quality of the experience of the early Church. However, being part of the Twelve involves more: it means having been present the whole time the Lord Jesus was exercising His ministry, and sharing the experience of the Paschal Mystery (Ac 1:21–22). A disciple is a *follower* of Jesus; an Apostle is one who is *sent* by Jesus. Most of the New Testament was written by eyewitnesses of Jesus or their disciples.

2.4 External Confirmation

2.4.1 Secular

Despite the fact that the Incarnation of the Son of God took place in the greatest humility, nevertheless secular historians, caught up by more stirring events and by famous personages, made passing but significant, references to Him.[4]

In his *Annals*, written between the years 115 and 120AD, Tacitus reports the burning of Rome in the year 64, falsely attributed by Nero to the Christians, and makes explicit reference to Christ: 'Yet no human effort, no princely largesse nor offerings to the gods could make that infamous rumour disappear that Nero had somehow ordered the fire. Therefore, in order to abolish that rumour, Nero falsely accused and executed with the most exquisite punishments those people called Christians, who were infamous for their abominations. The originator of the name, Christ, was executed as a criminal by the procurator Pontius Pilate during the reign of Tiberius.'[5] Suetonius also, in his biography of the Emperor Claudius, written around 121AD, informs us that the Jews were expelled from Rome because 'under the instigation of a certain Chrestus they stirred up frequent riots.'[6] This passage is generally interpreted as referring to Jesus Christ, who had become a source of contention within Jewish circles in Rome. To understand why the form *Chrestus* was used, it is necessary to know that in the first century, the Greek words *christòs* (meaning anointed) e *chrestòs* (meaning 'the best') were pronounced in the same way. Thus Suetonius probably made a mistake and thought that the head of this 'new sect' was called 'the best' rather than 'the anointed one.'

Also of importance as proof of the rapid spread of Christianity is the testimony of Pliny the Younger, the Governor of Bithynia, in his report to the Emperor Trajan, between the years 111 and 113: 'especially on account of the number of those that are in danger; for there are many of every age, of every rank, and of both sexes, who are now and hereafter likely to be called to account, and to be in danger; for this superstition is spread like a contagion, not only into cities and towns, but into country villages also, which yet there is reason to hope may be stopped and corrected.' Pliny the Younger said that the Christians themselves affirmed that 'they were wont, on a stated day, to meet together before it was light, and to sing a hymn to Christ, as to a god, alternately; and to oblige themselves by a sacrament [or oath], not to do anything that was ill: but that they would commit no theft, or pilfering, or adultery; that they would not break their promises, or deny what was deposited with them, when it was required back again; after which it was their custom to depart, and to meet again at a common but innocent meal.'[7]

Lucian of Samosata, the Greek satirist, wrote this rather scathing attack in The Death of Peregrine around AD 170:

> The Christians, you know, worship a man to this day
> – the distinguished personage who introduced their
> novel rites, and was crucified on that account... You
> see, these misguided creatures start with the general
> conviction that they are immortal for all time, which
> explains the contempt of death and voluntary
> self–devotion which are so common among them;
> and then it was impressed upon them by their
> original lawgiver that they are all brothers, from the
> moment that they are converted, and deny the gods
> of Greece, and worship the crucified sage, and live
> after his laws.[8]

2.4.2 Jewish

Some references to Christ are found for example in *The Antiquities of the Jews,* a work compiled in Rome between the years 93 and 94 by the historian Flavius Josephus

(37–110 AD), a Jewish historian, who was well disposed to the Romans, and served Vespasian and his son Titus, who both became emperors. He wrote various historical works in Greek, including *The Antiquities of the Jews*, which describes Jewish history from Abraham until the time of Flavius himself. A passage is to be found in book eighteen, which is cited also by St Eusebius of Caesarea:

> Now there was about this time (30 AD) Jesus, a wise man, if it be lawful to call him a man; for he was a doer of wonderful works, a teacher of such men as receive the truth with pleasure. He drew over to him both many of the Jews and many of the Gentiles. He was [the] Christ. And when Pilate, at the suggestion of the principal men amongst us, had condemned him to the cross, those that loved him at the first did not forsake him; for he appeared to them alive again the third day; as the divine prophets had foretold these and ten thousand other wonderful things concerning him. And the tribe of Christians, so named from him, are not extinct at this day.[9]

The Talmud is essentially the collection of Jewish oral traditions that were put into writing with additional commentary between the years of AD 70 and 200. From the Babylonian Talmud, we read:

> On the eve of the Passover Yeshu was hanged. For forty days before the execution took place, a herald went forth and cried, 'He is going forth to be stoned because he has practiced sorcery and enticed Israel to apostasy. Any one who can say anything in his favor, let him come forward and plead on his behalf.' But since nothing was brought forward in his favour he was hanged on the eve of the Passover![10]

The facts in this passage are somewhat difficult to assimilate. Although *Yeshu* refers to Jesus, the announcement that he was to be stoned is followed by the statement that he was hanged (crucified). One possible explanation is that the Jewish leadership's call for his stoning preceded his eventual arrest by at least those forty days. This would be consistent with Scripture's accounts of his numerous near–stonings (John 10:31–33, 11:8).

2.4.3 Christian

The fact that the Apostles spread the Christian faith so quickly and were willing to die for it, illustrated the words of St Paul: 'God's folly is wiser than human wisdom, and God's weakness is stronger than human strength' (1 Co 1:25). St John Chrysostom commented on this passage of Scripture and affirmed:

> What great labours did Plato endure, and his followers, discoursing to us about a line, and an angle, and a point, and about numbers even and odd, and equal unto one another and unequal, and such–like spider webs... How greatly did he labour, endeavouring to show that the soul was immortal! But the Cross wrought persuasion by means of unlearned men; yes, it persuaded even the whole world: and not about common things, but concerning God, and the godliness which is according to truth, and the evangelical way of life, and the judgment of the things to come. And of all men it made philosophers: the very rustics, the utterly unlearned. Behold how 'the foolishness of God is wiser than men,' and 'His weakness stronger?' How 'stronger?' Because it overran the whole world, and gripped all people, and while countless men were endeavouring to extinguish the Name of the Crucified, the contrary came to pass: that it flourished and increased more and more, but they perished and wasted away....For the noble things which publicans and fishermen were able to effect by the grace of God, these, philosophers, and rhetoricians, and tyrants, and in short the whole world, running ten thousand ways here and there, could not even form a notion of. For what did not the Cross introduce? The doctrine concerning the Immortality of the Soul; that concerning the

Resurrection of the Body; that concerning the contempt of things present; that concerning the desire of things future.

As Paul said, God's weakness is stronger than human strength. It is clear from this, that the Gospel is divine. How else could it have occurred to twelve ignorant men to attempt such great enterprises? Men who sojourned in marshes, in rivers, in deserts; who never at any time perhaps had entered into a city nor into a forum. Whence did it occur to them, to set themselves in array against the whole world? For that they were timid and unmanly, he shows who wrote of them, not apologizing, nor enduring to throw their failings into the shade: which indeed of itself is a very great token of the truth. What then does he say about them? That when Christ was apprehended, after so many miracles, they fled; and he who remained, being the leader of the rest, denied. How was it then that they who when Christ was alive, could not resist the attack of the Jews. Yet now that He was dead and buried, and as you say, had not risen again, nor had any talk with them, nor infused courage into them, whence did they set themselves in array against so great a world? Would they not have said among themselves, 'What does this mean? He Himself was not able to save, and will He protect us? He Himself did not defend us when He alive, and will He stretch out His hand to us now that He is dead? He Himself, when alive, did not subdue even one nation; and are we to convince the whole world by uttering His Name?' How, I ask, could all this be reasonable, I will not say, as something to be done, but even as something to be imagined? From this it is plain that had they not seen Him after He was risen, and received most ample proof of His power, they would not have risked so great a gamble.[11]

Early Church leaders such as Eusebius, St Irenaeus and Pope St Clement I of Rome (see *Epistle to the Corinthians*, a follow on from St Paul's letter), all writing before 250 AD, also shed light on the New Testament's historical accuracy. Eusebius, a friend of John the Apostle was an historian who preserved the writings of Papias, bishop of Heirespolis (130 AD), and wrote:

> The Elder (the Apostle John) used to say this also: 'Mark, having been the interpreter of Peter, wrote down accurately all that he [Peter] mentioned, whether saying or doing of Christ, not, however in order. For he was neither a hearer nor a companion of the Lord; but afterwards, as I said, he accompanied Peter, who adapted his teachings as necessity required, not as though he were making a compilation of the sayings of the Lord. So then Mark made no mistake writing down in this way some things as he mentioned them; for he paid attention to this one thing, not to omit anything that he had heard, not to include any false statement among them.'[12]

St Irenaeus was Bishop of Lyons (180 AD) and a student of Polycarp who was Bishop of Smyrna. Polycarp had been a Christian for 86 years and was a disciple of John the Apostle. Irenaeus wrote:

> Matthew published his gospel among the Hebrews in their own tongue, when Peter and Paul were preaching the gospel in Rome and founding the church there. After their departure, Mark the disciple and interpreter of Peter, himself handed down to us in writing the substance of Peter's preaching. Luke, the follower of Paul, set down in a book the gospel preached by his teacher. Then, John, the disciple of the Lord, who also leaned on his breast himself produced his gospel, while he was living at Ephesus in Asia.[13]

2.5 Archaeological Research verifies Scripture

It would be extremely difficult for the honest sceptic to dispute the overwhelming archaeological support for the historical accuracy of both the Old and New Testaments. Numerous items discussed in the Bible such as nations, important people, customary practices, and so forth have been verified by archaeological evidence. Bible critics have often been embarrassed by discoveries that corroborated Bible accounts they had previously deemed to be myth, such as the existence of the Hittites, King David, and Pontius Pilate, just to name a few. The noted Jewish archaeologist Nelson Glueck summed it up very well: 'It may be clearly stated categorically that no archaeological discovery has ever controverted a single biblical reference. Scores of archaeological findings have been made which confirm in clear outline or exact detail historical statements in the Bible.'[14]

When compared against secular accounts of history, the Bible always demonstrates amazing superiority. The noted biblical scholar R.D. Wilson, who was fluent in 45 ancient languages and dialects, meticulously analyzed 29 kings from 10 different nations, each of which had corroborating archaeological artefacts. Each king was mentioned in the Bible as well as documented by secular historians, thus offering a means of comparison. Wilson showed that the names as recorded in the Bible matched the artefacts perfectly, down to the last jot and tittle! The Bible was also completely accurate in its chronological order of the kings. On the other hand, Wilson showed that the secular accounts were often inaccurate and unreliable. Famous historians such as the Librarian of Alexandria, Ptolemy, and Herodotus failed to document the names correctly, almost always misspelling their names. In many cases the names were barely recognizable when compared to its respective artefact or monument, and sometimes required other evidence to extrapolate the reference.

One of the more overwhelming testimonies regarding the depth of archaeological evidence for the New Testament is in the account of the famous historian and archaeologist Sir William Ramsay. Ramsay was very sceptical of the accuracy of the New Testament, and he ventured to Asia Minor over a century ago to refute its historicity. He especially took interest in Luke's accounts in the Gospel of Luke and the Book of Acts, which contain numerous geographical and historic references. Dig after dig the evidence without fail supported Luke's accounts. Governors mentioned by Luke that many historians never believe existed were confirmed by the evidence excavated by Ramsay's archaeological team. Without a single error, Luke was accurate in naming 32 countries, 54 cities, and 9 islands. Ramsay became so overwhelmed with the evidence he eventually converted to Christianity. Ramsay finally had this to say: 'I began with a mind unfavourable to it...but more recently I found myself brought into contact with the Book of Acts as an authority for the topography, antiquities, and society of Asia Minor. It was gradually borne upon me that in various details the narrative showed marvellous truth.'[15] Ramsay added 'Luke is a historian of the first rank; not merely are his statements of fact trustworthy...this author should be placed along with the very greatest historians.'[16]

We will now consider four specific examples of how archaeology corroborates the New Testament. First, in John chapter five we read about Jesus healing a cripple at the pool of Bethesda. The text says (John 5:2) 'Now there is in Jerusalem near the Sheep Gate a pool, which in Aramaic is called Bethesda'. Furthermore, the text describes the pool as being 'surrounded by five covered colonnades.' Archaeological digs in Jerusalem are extremely difficult for two reasons. First, Jerusalem was destroyed by the Romans in 70 AD to quench a Jewish revolt and the new city was rebuilt over the old. Second, the high density of people in Jerusalem today means one cannot excavate easily. Nonetheless in 1888, a group of archaeologists digging in the northeast corner of the old city near St Anne's Church uncovered the pool of Bethesda right where it is predicted in the Gospel of John. The five colonnades as described by John are plainly seen.

Second, the Pool of Siloam has also been found, as recounted in John 9:1–7. The episode of Jesus and the blind man, as told by John, is well known. Jesus was fleeing the Temple to escape either the priests or an angry crowd when He encountered the man. His disciples asked Jesus who had sinned, the man or his parents, to cause him to be born blind. Jesus said that neither had sinned, but that the man had been born blind so that God's work might be revealed in him. With that, He spat in the dust to make mud, which He rubbed in the man's eyes before telling him to wash it off in the Pool of Siloam. When the man did so, he was able to see.

In June 2004 archaeologists Ronny Reich and Eli Shukron were digging in the area of the Gihon Spring where Hezekiah's Tunnel begins. Far to the south, between the end of the rock ridge that forms the City of David and a lush green orchard that is often identified as the Biblical King's Garden, is a narrow alley through which a sewer pipe runs carrying waste from the valley west of the City of David into the Kidron Valley east of the City of David. The Jerusalem city authorities needed to repair or replace this sewer and sent workers with heavy equipment to do some excavating. Shukron was watching the operation, when suddenly he saw two steps appear. He immediately halted the work, took a few pictures and wrote a report to the district archaeologist for Jerusalem. A quick response was called for because the winter rains were fast approaching and the sewer pipe had to be repaired or replaced. Ronny and Eli were quickly authorized to excavate the area on behalf of the Israeli Antiquities Authority. The more they excavated, the more steps they found, and the wider the steps became.[17] This biblical Pool of Siloam (in Hebrew *Breikhat Hashiloah*) is a freshwater reservoir that was a major gathering place for ancient Jews making religious pilgrimages to the city and the site where Jesus cured the man blind from birth, according to the Gospel of John. The waters of Siloam are mentioned by the prophet Isaiah, a contemporary of Hezekiah's, who refers to 'the gently flowing waters of Siloam' (Isaiah 8:6). When the exiles returned from Babylon and rebuilt the walls of Jerusalem, Nehemiah tell us that a certain Shallun rebuilt 'the wall of the Pool of Shiloah by the King's Garden' (Nehemiah 3:15).The pool was fed by the famous Tunnel of Hezekiah and is a much grander affair than archaeologists previously believed, with three tiers of five stone stairs, each separated by narrow landings, allowing easy access to the water. The pool was about 225 feet long, and they unearthed steps on three sides. They do not yet know how wide and how deep the pool was because they have not finished the excavation. The fourth side lies under a lush garden — filled with figs, pomegranates, cabbages and other fruits — behind a Greek Orthodox Church, and the team has not yet received permission to cut a trench through the garden. Some scholars had previously said that there wasn't a Pool of Siloam and that John was using a religious construct to illustrate a point. Now that the Pool of Siloam has been found exactly where John located it shows that his gospel which some academics thought to be only theology is now demonstrated to be grounded in history.

The pool of Jesus' time was built early in the first century BC and was destroyed by the future Roman Emperor Titus about AD 70. This may be the most significant and largest *miqveh* [ritual bath] ever found. The excavators have been able to date the pool fairly precisely because of two fortunate occurrences that implanted unique artefacts in the pool area. When ancient workmen were plastering the steps before facing them with stones, they either accidentally or deliberately buried four coins in the plaster. All four are coins of Alexander Jannaeus, a Jewish king who ruled Jerusalem from 103 to 76 BC. That provides the earliest date at which the pool could have been constructed. Similarly, in the soil in one corner of the pool, they found about a dozen coins dating from the period of the First Jewish Revolt against Rome, which lasted from AD 66 to 70. That indicates the pool had begun to be filled in by that time. Because the pool sits at one of the lowest spots in Jerusalem, rains flowing down the valley deposited mud into it each winter. It was no longer being cleaned out, so the pool quickly filled with dirt and disappeared.[18]

Third, before 1961, all historical reference to Pontius Pilate, who condemned Jesus to death, was believed to be due to the fact that the Gospels (or Flavius Josephus) referred to him. In other words there were no *archaeological* findings referring to Pontius Pilate. Then two Italian archaeologists excavated the Mediterranean port city of Caesarea. During the dig, they uncovered a two–by–three foot inscription in Latin. The inscription read, 'Pontius Pilate, Prefect of Judea, has presented the Tiberium to the Caesarians.' This was the first archaeological discovery of historical reference to the existence of Pontius Pilate.

Fourth, Capernaum was a large Galilean fishing village and busy trading centre. This place is of special interest to Christians because of its frequent mention in the history of Jesus Christ; Peter, Andrew, James and John also lived there. It played a unique and important part in Christ's life and ministry, and in His outreach to the people of Israel. The inhabitants of Capernaum, including various high ranking citizens, were given unique and abundant opportunities to hear Jesus Christ's message firsthand and witness His awesome power and love.

Capernaum stood 2.5 miles (4 km) from the Jordan River, on the north–western shore of the Sea of Galilee (modern Lake Kinneret, which the Bible also called the lake of Gennesaret, Sea of Chinnereth and the Sea of Tiberias). The ancient city of Capernaum was abandoned about a thousand years ago or more, and was rediscovered by archaeologists beginning in the 1800's. In modern times, it is called *Kefar Nahum* (Hebrew) and *Talhum* (Arabic). The Gennesaret area was one of the most prosperous and crowded districts of Palestine. Capernaum lay on the great Via Maris highway between Damascus (Syria) and

Caesarea Maritima on the Mediterranean Sea, and between Tyre and Egypt. Customs taxes were collected from travellers at this crossroads (Mt 9:9). This was the job of Levi, the tax collector, who became Christ's disciple and was later named Matthew. Jews criticized Jesus for befriending him and other tax collectors. Caravans stopped at Capernaum to resupply with produce and dried fish.

At the lake shore, where Peter and other fishermen worked, archaeologists discovered a fish sales area. This well–built structure measured 2 meters in width and 5 meters in length and contained two large, rather shallow, semicircular pools, one at each end, with a rectangular platform in the middle on which, presumably, the fish were cleaned and sold. The two pools had a thick coat of watertight plaster.[19]

After Our Lord's expulsion from Nazareth (Mt 4:13–16; Lk 4:16–31), Capernaum became His 'own city.' It was the scene of many acts and incidents of His life (Mt 8:5, 14,15; 9:2–6, 10–17; 15:1–20; Mk 1:32–34, and so forth). The New Testament tells us that a Roman centurion built a synagogue there for the Jews (Lk 7:1–5). His servant was later healed from severe palsy by Jesus (Mt 8:5–13; Lk 7:1–10). The remains of what must have been a beautiful basalt synagogue has been discovered by archaeologists. As expected for such a sacred building, it was found at the highest point in town. This is the synagogue where our Lord frequently taught (Jn 6:59; Mk 1:21; Lk 4:33). Here, Jesus cured a demon–possessed man (Mk 1:21–28) and delivered the sermon on the Bread of Life (Jn 6:25–59). He even restored the life of the daughter of one rulers of this synagogue (Mk 5:22; Lk 8:41). The synagogue is near the lake, and is built so that when the Jews prayed here, they faced Jerusalem. It was destroyed along with Jerusalem's temple, around 70 AD. Many years later, it was replaced with a white stone synagogue (perhaps 250–300 AD).

Only a few hundred feet from the synagogue, the stone house of the Apostle Peter has also been found at Capernaum. This is where Jesus healed Peter's mother–in–law and others (Mt 8:14–16). Jesus may have lived with Peter while staying in Capernaum. In the years following Jesus' death and resurrection, the house apparently became a house–church. Centuries later, Christians honoured the site by building a church here. It was destroyed in a later conquest of the city. Archaeologists have excavated both the church and the earlier house below. Literary sources and recent archaeological discoveries make the identification of the house of St Peter in Capernaum virtually certain. The house was built at the very end of the Hellenistic period (first century BC). In the second half of the first century AD some peculiar features set apart this building from all the others so far excavated in Capernaum. Here, in fact, the pavements was floored with lime several times. Significantly, many pieces of broken lamps were found in these thin layers of lime. One hundred and thirty–one inscriptions were found, written in four languages, namely: in Greek (110), Aramaic (10), Estrangelo (9), and Latin (2). The name of Jesus appears several times. He is called Christ, the Lord, and the Most High God. An inscription in Estrangelo mentions the Eucharist. There are also symbols and monograms, namely: crosses of different forms, a boat, the monogram of Jesus. The name of St Peter occurs at least twice: his monogram is written in Latin but with Greek letters. In another graffito, St Peter is called the helper of Rome. A third inscription mentions Peter and Berenike. This Peter, however, might be the name of a pilgrim. On several hundred pieces of plaster, decorative motifs appear. The colours employed are: green, blue, yellow, red, brown, white and black. Among the subjects one can distinguish floral crosses, pomegranates, figs, trifolium, stylized flowers and geometric designs such as circles, squares, and so forth. At the beginning of the fifth century, the house of St Peter was still standing, but it had been transformed into a church.[20]

Mary, the mother of Jesus, made her way to Capernaum

with her other relatives (Mt 12:46,48,49). It was here that Christ uttered the memorable words, 'Who is my mother? And who are my brethren? And he stretched forth his hand toward his disciples, and said, Behold my mother and my brethren!' Among the miracles of Christ that occurred at Capernaum are:

1. The raising from the dead of Jairus' daughter (Mark 5:22; Luke 8:41).

2. The liberation of a man possessed by an evil spirit (Mark 1:21–28).

3. The paralyzed man let down through the roof and healed (Mark 2:1–12).

4. The miraculous catch of fish by four disciples (Luke 5:1–11).

5. Tribute tax money needed by Peter supplied from a fish (Matthew 17:24–27).

6. The healing of the centurion's servant afflicted with palsy (Matt. 8:5–13).

7. The healing of the son of a nobleman in the King's court (Herod Antipas) (John 4:46–54).

8. The healing of many other people and casting out demons, as 'all the city was gathered together at the door' (Mark 1:29–34).

Despite the unique number of signs our Lord presented to them, many of the people of Capernaum remained unrepentant disbelievers. Because they turned so strongly away from the uniquely gracious light given, they were strongly judged: 'Much will be required of the person entrusted with much, and still more will be demanded of the person entrusted with more' (Lk 12:48). Thus, along with nearby Chorazin and Bethsaida, Capernaum received a very stern warning from Jesus: 'It will be more tolerable for the land of Sodom on the day of judgment than for you' (Mt 11:24). Ultimately, the cities were all destroyed, and Capernaum became virtually uninhabited ruins for centuries. Today,

Capernaum's inhabitants consist of a Franciscan Monastery and a nearby Greek Orthodox Church.

These and other data provide very strong evidence that the writings in the New Testament as we have them now are accurate, reliable, and authentic. The natural conclusion is that they are trustworthy as a source of Jesus' life and teaching. Sir Frederick Kenyon, the great classical scholar, former director and principal librarian of the British Museum and one of the foremost experts on ancient manuscripts, affirmed: 'The interval between the dates of original composition and the earliest extant evidence becomes so small as to be in fact negligible, and the last foundation for any doubt that the Scriptures have come down to us substantially as they were written has now been removed. Both the authenticity and the general integrity of the books of the New Testament may be regarded as finally established.'[21]

2.6 The Prophetic Evidence

Unlike any other book in the world, the Bible is the only one to offer specific predictions hundreds of years in advance of their literal fulfilment. The Bible contains nearly two thousand individual prophecies. The Bible is about 30 percent prophecy, and for this reason alone it is absolutely unique. There are no fulfilled prophecies in the Koran, in the Hindu Vedas or the Bhagavad–Gita, in the sayings of Buddha or Confucius, in the Book of Mormon, or anywhere else but in the Bible. Nor are there any prophecies concerning the coming of Buddha, Krishna, Mohammed, Zoroaster, Confucius, Joseph Smith, or any other founder or leader of a world religion. The Jewish Messiah is absolutely unique in this respect. His coming was foretold in dozens of specific prophecies which were fulfilled in the most minute detail in the life, death, and resurrection of Jesus Christ.

Figure 7: Prophecy and fulfilment

Messianic Prophecy	Old Testament	Fulfilment
He would be a descendent of Abraham	Genesis 12:3 and 17:9	Matthew 1:1, Galatians 3:16
He would be of the tribe of Judah	Genesis 49:10	Luke3:33, Hebrews 7:14
He would be of the house of David	2 Samuel 7:12	Matthew 1:20-24
He would be born of a Virgin	Isaiah 7:14	Matthew 1:21
He would be born in Bethlehem	Micah 5:1-2	Matthew 2:1, Luke 2:4-7
A messenger would go before Him	Isaiah 40:3, Malachi 3:1	Matthew 3:3, Mark 1:2-4
His ministry was to begin in Galilee	Isaiah 8:23-9:1	Matthew 4:13-16
His zeal for God would carry Him away	Psalm 69:9-10	John 2:17
He would perform miracles	Isaiah 35:5-6	Matthew 9:35
He would be rejected by the Jewish leaders	Psalm 118:22	1 Peter 2:7
He would be rejected by His own people	Isaiah 53:3	John 1:10-11; 7:5, 48
He would enter Jerusalem on a donkey	Zechariah 9:9	John 12:14-15
He would be betrayed for thirty pieces of silver	Zechariah 11:12-13	Matthew 26:14-15

Messianic Prophecy	Old Testament	Fulfilment
The money used in His betrayal would be thrown into the temple, and the Potter's field bought with it	Zechariah 11:13	Matthew 27:3-10
He would be silent before His accusers	Isaiah 53:7	Matthew 27:12-19
He would be mocked	Psalm 22:7-8	Matthew 27:39-40
His back would be struck	Isaiah 50:6	Mark 15:15
His face would be spat upon	Isaiah 50:6	Matthew 26:67; 27:30
He would be crucified, as described in the Old Testament centuries before the Romans adopted this method of execution	Psalm 22:13-18	Matthew 27:32-44; John 19:28-30
He would be put to death with criminals	Isaiah 53:12	Luke 23:33
He would pray for His persecutors	Isaiah 53:12	Luke 23:34
People would gamble for His clothes	Psalm 22:19	John 19:23-24
His side would be pierced and His bones would not be broken	Zechariah 12:10, Psalm 34:21	John 19:33-34
His Passion would be redemptive	Isaiah 53:5	1 Peter 2:24
He would be buried in a rich man's tomb	Isaiah 53:9	Matthew 27:57-60

Messianic Prophecy	Old Testament	Fulfilment
He would rise from the dead on the third day	Hosea 6:1-3; Isaiah 26:19; Psalm 16:10-11; Jonah 2:1	Luke 24:46; Matthew 12:40
Jesus will come again in glory as Judge	Daniel 7:13-14	Matthew 24:30; Luke 21:27

There are many prophecies concerning the Messiah that were fulfilled in Jesus Christ. Prophecy involves God teaching through history. There are many prophecies concerning the Messiah that were fulfilled in Jesus Christ. Since the coming of the Messiah is the theme of the Old Testament, the predictions fulfilled in Jesus Christ outnumber all others. These Old Testament prophecies, and their fulfilment as recorded in the New Testament, include the following prophecies concerning Christ the Messiah.

As well as these prophecies, there are also prefigurations of Christ, for example in the sacrifice of Abraham (Gen 22:1–19). Several features are unique about these prophecies, in contrast to all other examples of attempted predictions today. First, unlike the predictions of Nostradamus, these prophecies were very specific and detailed. For example, they gave the very name of the tribe, city, and time of Christ's coming. Second, none of these predictions failed, unlike those of the Jehovah's witnesses, and other sects, concerning the date of the end of the world. Third, these prophecies were written hundreds of years before Jesus was born. It was not a question of reading the trends of the times or simply making intelligent guesses. Fourth, many of these predictions were beyond human ability to arrange a fulfilment. For example, if Jesus were a mere human being, He would have had absolutely no control over when, where, or how He would be born, how He would die (especially since a foreign power, Rome, was to be the instrument of His death), or whether He would rise from the dead.

The best explanation for the fulfilment of such predictions, made hundreds of years earlier, is the existence of a transcendent God who knows all things, including 'the beginning from the end' (Isaiah 46:10). God's providence unfolds in the history of salvation. Sceptics sometimes claim equal authority for predictions from psychics. However, there is a quantum leap between the fallible human prognosticators and the unerring prophets of the Bible. Compare that with a study which revealed that top psychics were wrong 92% of the time.[22] Jean Dixon, for example, predicted that Jackie Kennedy would not remarry, but she married Aristotle Onassis the next day.[23]

Notes

1. W.F. Albright, *The Archaeology of Palestine and the Bible* (Revell, 1935), p. 127.
2. See B. Metzger, *The Text of the New Testament*, 1968, p. 86.
3. This idea is important also for chapter 4.
4. See Pope John Paul II, *Tertio Millenio Adveniente*, 5.
5. Tacitus, *Annales*, 15, 44.
6. Suetonius, *Vita Claudii*, 25, 4. The expulsion took place in the year 49 AD. See also Acts 18:42.
7. Pliny the Younger, *Epistle* 1, 96.
8. Lucian, *The Death of Peregrine*, 1113, in *The Works of Lucian of Samosata*, translated by H.W. Fowler and F.G. Fowler (Oxford: Clarendon, 1949), vol. 4.
9. Flavius Josephus, *The Antiquities of the Jews* Book 18, 63–64. See also Eusebius of Caesarea, *Ecclesiastical History* Book 1, chapter 11 in *PG* 20, 115–118 and *De demonstratione evangelica*, Book 3, n.5 in *PG* 22, 221–222.
10. *The Babylonian Talmud*, translated by I. Epstein (London: Soncino, 1935), vol. III, Sanhedrin 43a, p. 281.
11. St John Chrysostom, Homily 4 on First Corinthians.
12. Eusebius, *Ecclesiastical History*, Book 3, Chapter 39.
13. St Irenaeus, *Against the Heresies*, 3.1.1.

14. N. Glueck, *Rivers in the desert; a history of the Negev* (New York: Farrar, Straus and Cudahy, 1959), p. 136.
15. W. M. Ramsay (revised and updated by M. Wilson), *St Paul the Traveler and the Roman Citizen* (Grand Rapids, MI : Kregel Publications, 2001), p. 8.
16. Idem, *The Bearing of Recent Discovery on the Trustworthiness of the New Testament* (London: Hodder and Stoughton, 1915²), p. 222.
17. See H. Shanks, 'The Siloam Pool. Where Jesus Cured the Blind Man' in *Biblical Archaeological Review* 31/5 (September/October 2005), pp. 16–23.
18. See *ibid.*.
19. See H. Weiss, 'Recent Work at Capernaum,' in *Bible and Spade* 10/1 (Associates for Biblical Research, 1981), p. 24.
20. See S. Loffreda, 'Capernaum – Jesus' Own City,' in *Bible and Spade* 10/1 (Associates for Biblical Research, 1981), pp. 12, 7–8. See Idem, *Recovering Capharnaum* (Jerusalem: Edizioni Custodia Terra Santa, 1984).
21. Sir F. Kenyon, *The Bible and Archeology* (New York: Harper, 1940), pp. 288, 289.
22. A. Kole, *Miracle and Magic* (Eugene, OR: Harvest House, 1984).
23. *Ibid.*, p. 70.

3

New Testament Interpretation

Just as we have to seek gold in the earth, for the kernel in the shell, for the chestnut's hidden fruit beneath its hairy coverings, so in Holy Scripture we have to dig deep for its divine meaning.
St Jerome, On Ecclesiasticus

3.1 Christ and the Holy Spirit

3.1.1 Christ the Unique Word of Sacred Scripture

The Old Testament prefigures and prophecies Christ, and the New Testament reveals Him: 'All Sacred Scripture is but one book, and that one book is Christ, because all divine Scripture speaks of Christ, and all divine Scripture is fulfilled in Christ.'[1] In order to reveal Himself to men, in the condescension of His goodness, God speaks to them in human words: 'Indeed the words of God, expressed in the words of men, are in every way like human language, just as the Word of the eternal Father, when he took on himself the flesh of human weakness, became like men.'[2] Through all the words of Sacred Scripture, God speaks only one single Word, His one Utterance in whom He expresses Himself completely (Cf. Heb 1:1–3). As St Augustine wrote: 'You recall that one and the same Word of God extends throughout Scripture, that it is one and the same Utterance that resounds in the mouths of all the sacred writers, since He who was in the beginning God with God has no need of separate syllables; for He is not subject to time.'[3]

For this reason, the Church has always venerated the Scriptures as she venerates the Lord's Body. She never ceases to present to the faithful the Bread of life, taken from the one table of God's Word and Christ's Body. 'In the sacred books, the Father who is in heaven comes lovingly to meet his children, and talks with them.'[4] In Sacred Scripture, the Church constantly finds her nourishment and her strength, for she welcomes it not as a human word, 'but as what it really is, the word of God.'[5] The relationship between the oral and the written can be seen from St Paul's second letter to the Thessalonians: 'Therefore, brothers, stand firm and hold fast to the traditions that you were taught, either by an oral statement or by a letter of ours' (2 Th 2:15).

3.1.2 The Holy Spirit, Inspirer and Interpreter of Scripture

In Sacred Scripture, God speaks to man in a human way. To interpret Scripture correctly, the reader must be attentive to what the human authors truly wanted to affirm, and to what God wanted to reveal to us by their words. In order to discover the sacred authors' intention, the reader must take into account the conditions of their time and culture, the literary genres in use at that time, and the modes of feeling, speaking and narrating then current. 'For the fact is that truth is differently presented and expressed in the various types of historical writing, in prophetical and poetical texts, and in other forms of literary expression.'[6] However, since Sacred Scripture is inspired, there is another and no less important principle of correct interpretation, without which Scripture would remain a dead letter. 'Sacred Scripture must be read and interpreted in the light of the same Spirit by whom it was written.'[7] It is the same Holy Spirit who enlightens both author and reader.

The Second Vatican Council indicated three criteria for

interpreting Scripture in accordance with the Spirit who inspired it.[8] First, consistency and coherence need to be taken into account. The reader should be especially attentive 'to the content and unity of the whole Scripture'. Different as the books which compose it may be, Scripture is a unity by reason of the unity of God's plan, of which Christ Jesus is the centre and heart, open since His Passover (Cf. Lk 24:25–27, 44–46). The reader should relate each part to the whole. The phrase 'heart of Christ' can refer to Sacred Scripture, which makes known His heart, closed before the Passion, as the Scripture was still to be fulfilled and unfolded. However, the Scripture has been opened since the Passion; since those who from then on have understood it, consider and discern in what way the prophecies must be interpreted.[9]

Second, one should read Scripture in the context of the Church, or within 'the living Tradition of the whole Church'. According to a saying of the Fathers, Sacred Scripture is written principally in the Church's heart rather than in documents and records, for the Church carries in her Tradition the living memorial of God's Word, and it is the Holy Spirit who gives her the spiritual interpretation of the Scripture.[10]

Third, reading should be attentive to the analogy of faith (cf. Rm 12:6). By 'analogy of faith' we mean the relation of the truths of faith among themselves and within the whole plan of Revelation. Linking parts to the whole in the reading of the Scriptures helps us in the reconciliation of different interpretations, and also the study of difficult passages.[11]

3.2 Inspiration and truth of Sacred Scripture

Christian Tradition from the beginning believed in the divine origin of the Scriptures. St Augustine speaks of the Scriptures as 'God's handwriting' and adds: 'Letters have reached us from that city apart from which we are wandering; these letters are the Scriptures which exhort us to live well.' The Bible is a true and trustworthy account of God's revelation to man written down under the impulse and guidance of the Holy Spirit. In other words, the Bible is an inspired book. The word 'inspiration' appears when the Bible itself uses the expression 'divinely inspired' refers to the Sacred writers as 'inspired by the Holy Spirit.' Not only does the Bible claim to be inspired, but it also defines and describes what it means by inspiration. St Paul writes that 'All scripture is inspired by God and useful for refuting error, for guiding people's lives and teaching them to be upright' (2 Tm 3:16). St Peter adds that 'no prophecy ever came from human initiative. When people spoke for God it was the Holy Spirit that moved them' (2 Pt 1:21).

Jesus Christ and the writers of Scripture believed in the truthfulness and historical reliability of even the most disputed parts of the Old Testament. For example, while speaking to the Pharisees in the region of Judea beyond the Jordan, Jesus confirmed His belief in the real existence of an original couple created during the Creation (Mt 19:4; see Gn 2:24). In writing to the church at Corinth, Paul affirmed his belief in Adam as the first human (1 Co 15:45). Then, in his first letter to Timothy, he attested to the fact that Eve was created after Adam (2:13; see Gn 2:7, 21–25). St Paul regarded the serpent's deception of Eve as a historical event (2 Co 11:3; 1 Tm 2:13–14; see Gn 3). Both Jesus and the apostle St Peter held that Noah was a real person, and that the global Flood was a historical event (Mt 24:37–39; 2 Pt 2:5; 3:6; cf. Gn 6–8). Jesus and Peter also affirmed their belief in the historicity of Lot, and in the destruction of Sodom (Lk 17:28–32; 2 Pt 2:6–7; cf. Gn 19). St Paul attested to the Israelites' crossing of the Red Sea, and affirmed his belief in their drinking water from a rock (1 Co 10:1–4; see Heb 11:29 and Ex 14), while Jesus confirmed the miraculous healing of the Israelites who fixed their eyes on the bronze snake set up by Moses in the desert (Jn 3:14; cf. Num 21:4–9). Finally, unlike some people today, including some of those who exaggerate the symbolic aspect of the Bible at the expense of its divine inspiration, Jesus regarded the account of Jonah's three days and nights in the belly of a great fish as a historical event (Mt 12:39–40).

Inspiration in its strict sense denotes the supernatural influence of the Holy Spirit under which the Bible was written. In his Encyclical on Sacred Scripture, Pope Leo XIII writes that by supernatural power, the Holy Spirit so moved and impelled the sacred writers to write (He was so present to them) that the things which He ordered, and those only, they first rightly understood, then willed faithfully to write down, and finally expressed in apt words and with infallible truth.[12]

The Greek term underlying the word 'inspiration' (*theopneustos*) means 'God–breathed.' Thus, St Paul affirmed that Scripture is the product of the breath of God or God actually breathed out the Scriptures. Just as surely as God's breath brought the Universe into existence (Ps 33:6), so the Bible declares itself to be the result of God's out–breathing. Inspiration is the breathing of the Holy Spirit, a breath of Life. This shows very clearly how God is the author of Sacred Scripture: 'The divinely revealed realities, which are contained and presented in the text of Sacred Scripture, have been written down under the inspiration of the Holy Spirit.' Therefore, 'Holy Mother Church, relying on the faith of the apostolic age, accepts as sacred and canonical the books of the Old and the New Testaments, whole and entire, with all their parts, on the grounds that, written under the inspiration of the Holy Spirit, they have God as their author, and have been handed on as such to the Church herself.'[13] This guarantees a synthetic, unitary message. God inspired the human authors of the sacred books: 'To compose the sacred books, God chose certain men who, all the while he employed them in this task, made full use of their own faculties and powers so that, though he acted in them and by them, it was as true authors that they consigned to writing whatever he wanted written, and no more.'[14]

The Holy Spirit as principal Author of Sacred Scripture influenced the sacred writer in three ways. First, He illuminated the mind of the sacred writer. Under the enlightenment of the Holy Spirit the sacred writer formed a concept of what God wished him to write (history, prophecy, didactic literature) and of the single truths or facts which it was to contain. This illumination was not necessarily revelation since the sacred writer might have come to the knowledge of what was already revealed to others. But it enabled him to make correct use of his faculties, aided him in the gathering of materials, so that he correctly conceived in his mind all that God wished him to write.

Second, the Holy Spirit moved the will of the sacred writer. After the sacred writer had under inspiration formed in his mind an idea of the book and of its contents, the Holy Spirit moved the sacred writer's will to write freely, though infallibly, what God wished. Third, He aided the sacred writer in the work of composition. In this way, the Holy Spirit assisted the sacred author in carrying out his project, by watching over him and when necessary by positively directing him, lest he add or omit something and lest he fall into error. If certain writers made use of secretaries, and if these secretaries were instrumental in choosing the language and determining the mode of expression, they were inspired collaborators.

The inspired books teach the truth: 'Since therefore all that the inspired authors or sacred writers affirm should be regarded as affirmed by the Holy Spirit, we must acknowledge that the books of Scripture firmly, faithfully, and without error teach that truth which God, for the sake of our salvation, wished to see confided to the Sacred Scriptures.'[15]

To summarize, divine inspiration *excludes* erroneous elements, extraneous elements, which are true but not relevant. It also excludes embroidery or excessive detail which would drown the essential truth. Positively, inspiration *guarantees* the reliability of truth, as related to doctrine of the infallibility of the Church. This reliability of truth is known as inerrancy, meaning freedom from error. The inerrancy of Scripture is a consequence of its divine inspiration. Whatever the Bible teaches, God teaches, because God is the principal author of Scripture and His teaching is necessarily true. We attribute this quality of inerrancy in the first place to the original Biblical books written by the pen of the sacred writers themselves, and, secondly to reproductions of the Bible, but only in so far as these agree with the original sacred books. Though all the original copies of the books of the Bible have long disappeared and though certain copies of the Bible may contain errors due to copyists, translators, editors, and printers, yet in most cases the true reading can be established with the aid of the old copies and versions. This absolute inerrancy and authority of the Bible is taught by Sacred Scripture itself. Our Lord, the Apostles and Evangelists regarded any passage from Scripture as the word of God, as necessarily true, as a final and supreme authority. They affirm that 'Scripture cannot be broken' (Jn 10:35), that 'not the smallest letter or stroke shall pass from the Law until all is accomplished.' (Mt 5:18) and that the 'Scriptures shall be fulfilled' (Mt 26:54).

The Church has from the very beginning associated inerrancy with the divine inspiration of Scripture. There are few doctrines on which the agreement of the early Fathers and Christian writers was so unanimous and emphatic as the inerrancy of the Bible. The conviction of the Fathers on this point was not something which was apparent to them from a reading or study of the Scriptures, since the difficulties of the Bible present themselves even to a casual reader. Rather, it was a traditional teaching which they inherited from the Church with the Bible. Inspiration also guarantees the permanence of truth despite changing circumstances; the Scriptures thus endure as a living truth, guarding us against relativism. Recently, Pope Benedict XVI remarked: 'We must not yield to the temptation of relativism or of a subjectivist and selective interpretation of Sacred Scripture. Only the whole truth can open us to adherence to Christ, dead and risen for our salvation.'[16]

Still, the Christian faith is not only a 'religion of the book'. Christianity is the religion of the 'Word' of God, 'not a written and mute word, but incarnate and living.'[17] If the Scriptures are not to remain a dead letter, Christ, the eternal Word of the living God, must, through the Holy Spirit, 'open our minds to understand the Scriptures'(see Lk 24:45).

3.3 Interpretation and truth of Sacred Scripture

3.3.1 The Realist Perspective

In approaching the Scriptures, it is important to realise that faith is based on a realist understanding of creation and of history.[18] Realism is the metaphysical bridge which guarantees the true relation between the mind and reality and is thus the right approach to link reason with Christian belief in God. To highlight what is meant by realism, it is helpful to contrast it with nominalism, positivism, pragmatism, idealism and nihilism. Realism affirms the existence of universals against nominalism. Against positivism, realism proposes that reality extends beyond that which the natural sciences can measure It affirms the validity of objective truth in its own right against a merely pragmatist or utilitarian view. Realism affirms against idealism that the external world is not simply the projection of the mind. Against nihilism, realism affirms that the world makes sense and has meaning. In this realist perspective, we accept that the New Testament has a real relation to creation, to humankind, and to history.

3.3.2 Biblical criticism

The 'historical–critical method,' is the approach currently in use by the 'historical–critical school' of biblical interpretation. It is characterized by the way in which it uses literary–criticism and historical–criticism according to its own understanding of these terms. The method of 'literary–criticism' goes back to the Catholic Richard Simon (1638–1712), who examined repetitions (doublets), and various seeming discrepancies and incongruities of content and style in the Pentateuch in relation to the alleged Mosaic authorship of the whole, but it was afterwards developed mainly by a series of German Protestant exegetes. Literary–criticism is a search for the explanation of the many supposed cracks and contradictions in the sacred text of the Bible. Historical–criticism accepts the results of literary–criticism and goes on to seek 'the historical processes which gave rise to biblical texts.'[19] The acclaimed founder of the historical–critical school as such is Wilhelm de Wette (1780–1849), whose basic approach was to treat the events recorded in the Bible 'as phenomena comparable to other historical phenomena and subject to the same laws of historical research.'[20] What these 'laws of historical research' are has remained largely undefined by de Wette and his followers down to the present time. Historical–critics constantly use the terms 'historical science' and 'historical method,' which they identify with their particular approach and method, but their reasoning lacks a clear definition of terms.

The historical–critical method arose early in the nineteenth century on the basis of certain philosophical ideas emerging from the seventeenth and eighteenth centuries. In particular, we may find in the German Enlightenment (*Aufklärung*) of the eighteenth century a notable characteristic of modern study in general and liberal biblical exegesis in particular, namely the denial of the supernatural. Some of the philosophical antecedents of the method are the following.   First, the error of deism, or the idea that, although God created the universe, He left it to run on its own according to natural causes ever afterwards, so that there have never been nor ever will be any divine interventions or supernatural happenings; the belief that there is only a universal natural religion requiring belief in God and the performance of one's duty, while all positive religion was rejected. The freethinker Herbert of Cherbury (1581–1648), is considered the father both of English deism and of naturalism in religion, and this is not surprising, since his exclusion of any role of God in the history of the world easily led to the suggestion that God does not exist at all. In similar fashion, the exclusion by higher–critics of any formal and discernible role of divine inspiration in the composition of the books of the Bible easily led to the suggestion that there never was any divine inspiration at all. The second error can be termed naturalism, or the notion that everything in the world can be explained from natural causes alone; there is no supernatural reality. The third component is rationalism, or the error that human reason, based upon self–evident principles, is the sole judge of certified knowledge.

René Descartes (1596–1650) is recognized to be the father of modern rationalism because of his universal methodical doubt and his method of deduction solely from self–evident principles of human reason. Descartes actually excluded from his universal methodical doubt the truths of faith and morals,[21] and he accepted that man can know with certainty from the light of faith,[22] but the series of biblical critics who followed him in the eighteenth century turned his universal methodical doubt against the text of Sacred Scripture and left no place for a real light of faith either in the production of the Bible or in its interpretation. The fourth error is empiricism, or the notion that all certified knowledge is based upon verification by sense experience and experiment. Immanuel Kant (1724–1804) modified Cartesian reasoning in a theory of knowledge based on the belief that man cannot know external reality, but only his reasoning about what he experiences with his senses. The fifth error, subjectivism, as propounded by Kant, is the idea that man can know only the objects of his own thoughts and experiences (*phenomena*) but he cannot know reality external to his own mind (*noumena*). Based on Kant's theory of knowledge, critics would later adopt the belief that the sacred writers could have known only what they managed to figure out from their own limited experience. Georg Wilhelm Friedrich Hegel (1770–1831) modified the static philosophy of Kant with a dynamic philosophy according to which all reality is in constant development. Hegelian thinking also emphasized the belief that the supposedly Mosaic authorship of the Pentateuch must actually have been the result of a long process of development, as was the text of other books of the Bible. Under Hegel's influence, David Strauss (1808–1874) and Ferdinand Baur (1792–1860) 'developed a higher criticism of the Bible in which its supernatural elements were systematically explained away as products of mythology.'[23] Sixth, there is evolutionism, or the ideology that all reality is evolving as a whole in a vaguely upward direction and there are no immutable realities. Many of these errors can be combined under the global term of modernism: the belief that the outlook of modern man is superior to that of medieval and ancient man; and more specifically, the belief that all religion, including Christianity and the idea of God, arises from a preconceptual, subrational religious instinct dominant in primitive man, whose promptings are unacceptable to modern scientific man. The seven notions listed above contributed to the rise of higher–criticism, which later produced the historical–critical method.

Form criticism (*Formgeschichtliche Methode*) is a method of biblical criticism applied as a means of analyzing the typical features of texts, especially their conventional forms or structures, in order to relate them to their sociological contexts. Form criticism begins by identifying a text's genre or conventional literary form, such as parables, proverbs, epistles, or love poems. It goes on to seek the sociological setting for each text's genre; its 'situation in life' (in German, *Sitz im Leben*). For example, the sociological setting of a law is a court, or the sociological setting of a psalm of praise (hymn) is a worship context, or that of a proverb might be a father–to–son admonition. Having identified and analyzed the text's genre–pericopes, form criticism proceeds to ask how these smaller genre–pericopes contribute to the purpose of the text as a whole. Form criticism was originally developed for Old Testament studies, especially for the book of Genesis and the Psalms by Hermann Gunkel. It later came to be applied to the Synoptic Gospels by Karl Ludwig Schmidt, Martin Dibelius and Rudolf Bultmann, among others.[24] A key concept of form criticism is the creative power of the community, and this postulate leaves little room for the role of the eye–witness. Here, as elsewhere, the method is subject to an ideological prejudice. For the creative role of the community is a concept ultimately founded on Hegelian philosophy: the idea immanent in humanity is expressed especially in a collective fashion. Hence, the primacy is accorded to the community at the expense of the individual. Also, the form critics tend to focus on the Christ of faith, ignoring the Jesus of history. Added to this, Bultmann proposed, from his own existentialist perspective, that the New Testament need to be demythologized. In this context, for Bultmann knowledge of the historical Jesus is not essential to Christian faith: in order to believe it is sufficient to meet Him in our experience as He comes to us as a proclamation (kerygma) in a living, present challenge.

Redaction criticism (*Redaktionsgeschichte*) is a more recent critical method for the study of the Bible, especially the Gospels and other books whose contents have overlap. Redaction criticism is a historical discipline which is concerned to discover the intended purpose of the final author or editor of a book. Whereas form criticism has made us aware of the pre–Gospel tradition, but often at the expense of the role of the evangelists, redaction criticism has drawn our attention to their contribution. Unlike its parent discipline, form criticism, redaction criticism does not look at the various parts of a narrative to discover the original form. Instead, it focuses on how the author or editor has shaped and moulded the material in his sources to express his literary goals for the work, namely the reasons he is writing his work. Redaction criticism sees the author or editor not as a mere 'cut–and–paste' collector of stories, but as a theologian who is trying to meet his theological agenda by shaping the sources he uses. Three scholars in particular have contributed to Redaction criticism, namely G. Bornkamm, W. Marxsen, and H. Conzelmann.[25]

The redaction critic detects editorial activity in the following ways. First, through the repetition of common motifs and themes (for example, in Matthew's Gospel, with the fulfilment of prophecy). Second, using comparison between two accounts. Does a later account add, omit, or conserve parts of an earlier account of the same event? The third consideration is the vocabulary and style of a writer. Does the text reflect preferred words for the editor, or are there words that he rarely uses or attempts to avoid using? If the wording reflects the language of the editor, it points toward editorial reworking of a text, while if it is unused or avoided language, then it points toward being part of an earlier source. From these considerations, redaction critics can sketch out the distinctive elements of an author or editor's theology. If a writer consistently avoids reporting, for example, the weaknesses of the Twelve, even when he has earlier sources that provide fine details of their follies, one could draw the conclusion that the later editor or author held the Twelve in higher esteem, either because of his own presuppositions, or because he perhaps is trying to reinforce the legitimacy of those chosen by Jesus to carry on his work. Through tracking the overall impact of this editorial activity, one can come away with fairly strong picture of the purpose of a particular writing.

The advantages of redaction criticism can be summarized as follows. First, it emphasizes the creative role of the author. Second, redaction critics from disparate traditions and presuppositions can still find wide agreement on their work since the purpose of an author or editor is largely still recoverable. Third, it can show us some of the environment in the communities to which works were written. If an author is writing a Gospel, he is probably trying to correct or reinforce some issue in the social setting of the community to which he is writing. Fourth, it shows that historical narratives in the Bible are not primarily concerned with chronological accounts of historic events, but have theological agendas, though this does not justify the notion that the accounts are non–historical. Against redaction criticism, we can say that in Gospel studies, it assumes Markan priority, which, while widely agreed, is not unanimously accepted. Next, it tends perhaps to lay too much store on the creativity of the author. Third, sometimes it is asserted that what has been added or modified in a text is unhistorical, when it could simply be the addition of another source or perspective. Fourth, there has also been a tendency to see only what an author has modified as being the important aspects of his theology, while ignoring the possible importance of those items which he has preserved. Fifth, sometimes redaction critics make too much out of minor differences in detail.

It is not infrequent that, in some mistaken biblical exegesis, one finds assertions that certain aspects of the life of Christ as recorded in the Gospels are unhistorical. With striking confidence it is declared that particular events and teachings are the outgrowth of the evangelists' imagination, or a retrospective projection of events and sayings, which amplify the personality of Christ in the light of the Resurrection. Thus it is alleged, for example, that the infancy narratives in Luke and Matthew are creations of the sacred writers in the light of some parallel Old Testament events, and that this is a literary device to give status to the birth of Jesus. Consequently, according to some exegetes, there is no historical basis for the message of the angels to the shepherds, or the visit of the Magi to Bethlehem. The historical authenticity of central doctrines of the faith such as the virginal conception of Christ, Jesus' self–knowledge as the pre–existing Son of God, the fact that He instituted the priesthood and the episcopate is sometimes undermined, doctrines the certainty of which the Church has always seen affirmed in the Gospel accounts.

The problem here is essentially a denial of the fundamental historical character of the gospels. It is an attitude of mind which is nourished by several different influences. At one level there is an implicit denial of the supernatural character of the Incarnation. The tendency, begun in liberalism and modernism which reduces faith to a mere idea, culminated in R. Bultmann's approach. The continuing influence of M. Dibelius and R. Bultmann, the principal founders of the form–critical phase of historical–critical interpretation, continues to have a great impact on modern exegesis. The Bultmannian school postulates a complete discontinuity between the Jesus of history and the Christ of faith, with the consequent need to 'demythologize' the gospel accounts to get to the basic kerygma, or proclaimed message. To explain the genesis of the gospels, form criticism affirmed that the environment in which the gospels crystallized was the primitive Christian community. This community, the form critics say, was 'anonymous' and 'creative,' and was influenced by contiguous pagan cultures in such a manner that it provided the type of popular setting in which legends are born. The gospel stories are thus a product of 'faith' and not of history, because faith and scientific history are incompatible. This exegetical approach, as can be clearly seen, undermines both the historicity of the Gospels and the doctrine of the divine inspiration of Scripture as the Church has always understood them. Bultmann's conclusions are not the scientific result of historical findings but emerge from a framework of systematic presuppositions, involving the use of an evolutionist model of natural science within biblical theology, as well as an existentialist philosophy.[26] This liberal or modernist approach to Scriptural interpretation exaggerates the role of human techniques in the formation of the Bible and in its exegesis. In a rationalist way, it seeks to reduce to merely symbolic or mythological meanings that which in fact Scripture teaches as true at the deepest level. Both Catholic and Protestant theologies have at various times suffered the ravages of modernist reductionism.

The Church has pointed out that form criticism may be used, but with due caution. The reason is that dubious philosophical and theological principles have often come to be mixed with this method, which not uncommonly have undermined the method itself as well as the conclusions in the literary area. 'For some proponents of this method have been led astray by the prejudiced views of rationalism. They refuse to admit the existence of a supernatural order and the intervention of a personal God in the world through strict revelation, and the possibility and existence of miracles and prophecies. Others begin with a false idea of faith, as if it had nothing to do with historical truth, or rather were incompatible with it. Others deny the historical value and nature of the documents of revelation almost a priori. Finally, others make light of the authority of the apostles as witnesses to Christ, and of their task and influence in the primitive community, extolling rather the creative power of that community. All such views are not only opposed to Catholic doctrine, but are also devoid of scientific basis and alien to the correct principles of historical method.'[27]

3.3.3 Hermeneutics: Understanding Revelation

In all human communication, the receiver must extract meaning from the symbols (the message) used by the communicator. Hermeneutics (from the Greek word ἑρμηνεία which means speech or interpretation) is used to describe the process of understanding or of discovering meaning from the Bible. It refers to four stages. First, the passage from mind to language on the part of the writer, as language interprets the mind. Second, the process of translation from an ancient language to a modern one (see 1 Co 12:10, which actually uses the word interpretation, or ἑρμηνεία). Third, interpretation is carried out by commentary and explanation on the part of the teaching Church. Fourth, the receiver of the message also interprets the message.

Hermeneutics is a very general term, but in classical biblical studies it is divided into three constituent disciplines: *noematics*, the general study of the various meanings of Scripture; *heuristics*, which studies the specific meanings of texts by using certain literary and doctrinal criteria; and *prophoristics*, which is the exposition of biblical materials for the general public. *Exegesis* is the study of the meaning of a text in relationship to theology and the Church as a whole, and embraces the subject matter of heuristics and prophoristics; it includes the historical and literary study of a text, a determination of the text's meaning within the context of the wider canon of Scripture, and its application to the Church's life today.

In order to interpret the Bible in a scholarly manner, its twofold character must always be kept in view: it is a Divine book, in so far as it has God for its author; it is a human book, in as far as it is written by men for men. In its human character, the Bible is subject to the same rules of interpretation as other books; but in its Divine character, it is given into the custody of the Church to be kept and explained, so that it needs special rules of hermeneutics. Under the former aspect, it is subject to the laws of the literary and historical interpretation; under the latter, it is bound by the precepts of what we may call the Catholic explanation.

Exegesis as the study of a text or book in the light of other revealed truths is at the service of the Church. Essential to the success of any exegete is that he possess the proper dispositions for studying the Bible. The New Testament is much more than an ancient document that can be grasped by the principles of human scholarship alone. Rather, Scripture has a Divine Author and conveys a truth that transcends human reason. The exegete must therefore have faith in order to study God's Word properly. Since God is also goodness, there must be moral rectitude in the exegete's will. If these are lacking, a biblical researcher will stay only on the surface of texts and never grasp their full meaning. Faith entails the acceptance of a biblical text as containing an infallible truth and not simply a human thought or opinion. Faith connects the scholar with the entire context of Scripture and indeed with Revelation as a whole. It gives him a greater penetration into the real meaning and import of the sacred texts, and opens him to the Holy Spirit's gift of understanding. Without faith that God can truly elevate the human intellect and move the will, one would miss the whole message of the prophetic, sapiential, and psalmist literature. Without faith that God can truly intervene in history, the scholar would not be able to grasp even the literal meaning of a biblical narrative, and what the author, as a man of faith, was trying to say.

The moral virtues that open the exegete to the true Word of God are: humility, by which he recalls the limited value of his own mind or ideas before the holy text; charity, by which he recalls that Scripture is really a manifestation of God's love for us and an invitation to enter into His intimate life; and patience, by which he avoids rash conclusions and reflects upon his material in the light of a higher truth. It is appropriate for the researcher to pray to the Holy Spirit before he studies, especially asking for His gifts: wisdom, so that he might consider the text in the light of God's providence and loving plan for mankind; understanding, so that he can connect his research with other truths of faith; fortitude, so that he not be discouraged by the difficulty or obscurity of a given Hebrew or Greek text or the many theories about it; fear of God, so that he revere and appreciate the power and justice of God in the texts he studies, and not become proud in his own conceptions; and finally, piety, by which he recognizes the sacred text as just that – sacred – to which he owes a great reverence.

Christians must discover the meaning intended by the authors of the books of the Bible to understand what God is revealing. All Christians recognize that how we approach the Bible determines often what we take from it. Understanding what God would have us know from the Bible involves comprehending the following points. First, the Bible contains some very ancient books with a timeless message. Next, sometimes it is not even known who the author of a book really was. Furthermore, since many authors were ancient Semites, their way of thinking and manner of expressing themselves differ in some ways from our own; for example, the concept of the 'heart'.[28] There are also linguistic challenges. Also, since we do not possess any original manuscripts of the books of the Bible, we have to contend with copying and editing which occurred over time, but which we know is reliable.[29] Then there is the issue of the multiplicity of human authors and editors complicates our understanding. Finally, the fact of both a divine and a human author makes understanding a challenge. The Catholic Church has been solicitous over the way in which the Bible is interpreted. Experience teaches us that it is easy to find even contradictory meanings from the same Scripture with a careless approach to reading and interpreting the Bible.

3.3.3.1 Interpreting Difficult passages

The Raising of Jairus' Daughter

Let us consider the difficulty raised by the accounts of the raising of Jairus' daughter (Matthew 9:18; Mark 5:21; Luke

8:40). Mark and Luke assert that Jairus approached Jesus when He and the disciples got out of the boat near Capernaum, as crowds came rushing up to Him. Matthew, on the other hand, states that it was while John the Baptist's disciples were talking with Jesus at Matthew's house that Jairus approached Him. Some commentators have wrestled with this apparent contradiction, and some have even concluded that the event must have happened twice – that Jairus' daughter died and was raised by Jesus on two different occasions![30]

Liberal scholars, of course, see evidence here of conflicting oral traditions: 'This may be because Matthew is drawing upon an independent tradition (e.g., the Galiliean tradition, proposed by Lohmeyer), or it may be an instance of Matthew's simplification of a story in the interests of catechetical use.'[31] Surprisingly, Evangelicals sometimes offer a similar solution: 'We can probably explain this difference in order by assuming that in the oral period the account of Jesus' raising of Jairus' daughter circulated as an independent unit whose meaning was complete in itself.' They would go on to say that individual pericopes like the healing of Jairus' daughter 'are often best interpreted as self–contained units whose connection with the surrounding materials should not be pressed.'[32]

However, Matthew makes the explicit assertion that there is a connection. In Matthew's account, Jesus arrives in Capernaum, heals a paralytic, calls Matthew and attends his dinner, then gets into a discussion with John the Baptist's disciples at that dinner about fasting. Matthew states that it was while He was talking with John's disciples that Jairus approached Him. Mark, however, writes that it was when Jesus arrived in the boat that a great multitude approached Him – such a great multitude that Jesus was unable to move away from the seashore. Then Jairus approached Him. In this case, merely saying that the order is not important hardly solves the problem. The text makes clear assertions about order. So which is it? Did Jairus approach Jesus at the seashore or at Matthew's dinner? We need to work methodically through the principles of harmonization.

The synoptics are all describing the same event. We are given details such as Jairus' name, the age of his daughter, her name, the cynical reaction of the mourners, and numerous other significant details. Most importantly, all three synoptics record the story of the healing of woman with the haemorrhage that occurred on the way to Jairus' house. That all of these details and events would happen twice is hard to believe.

The authors provide details in the narrative that infer a sequence. Mark and Luke make mention of a huge crowd that greeted Jesus at the seashore, and then they also mention that a crowd followed Jesus on the way to Jairus' house. They seem to infer that this was the same crowd, and thus that Jairus' approach to Jesus occurred soon after He arrived in the boat and was met by the crowd. Are the authors explicitly indicating sequential connection to other events? Matthew definitely does this by stating that 'while He was saying these things to them, behold, there came a synagogue official, and bowed down before Him, saying, "My daughter has just died..."'(Mt 9:18). To assert that Jairus approached Jesus at any other time would raise questions about the inerrancy of Matthew 9:18, for he makes an explicit assertion about the sequence of events.

Mark does not make an explicit statement of sequence, but gives a strong impression that it was while Jesus was gathering about Jesus at the seashore: 'And when Jesus had crossed over again in the boat to the other side, a great multitude gathered about Him; and He stayed by the seashore. And one of the synagogue officials named Jairus came up, and upon seeing Him, fell at His feet' (Mk 5:21). Luke is the least specific: 'And as Jesus returned, the multitude welcomed Him, for they had all been waiting for Him. And behold, there came a man named Jairus' (Lk 8:40).

We would have to answer then, that Matthew does make

an explicit sequential connection, whereas Mark and Luke do not. So in this case, although Matthew is the least chronologically–concerned of the three synoptics, we must first accept that in this case Matthew's account is chronologically accurate. How then can we explain the sequence that Mark and Luke infer?

Mark seems to indicate strongly that Jesus was by the seashore when Jairus approached him. Some exegetes say that this is Mark's intent: 'Jesus was again to be found 'beside the sea,' near Capernaum; with a large crowd assembled about him, as usual. It was then that Jairus fell prostrate at his feet.'[33] In fact, as we open the various commentaries written on the Book of Mark, one after the other, each commentary understands Mark to portray Jesus by the lakeshore, surrounded by throngs, with Jairus talking to Him. Yet none of them addresses the problem this creates when compared with Matthew's account.[34]

What is important here is that neither Mark nor Luke make specific statements about when Jairus approached Jesus. Both describe the scene at Jesus' arrival, and then move on to the story of Jairus without necessarily connecting the two scenes. As one scholar says of Mark's account, 'Whether the incident of Jairus' daughter takes place on the day of landing is not said; it is represented as the next event of importance.'[35] Luke is even more vague – he simply states that when Jesus arrived, the multitudes welcomed Him and had been waiting for Him. We can fairly conclude that Mark has omitted several events that actually occurred between Mark 5:21 and 22, and that Luke has followed Mark in this omission. Concerning the issue of the crowds, there were always crowds that followed Jesus during this period. Matthew's account of these events shows that the multitudes were following Jesus each step of the way. So to argue that the crowd that met Jesus at the seashore and the crowd that followed Him to Jairus' house are the same is unfounded textually.

Upon Jesus' return from across the lake, the Gospels

reveal a general sequence we can follow.

1. Jesus was greeted at the seashore by a crowd.

2. Jesus healed a paralytic before a huge crowd.

3. Jesus called Matthew and went to a dinner at his house.

4. Jesus had a discussion with the Pharisees, and then the disciples of John.

5. Jairus approached Jesus about his dying daughter.

6. Jesus healed the woman with the haemorrhage.

7. Jesus raised Jairus' daughter.

The resolution of the apparent paradox runs like this. Matthew records all these events in this sequence. Mark and Luke record event 1, and then jump to event 4. Mark and Luke have placed events 2–4 at an earlier part of their gospels. In this case, it is most likely that Mark and Luke have rearranged the order for two reasons. One, Matthew makes more explicit statements about the sequence of these events, whereas Mark and Luke are more vague. Second, Matthew was an eyewitness to these events. These events surrounded the calling of Matthew to discipleship and the ensuing dinner he gave for Jesus at his house. He would have been present when Jairus approached Jesus at his dinner. These were undoubtedly events Matthew remembered well.

The Anointing of Jesus

The anointing of Jesus is an event reported by the Synoptic Gospels and the Gospel of John, in which a woman pours the entire contents of an *alabastron* of very expensive perfume over the head of Jesus. This event is a subject of considerable debate, as many scholars hold that it is actually two separate events: one occurring at the beginning of Jesus' ministry in which He offered forgiveness to a repentant woman, and the other in which He is anointed in preparation for His burial. Luke's Gospel speaks of Jesus' feet being anointed by a woman had been sinful all her life, and who was crying; and when her tears started landing on the feet of Jesus, she wiped His feet with her hair (Lk 7:36–50). Many biblical historians hold that this episode could not have occurred only a few days prior to the crucifixion, due to the numerous events that followed in Luke's Gospel. John 12:1–8 names her Mary, and the text assumes her to be Mary, a sister to Lazarus, as it also identifies her sister Martha. Although the woman's act has traditionally been associated with Mary Magdalene, there is no biblical text identifying her as such. According to the Gospel of Mark 14:3 the perfume in his account was the purest of spikenard oil.

The passage in Luke is similar to another episode of Jesus being anointed by a woman, and is often confused with it. So if we are to understand the story of Jesus anointed by a sinful woman, we need to disentangle it from the story of Jesus' anointing at Bethany near the end of His ministry (Matthew 26:6–13; Mark 14:1–11; John 12:1–10). The two events are confused easily enough because of several similarities: Jesus is anointed with expensive perfume, He is anointed by a woman, and the anointing takes place in the house of a man named Simon.

However, the differences between the accounts show that the passage in Luke 7:36–50 is really a different incident from that found in Matthew 26:6–13; Mark 14:1–11; John 12:1–10. The anointing at Bethany differs in that it takes place at the home of Simon the Leper, not Simon the Pharisee. The woman doing the anointing at Bethany is not spoken of as sinful, but actually appears to be Mary, Lazarus' sister. Furthermore, the meaning of the anointing at Bethany is to prefigure Jesus' burial. Also, the anointing is on the head in Matthew and Mark, although on the feet in John. The criticism is by disciples, especially Judas, over the value of the perfume that is 'wasted', rather than a criticism of the morals of the woman doing the anointing.

In John the use of the word 'dinner' refers exclusively to

Jesus' Last Supper with His disciples. This dinner has echoes of that meal. John's version of the story combines elements from both Luke and Mark, namely Mary anoints Jesus' feet (Luke) but this is linked with Jesus' burial (Mark). In John the verb 'to wipe' is the same verb used to describe Jesus' wiping of His disciples' feet at the foot–washing in John 13:5. Mary's anointing and wiping of Jesus' feet thus point toward Jesus' foot–washing at the Last Supper.

A possible conclusion is that the four Gospels represent two anointing incidents. The first chronologically is seen in Luke 7:36–50. The second chronologically is represented by Mark 14:1–11, upon which Matthew 26:6–13 is totally dependent. The episode in John 12:1–8 is an amalgamated story, incorporating details from both incidents and adding details from Luke 10:38–42. It is significant that by actually replacing the original location of the pouring of the 'costly ointment of pure nard' from Jesus' head (Mk 14:3=Mt 26:7), originally understood as a prophetic act of messianic character, parallel to St Peter's confession at Caesarea Philippi (Mk 8:27ff and parallels), to Jesus' feet (Jn 12:3), John made a woman proleptically anticipate the incident of the washing by Jesus Himself of His disciples' feet. By so doing, John changed even an act of 'witness' into an act of 'diakonia'. The mystical significance of St John's account of the anointing is further underlined by the mention of Mary's action in John 11:2. This verse constitutes a *prolepsis* – a rhetorical figure consisting in the anticipation of a future event.[36] From the Synoptic Gospels, Christians of John's day already knew about Martha and Mary from Luke 10:38–42. Therefore John's reference in John 11:2 to Mary's anointing of Jesus in John 12:2 is clearly understandable as underlining the mystical importance of Mary's action in John chapter 12, by anticipating it in John chapter 11. Moreover, the context of John chapter 11 is the raising of Lazarus which itself prefigures the Resurrection of Jesus Christ.

3.3.4 An Introduction to Biblical Genres

In general terms, we may define a *genre* as a category or type of literature (or of art, music, and so forth) character-ized by a particular form, style, or content. This definition stems from the fact that there are many possible ways to classify or categorize human communications. One could start by distinguishing between *verbal* and *non–verbal* communications. Then, verbal communications (using words) could be *oral* (spoken and heard) or *written* (reading and writing). Non–verbal communications can include signs and symbols, body–language, paintings. Next, the largest division of literary works is between *poetry* and *prose*; but one could also consider rhetoric, film, drama, comedy, laws, and so forth as separate divisions. One might also distinguish *how* or *where* the material is published, such as books, journals, magazines, newspapers, newsletters, flyers, posters, letters, internet. There are many different *large literary genres* (whole books), like biographies, histo-ries, technical manuals, textbooks, poetic anthologies, legal codes, novels. There are also many *smaller genres* or *subgroups* within each of these larger categories, such as the fact that newspapers contain news articles, editorials, sports results, financial reports, obituaries, comics, classified ads, movie reviews, and so forth.

The biblical scholar classifies the various literary genres, studies their features, and considers how and where such forms were actually used in the 'life setting' of the religious communities. We may consider an analogy with biology. Modern biologists classify plants and animals into differ-ent classes, orders, families, genus, and species. They describe each category in detail, and study how one genus or species differs from another. They also consider how each genus or species interacts with and is affected by its environment. Biblical scholars do similar things in classi-fying each biblical text as part of a certain genre or sub–genre. They describe each genre or form, and study the characteristics that distinguish one form from another. They also consider when and where ancient Jews or Christians first used such materials. The principle is that understanding the parts, we may better understand the whole.

Several major genres are present within the New Testament. First, *Gospels* or proclamations of the 'good news' about Jesus intended to establish and strengthen people's faith in him; these are quasi–biographical, historical portraits of the life, teachings, death and Resurrection of Jesus. This genre comprises the Gospels of Matthew, Mark, Luke, and John. Next we find the genre of *Acts*, a partial narrative account about the beginnings and the growth of early Christianity; this is not a complete history of the early Church, since it focuses on the essential actions of a few missionary leaders. In this genre we find the Acts of the Apostles.

The third type of genre we find is that of *Letters*, or literary structures addressing practical and theological issues relevant to particular communities. Under this heading are found St Paul's Letters to Christian communities in the various cities: Romans, 1 Corinthians, 2 Corinthians, Galatians, Ephesians, Philippians, Colossians, 1 Thessalonians, 2 Thessalonians. The fourth genre is that of *Letters to individual Christian leaders*, which include 1 Timothy, 2 Timothy, Titus and Philemon. These Letters also contain collections of instructions for the practical organization of religious communities. The first three Letters are called the 'Pastoral Letters'. Also, 2 Timothy is sometimes seen under the sub–genre of a *Testament*, or a document that gives a dying person's last wishes and instructions for his successors. The fifth genre is that of *Homily*, a Biblical 'Sermon' which interprets Jesus in light of the Old Testament; the only example is the Letter to the Hebrews of which neither the author nor the audience is explicitly mentioned. The sixth genre is that of the seven *Catholic Epistles*. These are attributed to early Apostles, and were written to broader audiences, hence the expression 'Catholic' signifying 'general' or 'universal'. Here we find the Letter of James, 1 Peter, 2 Peter, 1 John, 2 John, 3 John, and Jude. Here again we can form sub–genres. The Letter of James can be regarded as a *Wisdom Collection,* a collection of general instructions on how to live a good Christian life. Also 1 Peter, 2 Peter, and 1 John can be termed *Encyclical Letters,* or more stylized literary works in letter format, intended for broader audiences. The seventh genre is that of *Apocalypse,* a vividly symbolic narrative that reveals God's fulfilment of history. Current historical problems become a springboard for looking forward to God's present and future action in history, especially at the End Times, with Christ's Second Coming, and the New Heavens and New Earth. Struggles between good and evil also characterize this genre. The example of an *Apocalypse* is the Book of Revelation.

The lists described above are *not comprehensive,* but include only the more prominent categories of New Testament biblical literature. There are many other *smaller genres* found within the various books. For example, the New Testament Gospels contain narrative materials, discourse materials, and some mixed genres. *Narrative* genres include genealogies; narrator's introductions; transitions and summary passages; miracle stories; call stories; conflict or controversy stories; vision reports, and so forth. *Discourse* genres include parables and allegories; hymns and prayers; laws and legal interpretations; exhortations, short individual sayings or proverbs; longer speeches, discourses or monologues, and so forth. *Mixed* genres include longer narratives that contain extended dialogues, and 'pronouncement stories' or 'apothegms' (short narratives that climax in a short saying or proverb). Many of these sub–genres can also be *further sub–divided.* For example, 'miracles' can include healings, exorcisms, restoration miracles, nature miracles, and so forth. Among the miracles, there are three episodes when Jesus raised someone from the dead: the Widow's son in Luke 7:11–17, Jairus' daughter in Matthew 9:18–26, and Lazarus in John 11:1–44.

3.3.5 The senses of Scripture

Interpretation of the inspired Scriptures must be attentive above all to what God desires to reveal through the sacred authors for our salvation:

> It is the task of exegetes to work, according to these rules, towards a better understanding and explanation of the meaning of Sacred Scripture in order that their research may help the Church to form a firmer judgement. For, of course, all that has been said about the manner of interpreting Scripture is ultimately subject to the judgement of the Church which exercises the divinely conferred commission and ministry of watching over and interpreting the Word of God.[37]

What comes from the Spirit is not fully 'understood except by the Spirit's action.'[38] Or, in the words of St Augustine: 'But I would not believe in the Gospel, had not the authority of the Catholic Church already moved me.'[39] According to an ancient tradition, one can distinguish between two senses of Scripture: the literal and the spiritual, the latter being subdivided into the typical, moral (or tropological) and anagogical senses. The profound concordance of the various senses guarantees all its richness to the living reading of Scripture in the Church. We analyze biblical texts in order to synthesize the truth which they contain. A sense can be understood as a 'layer of meaning'.

3.3.5.1 Literal Sense

The starting point then for understanding the Bible is the *literal sense*. The Catholic Church teaches that the first principle of hermeneutics is the literal meaning of the text. St Jerome wrote that all interpretation rests on the literal sense.[40] St Thomas Aquinas pointed out: 'All other senses of Sacred Scripture are based on the literal.'[41] Pope Pius XII declared:

> Let the interpreters bear in mind that their foremost

and greatest endeavour should be to discern and
define clearly that sense of the biblical words which
is called literal. Aided by the context and by
comparison with similar passages, let them
therefore by means of their knowledge of languages
search out with all diligence the literal meaning of
the words.[42]

We may define the literal sense of Scripture as the meaning
which the human author, under divine inspiration, directly
intended and which the author's words convey. This literal
sense is the meaning conveyed by the words of Scripture
and discovered by exegesis, following the rules of sound
interpretation.

The are certain useful criteria to understand the literal
sense. The literary form or genre that the author used is the
first aid in determining what the author meant. If the author
wrote poetry instead of history, then the literary form of
poetry assists in determining the meaning intended by the
author. Some other literary forms of the Bible include
history, law, songs, love stories, parables, and so forth. One
should remember, however, that the form is a vehicle for
the content. Next, the literary history of the biblical book or
of the section of the Bible that contains the book also aids in
determining the meaning intended by the author. Literary
history of a book includes what is known about the author,
his background, his historical period.

As an example of the Church exploring the literal sense
of a scripture passage in order to understand what meaning
should be seen from it, we can consider the sixth chapter of
the Gospel according to John. One should bear in mind that
John's Gospel is very Eucharistic. The literary form of John
6:25–69 is that of a discourse. It was preceded by two important miracles which have Eucharistic connotations, namely
the Wedding Feast at Cana (Jn 2:1–12), and the Multiplication of the Loaves (Jn 6:1–15), which occurred near Passover
(Jn 6:4) just like Last Supper (Jn 13:1). Most scripture scholars today affirm that John's Gospel is historical in nature.

Hence we believe that John strove to preserve both the words and actions of Jesus. Unlike the Synoptics, John wrote through the eyes of the faith of the late Apostolic Church in light of the way that faith translated into practice and worship.

Now we can move to our interpretation of John 6:25–69. Following the details of the multiplication of the loaves and fishes, Jesus walks on the sea and then He reacts to the crowds' need for signs. Jesus takes them from manna, bread from heaven, to 'true bread from heaven (v. 32)' ... 'I am the bread (v. 35).' 'I am the bread that came down from heaven (v. 41).' Jesus is saying this: 'I am the bread that came down from heaven.' The best way a person can make a clear literal point is repetition (a literary form which emphasizes the literal meaning) of the same message in different ways. This is important, because the New Testament is economical. We have the sub–genre of repetition which points to a literal interpretation. Five times in different verbal expressions, Jesus confirmed the reality of the meaning he intended. First, He proclaimed: 'I am the living bread that came down from heaven; whoever eats this bread will live forever; and the bread that I will give is my flesh for the life of the world' (Jn 6:51). Then in verse 53, He affirmed: 'Amen, amen, I say to you, unless you eat the flesh of the Son of Man and drink His blood, you do not have life within you.' 'Amen, amen, I say to you' is a solemn mode of emphasis which further highlights this point and is sometimes rendered 'I tell you most solemnly.' In verse 54, Jesus stated: 'Whoever eats my flesh and drinks my blood has eternal life, and I will raise him on the last day.' In John 6:55, He said 'For my flesh is true food, and my blood is true drink.' Then in verse 56, He added: 'Whoever eats my flesh and drinks my blood remains in me and I in him.' The use of the word 'flesh' links with John 1:14, 'The Word was made flesh,' referring to the Incarnation. Thus the Eucharist is the extension of the Incarnation. Confirmation of this Eucharistic sense of the passage is further bolstered by reading John 6:60, 66: 'Then many of His disciples who were listening said, "This saying is hard; who can accept it?" ... As a result of this, many (of) His disciples returned to their former way of life and no longer accompanied Him.' Had these disciples mistaken the meaning of His words, Jesus, knowing their thoughts and their error, would surely have known and corrected them. He didn't do this, so they had clearly understood His meaning. Jesus' flesh was to be really eaten; His blood to be really drunk. This observation leads to the Fuller sense which is necessary for understanding John 6:51–56. Significantly, St Peter makes his profession of faith at the end of this passage (Jn 6:67-69).

This Fuller sense is obtained by considering other passages in the New Testament to provide a synthetic and unitary picture. The various New Testament accounts of Jesus feeding the Multitudes, the Last Supper of Jesus with the Disciples, and the early Christian Church's commemoration of the Lord's Supper (also called the Breaking of the Bread), contain similar patterns of four key verbs, again making a clear literal point with *repetition*. These miracles and the accounts of the institution of the Eucharist are linked by a common literary form, which helps to set the miracles in a Eucharistic context. If we consider the Feeding of the 5000 (in all four Gospels), we find a common literary form with the use of four verbs being repeated, namely taking, blessing, breaking, giving. In Mark 6:41, we read: '*Taking* the five loaves and the two fish, He looked up to heaven, and *blessed* and *broke* the loaves, and *gave* them to His disciples to set before the people; and He divided the two fish among them all.' In Matthew 14:19, we read: '*Taking* the five loaves and the two fish, He looked up to heaven, and *blessed* and *broke* the loaves, and *gave* them to the disciples, and the disciples gave them to the crowds.' In Luke 9:16, we read: 'And *taking* the five loaves and the two fish, He looked up to heaven, and *blessed* and *broke* them, and *gave* them to the disciples to set before the crowd.' Finally, in John 6:11, the text reads 'Then Jesus *took* the loaves, and when He had *given thanks*, He *distributed* them to those who were seated; so also the fish, as much as they wanted.'

Turning to the episode of the Feeding of the 4000 (only in Mark and Matthew, not in Luke or John), we find the same dynamic. Mark recounts that 'He *took* the seven loaves, and after *giving thanks* He *broke* them and *gave* them to His disciples to distribute; and they distributed them to the crowd' (Mk 8:6). Similarly, Matthew recounts that 'He *took* the seven loaves and the fish; and after *giving thanks* He *broke* them and *gave* them to the disciples, and the disciples gave them to the crowds' (Mt 15:36).

Accounts of the Last Supper are to be found in the Synoptic Gospels, and in Paul, but in a very different form in John. In fact, the whole of St John's Gospel is eucharistic. St Mark recounts that 'While they were eating, He *took* a loaf of bread, and after *blessing* it He *broke* it, *gave* it to them, and said, "Take; this is my body." Then He *took* a cup, and after *giving thanks* He *gave* it to them, and all of them drank from it. He said to them, "This is my blood of the covenant, which is poured out for many" (Mk 14:22–24). Similarly St Matthew states: 'While they were eating, Jesus *took* a loaf of bread, and after *blessing* it He *broke* it, *gave* it to the disciples, and said, "Take, eat; this is my body." Then He *took* a cup, and after *giving thanks* He *gave* it to them, saying, "Drink from it, all of you; for this is my blood of the covenant, which is poured out for many for the forgiveness of sins"' (Mt 26:26). Luke's account runs: 'Then He *took* a cup, and after *giving thanks* He said, "Take this and *divide it* among yourselves";... Then He *took* a loaf of bread, and when He had *given thanks*, He *broke* it and *gave* it to them, saying, "This is my body, which is given for you. Do this in remembrance of me." And He did the same with the cup after supper, saying, "This cup that is poured out for you is the new covenant in my blood"'(Lk 22:17, 19–20). St Paul's account inserts the Eucharist into tradition:

> For I received from the Lord what I also handed on

to you, that the Lord Jesus on the night when He was betrayed *took* a loaf of bread, and when He had *given thanks*, He *broke* it and said, 'This is my body that is for you. Do this in remembrance of me.' In the same way He *took* the cup also, after supper, saying, 'This cup is the new covenant in my blood. Do this, as often as you drink it, in remembrance of me.' For as often as you eat this bread and drink the cup, you proclaim the Lord's death until He comes (1 Co 11:23–26).

Another example of the same dynamic, found only in St Luke's Gospel, relates to the Supper at Emmaus: 'When He was at table with them, He *took* bread, *blessed* it, and *broke* it, and *gave* it to them. Then their eyes were opened, and they recognized Him; and He vanished from their sight... That same hour they got up and returned to Jerusalem; and they found the eleven and their companions gathered together... Then they told what had happened on the road, and how He had been made known to them in the breaking of the bread' (Luke 24:30–31, 33, 35). Accounts of the early Christian Eucharist refer to it as the breaking of the bread, as we see from the Acts of the Apostles: 'They (the community of believers and converts in Jerusalem) devoted themselves to the apostles' teaching and fellowship, *to the breaking of bread* and the prayers' (Ac 2:42).

In the Mass, the Church adopts the very same Words of Institution as Jesus Christ used at the Last Supper. Throughout the centuries, during the celebration of the Mass, the priest speaks such words as these, based on the above New Testament texts:

Before He was given up to death, a death He freely accepted, Jesus *took* bread, and *gave you thanks*. He *broke* the bread, *gave* it to his disciples and said: 'Take this, all of you, and eat it: This is my body which will be given up for you.' When supper was ended, He *took* the cup. Again He *gave you thanks* and praise, *gave* the cup to His disciples, and said: 'Take this, all of you, and drink from it: This is the cup of my blood, the blood of the new and everlasting covenant. It will be shed for you and for all, so that sins may be forgiven. Do this in memory of me.'[43]

3.3.5.2 Fuller Sense

St Jerome also said that we must not stop at the simple literal sense: 'Just as we have to seek gold in the earth, for the kernel in the shell, for the chestnut's hidden fruit beneath its hairy coverings, so in Holy Scripture we have to dig deep for its divine meaning.'[44] We must seek the fuller sense which is like finding the root of a plant. The Bible has God, a divine author, besides the human author. The Church teaches that there exists a more–than–literal meaning for understanding the Bible: *a fuller sense*. This sense, which goes beyond the face value, is connected with the important idea of *synthesis*, namely connection with other facets of faith and theology to make a global whole. The definition of the fuller sense is: 'The deeper meaning intended by God as divine author.' The fuller sense of Scripture, since it is the meaning intended by God, may not have been clearly known and intended by the human author.

The following criteria are helpful to establish the fuller sense. First, because the Catholic Church holds that there are sources of Divine Revelation, Scripture and Tradition, both under the authority of the Holy Spirit, the fuller sense of the Bible can be found in the authoritative interpretation of those revealed sources. Some of these authorities are the New Testament itself, the Fathers of the Church, the Church in Council (see the early Church model in Acts 15), the 'faithful people' faithful to what was handed down to them, all guided and guaranteed by the Magisterium. Second, the fuller sense of any Scripture text has to be in agreement with the literal sense of the words. This fuller sense must be a consequential development of what the human author of the text intended to say under divine inspiration. The fuller sense goes in the same direction as the literal sense, but gives a more complete picture.

An example of the fuller sense in the interpretation of Scripture is found by looking at the following New Testament passage. In the Gospel according to Matthew, Chapter 1, verse 23, Matthew says that the conception of Jesus by Mary was a virginal conception and took place so that the words of the prophet Isaiah (7:14) might be fulfilled. Matthew, under the inspiration of the Holy Spirit, gives an interpretation of Isaiah which goes beyond the literal to the fuller sense. Matthew clearly interprets Isaiah in a fuller sense: the unmarried woman is the Virgin Mary, and God–with–us is Jesus Christ. The Fuller sense enriches the picture, because passages of the Bible are complementary. Parallel texts furnish a complementary picture, leading to the fuller sense. For example, as regards the Eucharist, see Matthew 26:26–30; Mark 14:22–26; Luke 22:14–23.; Acts 2:42; 1 Corinthians 11:23–26.

3.3.5.3 *Other Senses*

A medieval couplet summarizes the significance and relation of the various senses: 'The Letter speaks of deeds; Allegory to faith; The Moral how to act; Anagogy our destiny.'[45] St Thomas Aquinas defined these four senses of Sacred Scripture in his *Summa Theologiae.*[46]

Allegorical and typical senses

Two basic figures of speech are simile and metaphor. In *simile*, one thing is compared to another of a different kind and the similarity is expressed by the words 'like' or 'as'. For example, Jesus sends out His disciples *as* lambs among wolves (Lk 10:3). (Like things are employed). In *metaphor*, (from the Greek *metapherein*, carrying over), a more literary figure, the qualities of one thing are directly ascribed to another without an explicit point of comparison. For example, Jesus said: 'You are the salt of the earth' (Mt 5:13). (Unlike things are employed).

In general, a *parable* (from the Greek *parabolē*, placing

things side by side for comparison) is a *developed simile,* where the story while abstract is still true to life (in contrast to fable). The object of the parable is the total vision. Thus the kingdom is not simply like the net, but like the catch of fish and the separation of the good from the bad. (Mt 13:47). *Allegory* is a *developed metaphor* or series of metaphors, less clear and more elusive than parable. In allegory each detail or character is significant, often with a hidden meaning. For example see Mark 4:1–20, which is an allegorized parable of the sower and the seed.

While the allegorical sense is *imaginative,* involving the use of a story, typology is based on *historical connections.* Following the lead of Paul himself (see Rom 5:14) there is another way for seeing meaning in the Bible: *the typical sense.* Also St Peter points this out in his First Letter (1 Pt 3:20–21). The definition of the *typical sense* of Bible texts is the deeper meaning that some elements (persons, places, things and events) of the Bible have because God, the divine author of the Bible, intended that these elements fore-shadow (or prefigure) further things. The typical sense is an indication of the divine inspiration of texts.

We can acquire a more profound understanding of events by recognizing their significance in Christ; thus the crossing of the Red Sea is a sign or type of Christ's victory and also of Christian Baptism. Cf. 1 Co 10:1–2. Originally a type (*tupos*) meant a 'model' or 'pattern' or 'mould' into which clay or wax was pressed, that it might take the figure or exact shape of the mould. The word 'type' is generally used to denote a resemblance between something present and something future, which is called the 'antitype.' We find in the first letter of St Paul to the Corinthians the Scriptural basis for the idea of types: 'Now these happen-ings were examples (τύποι), for our benefit, so that we should never set our hearts, as they did, on evil things' (1 Co 10:6).

In our case, a type means an Old Testament person, place, thing, or event that prefigures a person, place, thing,

or event in the New Testament called the *antitype*. The antitype means 'in place of the *tupos* or type.' Type is inferior to
antitype, in that it is only a shadow. However the type has
real existence. The type is always temporal; the antitype is
eternal. The type is different than a symbol in that it foreshadows. God himself must have established the relation
of the type to its antitype through salvation history; this
excludes objects which are naturally related to others. As
examples of types and antitypes, we can consider the
prefiguration of the Sacrifice of Christ. Here the type is
Abraham offering his son Isaac (Gen 22:1–14). The antitype
is God offering His son Jesus. The foreshadowing of the
Holy Eucharist is another example. The type is the gift of
manna from God in the desert to the Israelites   (Ex
16:11–35). The antitype is the Gift of Christ, the true bread
from heaven (see Jn 6).

   Some criteria for understanding the typical sense would
include the following concepts. First, the typical sense of
the Bible is created by continuing revelation or growth in
the understanding the Word of God. Post–biblical growth in
understanding the Word of God is evidenced in the growth
and development of the understanding of the Trinity, the
Incarnation, and other doctrines. Types (or the typical
sense) are discovered in the New Testament, or in the agreement among members of the Church faithful to what was
handed down to them, in the Fathers of the Church, in
worship and the liturgy, and its development through the
ages, in the documents of the Church, and so forth. The
Catholic Church believes that the Holy Spirit is a revealing
authority in the Church and reveals Himself to 'faithful
people' in all ages. The other criterion for discovering the
typical meaning of Scripture is to understand that any type
found in the text of the Bible has to be related to the
anti–type (for example, Adam to Christ). This confirms that
God planned the relationship of the type to the anti–type.

   An example of the typical meaning in the Bible is in
Paul's writings. Paul appears to delight in establishing types

between the New Testament and the Old Testament. In 1 Corinthians 10:6 Paul typifies those events which occurred to the Israelites in the desert of Sinai throughout the Exodus to those things that happen to Christians. Another example of a type, the typical meaning in the Bible, is the bronze serpent raised by Moses in the desert. The evangelist John presents raising the bronze serpent as a type of Christ crucified (Jn 3:14).

The moral sense

The moral sense is also called the tropological sense, and deals with how the events reported in Scripture inspire us to act justly. As St Paul says, they were written 'as an example.' (1 Co 10:6–11; cf. Heb 3:1 –4:11). As St Peter also affirms: 'For to this you have been called, because Christ also suffered for you, leaving you an example that you should follow in His footsteps' (1 Pt 2:21). A further example of the tropological sense is to see how St John in his Gospel interprets Christ's miracles as the actions of Christ also in the Church here and now.

The anagogical sense

The anagogical sense is also called the eschatological sense, and derives from the Greek expression *anagoge* (meaning 'leading'). Here, we can view realities and events in terms of their eternal significance, leading us toward our true homeland: thus the Church on earth is a sign of the heavenly Jerusalem. Examples of texts which are germane to this interpretation are: Matthew 13: 24–30; 36–43; Revelation 21:1 – 22:5. In summary, we may say that, as regards the time sequence, the literal sense deals with the past. The typical sense links past and present, or the remote past with the recent past. The moral sense deals with the present, asking how we actualize the New Testament in our own lives. The anagogical sense deals with the future. The profound concordance and complementarity of the various senses of the New Testament guarantees a great richness to the living reading of Scripture in the Church.

As an example of the four senses of Scripture, we can consider the parable of the Good Samaritan, in Luke 10:30–37:

> Jesus replied and said, 'A man was going down from Jerusalem to Jericho, and fell among robbers, and they stripped him and beat him, and went away leaving him half dead. And by chance a priest was going down on that road, and when he saw him, he passed by on the other side. Likewise a Levite also, when he came to the place and saw him, passed by on the other side. But a Samaritan, who was on a journey, came upon him; and when he saw him, he felt compassion, and came to him and bandaged up his wounds, pouring oil and wine on them; and he put him on his own beast, and brought him to an inn and took care of him. On the next day he took out two denarii and gave them to the innkeeper and said, 'Take care of him; and whatever more you spend, when I return I will repay you.' Which of these three do you think proved to be a neighbour to the man who fell into the robbers' hands?' And he said, 'The one who showed mercy toward him.' Then Jesus said to him, 'Go and do the same.'

The literal sense is contained in the bare meaning of the words. It is that a Samaritan helps a traveller who has fallen among thieves. Among the Fathers, including Origen, St Ambrose and St Augustine, the parable of the Good Samaritan is given an allegorical interpretation. The man who fell among robbers represents Adam and his descendents. Jerusalem is the place of peace and original integrity, which man leaves by going down to Jericho which is the state of trouble and sin. Normally a person would go *towards* Jerusalem. The robbers symbolize the devil and his fallen angels who stripped man, following his original sin, of his supernatural faculties and left him wounded in his natural faculties. The priest and the Levite represent the Old Law which was incapable of really helping man. The

Samaritan represents Christ and the beast His Sacred Humanity. The wine which the Samaritan uses to heal man is the sacrament of the Eucharist, and the oil, His mercy. The inn symbolizes the Church, the innkeeper signifies St Peter and his successors, and the Bishops and priests of the Church. The coins represent the Gospel and the Sacraments. The moral sense is contained in the command of Jesus 'Go and do the same', an invitation to help others in Jesus' name. The anagogical sense is found in the return of the Samaritan (Christ) at the end of time to collect man who has been redeemed. The fuller sense is arrived at by consideration of all the other senses together.

A study of the Jerusalem temple provides a further classic example to demonstrate the four senses of Scripture. In the literal sense, the temple was the actual building that once stood in Jerusalem. There, the Israelite priests offered sacrifice, the people worshipped, and God dwelt in the Holy of Holies. This temple of the Old Testament has greater importance because God uses it as a sign to reveal important realities in the New Testament: Jesus and the Christian life. Allegorically, the temple points to Jesus, Who said He was the true Temple which would be destroyed and raised up in three days (Jn 2:19–21). Just as the Jerusalem temple was the place of sacrifice for the Jews, so does Jesus' Body house the everlasting sacrifice on Calvary for all humanity. The moral sense of the temple is found in the Christian, whose body is 'a temple of the Holy Spirit' (1 Co 6:19). Just as the temple contained the awesome presence of God, so do the bodies of Christians hold the presence of the Holy Spirit by virtue of their Baptism. Anagogically, the Jerusalem temple finds its eschatological meaning in the heavenly sanctuary, where God will dwell among us in our eternal home, as described in Book of Revelation (Rev 21:22).

Notes

1. Hugh of St Victor, *De arca Noe*, 2, 8 in PL 176, 642
2. Vatican II, *Dei Verbum*, 13. See John 1.
3. St Augustine, *Enarratio in Ps. 103*, 4, 1 in PL 37, 1378; cf. Ps 104; Jn 1:1.
4. Vatican II, *Dei Verbum*, 21.
5. 1 Th 2:13; cf. Vatican II, *Dei Verbum*, 24.
6. Vatican II, *Dei Verbum*, 12.
7. *Ibid.*.
8. *Ibid.*.
9. See St Thomas Aquinas, *Exposition on Psalm 21, 11*; cf. Ps 22:14.
10. See Origen, *Homilia in Lev.* 5, 5 in *PG* 12, 454: 'according to the spiritual meaning which the Spirit grants to the Church.'
11. As examples of difficult passages, consider the relationship between Matthew 10:34–36 and John 14:27, dealing with peace, and also between Luke 14:26 and Matthew 15:4–6, dealing with love of family.
12. Pope Leo XIII, *Providentissimus Deus*, 20.
13. Vatican II, *Dei Verbum*, 11. Cf. Jn 20:31; 2 Tm 3:16–17; 2 Pt 1:19–21; 3:15–16.
14. Vatican II, *Dei Verbum*, 11.
15. Vatican II, *Dei Verbum*, 11.
16. Pope Benedict XVI, *Homily at Mass in Piłsudski Square, Warsaw* (26 May 2006).
17. St Bernard, *Super missus est*, Homilia 4, 11 in *PL* 183, 86.
18. See Pontifical Biblical Commission, *Instruction Concerning the Historical Truth of the Gospels* (April 21, 1964). This is the English translation of Pontifical Biblical Commission, *Instructio de historica Evangeliorum veritate* in *AAS* 56 (1964), pp.712–718.
19. Pontifical Biblical Commission, *The Interpretation of the Bible in the Church* (Vatican City, 1993), I, A, 2.
20. A. Suelzer & J. Kselman, 'Modern Old Testament Criticism,' in *The New Jerome Biblical Commentary* (Englewood Cliffs: Prentice Hall, 2000), p. 1117.
21. See R. Descartes, 'Reply to the Fourth Set of Objections,' in R.M. Hutchins et al., *The Great Books of the Western World*, vol. 31, p. 162.

22. Cf. Descartes, 'Reply to the Second Set of Objections,' in Hutchins et al., *The Great Books of the Western World*, vol. 31, p. 125.

23. B. Blanshard, 'Rationalism,' in *The Encyclopedia Americana* (1967), vol. 23, p. 230c.

24. See K. L. Schmidt, *The place of the Gospels in the general history of literature* (Columbia: University of South Carolina Press, 2002); R. Bultmann, *The history of the synoptic tradition* (Oxford: Blackwell, 1972); M. Dibelius, *From tradition to Gospel* (Cambridge : James Clarke, 1971).

25. See G. Bornkamm, *The New Testament : A guide to its writings* (Philadelphia: Fortress Press, 1978); W. Marxsen, *Introduction to the New Testament: an approach to its problems* (Oxford: Blackwell, 1968); H. Conzelmann, *History of primitive Christianity* (London : Darton, Longman & Todd, 1973).

26. See J. Ratzinger, 'L'interpretazione della Bibbia in conflitto' in I. de la Potterie (ed.), *L'esegesi cristiana oggi* (Casale Monferrato: Piemme, 1991), pp. 104–111.

27. Pontifical Biblical Commission, Instruction Concerning the Historical Truth of the Gospels, (April 21, 1964), V.

28. In the Hebrew mentality of the Scriptures, the heart (lēb) does not represent, as one may think at first sight, the centre of love and emotions, but rather of the mind and the will together. The heart is thus the organ of thought rather than of feeling. For the Semitic mentality considered the human being as a unity, an animated body, while the Greeks tended to the idea of an incarnate spirit. See J. L. McKenzie, 'Aspects of Old Testament Thought' in R. E. Brown, J. A. Fitzmeyer, R. E. Murphy (eds.), *The New Jerome Biblical Commentary* (London: Geoffrey Chapman, 2000), p. 1295.

29. We dealt with this in chapter two, section 2.2 above.

30. R. H. Stein, *The Synoptic Problem: An Introduction* (Baker, 1987), p.218.

31. D. Hill, *The New Century Bible Commentary: The Gospel of Matthew* (Eerdmans, 1972), p. 178

32. R. H. Stein, *The Synoptic Problem: An Introduction* (Baker, 1987), p.219.

33. W. Hendriksen, *Exposition of the Gospel According to Mark* (Baker, 1979), p.202.

34. There are many liberal scholars who have no problem with the notion that Matthew, for instance, fabricated the setting and location of the story for didactic purposes. Yet even conservative or evangelical scholars have little to say about this apparent contradiction.

35. V. Taylor, *The Gospel According to St Mark* (London: Macmillan & Co., 1952), p.286.

36. See G. Van Belle, 'Prolepsis in the Gospel of John' in *Novum Testamentum* 43/4 (2001), pp. 334–347.

37. Vatican II, *Dei Verbum*, 12.

38. Cf. Origen, *Hom. in Ex.* 4, 5 in *PG* 12, 320.

39. St Augustine, *Contra epistolam Manichaei* 5, 6 in *PL* 42, 176.

40. Cf. St Jerome, *In Ezech.*, 38:1, 41:23, 42:13; *In Marc.*, 1:13–31; *Epist. ad Dardanum*, 129, 6, 1.

41. St Thomas Aquinas, *Summa Theologiae*, I, a.1, q.10, ad I.

42. Pope Pius XII, Encyclical *Divino Afflante Spiritu*, 23.

43. *Roman Missal*, Eucharistic Prayer II.

44. St Jerome, *In Eccles.*, 12:9. See also *Epist. ad Paulinum*, 58, 9, 1, where he remarks: 'Everything we read in the Sacred Books shines and glitters even in its outer shell; but the marrow of it is sweeter. If you want the kernel you must break the shell.'

45. It rhymes better in Latin:
    'Lettera gesta docet,
    quid credas allegoria,
    moralis quid agas,
    quo tendas anagogia.'

46. St Thomas Aquinas, *Summa Theologiae*, I, q. 1, a. 10.

4

The Church's role

This heaven–sent treasure Holy Church considers as the most precious source of doctrine on faith and morals. No wonder therefore that, as she received it intact from the hands of the Apostles, so she kept it with all care, defended it from every false and perverse interpretation and used it diligently as an instrument for securing the eternal salvation of souls, as almost countless documents in every age strikingly bear witness.

Pope Pius XII, Divino Afflante Spiritu

4.1 The formation of the New Testament

There are essentially three stages of tradition (handing–on) by which the doctrine and the life of Jesus have come down to us. First, Christ our Lord joined to Himself chosen disciples (Mk 3:14; Lk 6:13), who followed Him from the beginning (Lk 1:2; Acts 1:21–22), saw His deeds, heard His words, and in this way were equipped to be witnesses of His life and doctrine (Lk 24:48; Jn 15:27; Acts 1:8; 10:39; 13:31). When the Lord was orally explaining His doctrine, He followed the ways of reasoning and of exposition which were current at the time. He accommodated Himself to the mentality of His listeners and saw to it that what He taught was firmly impressed on the mind and easily remembered by the disciples. These men understood the miracles and other events of the life of Jesus correctly, as deeds performed or designed that men might believe in Christ through them, and embrace with faith the doctrine of salvation.

Second, the apostles proclaimed above all the death and resurrection of the Lord, as they bore witness to Jesus (Lk 24:44–48; Acts 2:32; 3:15; 5:30–32). They faithfully explained His life and words (Acts 10:36–41), while taking into account in their method of preaching the circumstances in which their listeners found themselves.[1] After Jesus rose from the dead and His divinity was clearly perceived (Acts 2:36; Jn 20:28), faith, far from destroying the memory of what had transpired, rather confirmed it, because their faith rested on the things which Jesus did and taught (Ac 2:22; 10:37–39). Nor was He changed into a 'mythical' person and His teaching deformed in consequence of the worship which the disciples from that time on paid Jesus as the Lord and the Son of God. There is no reason to deny that the apostles passed on to their listeners what was really said and done by the Lord with that fuller understanding which they enjoyed (Jn 2:22; 12:16; 11:51–52; cf. 14:26; 16:12–13; 7:39), having been instructed by the glorious events of the Christ and taught by the light of the Spirit of Truth (Jn 14:26; 16:13). So, just as Jesus Himself after His resurrection 'interpreted to them'(Lk 24:27) the words of the Old Testament as well as His own (Lk 24:44–45; Acts 1:3), they too interpreted His words and deeds according to the needs of their listeners. 'Devoting themselves to the ministry of the word,' (Acts 6:4) they preached and made use of various ways of speaking which were suited to their own purpose and the mentality of their listeners. For they were debtors (1 Co 9:19–23) 'to Greeks and barbarians, to the wise and the foolish' (Rom 1:14). However, these ways of speaking with which the preachers proclaimed Christ must be distinguished and properly assessed: catecheses, stories, testimonies, hymns, doxologies, prayers, and other literary forms of this sort which were in Sacred Scripture and were accustomed to be used by men of that time.

Third, this primitive instruction, which was at first passed on by word of mouth and then in writing–for it soon happened that many tried 'to compile a narrative of the things' (Lk 1:1) which concerned the Lord Jesus–was committed to writing by the sacred authors in four Gospels for the benefit of the churches, with a method suited to the peculiar purpose which each author set for himself. From the many things handed down they selected some things, reduced others to a synthesis, still others they explicated as they kept in mind the situation of the churches. With every possible means they sought that their readers might become aware of the reliability (Lk 1:4) of those words by which they had been instructed. Indeed, from what they had received the sacred writers above all selected the things which were suited to the various situations of the faithful and to the purpose which they had in mind, and adapted their narration of them to the same situations and purpose. Since the meaning of a statement also depends on the sequence, the Evangelists, in passing on the words and deeds of our Saviour, explained these now in one context, now in another, depending on (their) usefulness to the readers. Consequently, let the exegete seek out the meaning intended by the Evangelist in narrating a saying or a deed in a certain way or in placing it in a certain context. For the truth of the story is not at all affected by the fact that the Evangelists relate the words and deeds of the Lord in a different order, and express his sayings not literally but differently, while preserving their sense.[2] For, as St Augustine says,

> It is quite probable that each Evangelist believed it to have been his duty to recount what he had to in that order in which it pleased God to suggest it to his memory in those things at least in which the order, whether it be this or that, detracts in nothing from the truth and authority of the Gospel. But why the Holy Spirit, who apportions individually to each one as He wills (1 Co 12:11), and who therefore

undoubtedly also governed and ruled the minds of
the holy writers in recalling what they were to write
because of the pre–eminent authority which the
books were to enjoy, permitted one to compile his
narrative in this way, and another in that, anyone
with pious diligence may seek the reason and with
divine aid will be able to find it.[3]

The formation and transmission of the New Testament can
be considered as a ten–stage process, with considerable
chronological overlap, continuing down to today. The starting point is the historical Person of Jesus Christ. Words are
spoken and deeds are performed by Jesus Himself during
His lifetime on earth. As regards the life and teaching of
Jesus, the Church holds firmly that the four Gospels, whose
historicity she unhesitatingly affirms, 'faithfully hand on
what Jesus, the Son of God, while He lived among men,
really did and taught for their eternal salvation, until the
day when He was taken up.'[4] Contact with Jesus inspired
the writers, and the Holy Spirit 'guided them to the
complete truth' (Jn 16:13–15). The second stage is the Oral
Tradition, whereby traditions and beliefs about Jesus are
developed and passed on by early Christian communities.
'For, after the Ascension of the Lord, the apostles handed on
to their hearers what He had said and done, but with that
fuller understanding which they, instructed by the glorious
events of Christ and enlightened by the Spirit of truth, now
enjoyed.'[5] The impact of Pentecost is crucial in this regard.
Third, written sources are elaborated, constituting an
expression of written Tradition. Some of the miracles and
sayings of Jesus are compiled and recorded in early written
documents, formed from oral and written tradition. Fourth,
complete written texts are produced: individual letters, full
Gospels, and so forth, are written with particular messages
for particular situations. 'The sacred authors, in writing the
four Gospels, selected certain of the many elements which
had been handed on, either orally or already in written
form; others they synthesized or explained with an eye to

the situation of the churches, the while sustaining the form of preaching, but always in such a fashion that they have told us the honest truth about Jesus.'[6] St Luke describes this process in his Gospel:

> Inasmuch as many have undertaken to compile an account of the things accomplished among us, just as those who from the beginning were eyewitnesses and ministers of the word have handed them down to us, it seemed fitting for me as well, having investigated everything carefully from the beginning, to write it out for you in consecutive order, most excellent Theophilus; so that you might know the exact truth about the things you have been taught (Lk 1:1–4).

The fifth phase involves distribution, whereby some writings (immediately recognized as sacred and special) are copied and shared with other Christian communities throughout the Mediterranean. The sixth aspect was collection, in which certain Christians began gathering together several different Gospels and collecting the letters of Paul. Then, the seventh step was Canonization whereby four Gospels, several collections of letters, and a few other texts are accepted as authoritative Scriptures, making the 27 books of the New Testament. The Church was inspired in deciding which books are canonical. An eighth phase is that of translation in which biblical texts are translated from the Greek original into other ancient and modern languages: Latin, Syriac, Coptic, Armenian, Slavonic and various others. The ninth aspect involves interpretation in which the meaning of the scriptures is investigated on various levels: literal, spiritual, historical, social, and so forth. Finally, the tenth phase is that of application, and here Christian communities and individuals live out the New Testament in their daily lives: liturgical, moral, sacramental, and theological aspects are at play here, as well as personal spiritual reflection and growth.

Within this process, the Gospel writers enjoyed a particular five–fold role. First, they were selectors: from among the many things Jesus said and did, they chose under divine inspiration what to include and emphasize, as seen in John 21:25. They were also arrangers, in that they organized the material, from oral and written traditions, into sections, not necessarily always chronologically, but often thematically. Third, they were shapers, since they moulded their material and recounted the episodes of the New Testament in ways that would emphasize the essential message in a coherent whole. Fourth, they were theologians, since they reflected on the meaning and significance of the events in the light of their belief in Jesus Christ. Finally, they were proclaimers, as they preached the 'Good News' about Jesus Christ, true God and true Man, in ways appropriate to their own audiences. The Gospels are alive and valid for all time.

4.2 The Synoptic Problem

The first three Gospels are frequently called the Synoptics (from the Greek terms *syn* 'together,' and *opsis* 'view'). When placed side by side and brought under one view, these three Gospels present a striking resemblance and appear as one narrative. The Synoptic Gospels according to Matthew, Mark, and Luke, are so similar to each other that, in a sense, they view Jesus 'with the same eye,' in contrast to the very different picture of Jesus presented in the Fourth Gospel of John. Yet there are also many significant differences between the three Synoptic Gospels. First, it is interesting to note the unique materials in the various synoptic Gospels.

In St Mark's Gospel, the following items are unique:

- 1:1 – Introductory Verse
- 3:19b–21 – Jesus' Family Tries to Restrain Him
- 4:26–29 – The Parable of the Seed Growing of Itself

•7:31–37 – Jesus Heals a Deaf Man in the Decapolis

•8:22–26 – Jesus Gives Sight to the Blind Man of Bethsaida

•14:51–52 – A Young Man Runs Away Naked after Jesus' Arrest

•16:14–18 – The Commissioning of the Eleven

In St Matthew's Gospel, the following items are unique:

•1:1 – Introductory Verse

•1:18—2:23 – The Infancy Narrative (incl. Dreams of Joseph, Birth of Jesus, Visit of the Magi, Flight into Egypt, Massacre of the Infants of Bethlehem, Return from Egypt)

•5:17–20, 21–24, 27–29, 31, 33–38, 43 – Jesus Teaches about the Law, Anger, Adultery, and Oaths

•6:1–8, 16–19 – Teaching about Almsgiving and about Fasting

•7:6, 15–17 – Sayings about Pearls before Swine, and False Prophets

•7:28–29 – Conclusion to the Sermon on the Mount

•9:27–31 – The Healing of the Two Blind Men (cf. 20:29–34)

•9:35–38 – A Summary of the Compassion of Jesus

•10:22–23 – Part of Jesus' Teaching about Upcoming Persecutions

•11:1 – Narrator's Conclusion to Jesus' Missionary Discourse

•11:28–30 – The Gentle Mastery of Christ

•13:24–30 – The Parable of the Weeds among the Wheat

•13:36–43 – The Explanation of the Parable of the Weeds

- •13:44–52 – Three More Parables and a Concluding Dialogue

- •14:28–31 – Peter Attempts to Walk on Water

- •16:17–19 – Jesus' Response to Peter's Confession

- •17:24–27 – Dialogue about Payment of the Temple Tax

- •18:15–20, 21–35 – A Brother Who Sins, and The Parable of the Unforgiving Servant

- •19:10–12 – The Disciples React to Jesus' Teaching on Divorce

- •20:1–16 – The Parable of the Workers in the Vineyard

- •21:28–32 – The Parable of the Two Sons

- •Almost all of chapter 23 – Prohibition of Titles, Woes to the Scribes and Pharisees

- •25:1–13 – The Parable of the Ten Bridesmaids

- •25:31–46 – The Parable of the Sheep and the Goats

- •27:3–10 – The Death of Judas

- •27:24–25 – Pilate Washes His Hands

- •27:52–53 – Resuscitation of the Saints

- •27:62–66 – The Guard Posted at the Tomb

- •28:11–15 – The Report of the Guard

- •28:16–20 – The Commissioning of the Disciples

Material common to other Gospels is also to be considered, but rendered in a significantly different manner in Matthew:

- •1:2–17 – The Genealogy of Jesus

- •Most of chapters 5–7 – The Sermon on the Mount (especially 5:3–12; 6:9–15; 7:15–20)

- •Most of chapter 10 – The Missionary Discourse

• 12:33–37 – The Tree and Its Fruit

• 16:13–23 – Peter's Confession about Jesus

• Much of chapter 18 – The Community Discourse

• 22:1–14 – The Parable of the Wedding Feast

• 25:14–30 – The Parable of the Talents

In St Luke's Gospel, the following items are unique:

• 1:1–4 – The Literary Prologue (Dedication to Theophilus)

• 1:5—2:52 – The Infancy Narrative (including the Announcement of John's Birth, Announcement of Jesus' Birth, Mary Visits Elizabeth, Canticle of Mary, Birth of John, Canticle of Zechariah, Birth of Jesus, Visit of the Shepherds, Circumcision and Naming of Jesus, Presentation at the Temple, Return to Nazareth, and Boy Jesus in the Temple)

• 3:10–14 – John the Baptist Replies to Questioners

• 4:14–30 – Jesus Preaches and is Rejected at Nazareth

• 5:1–11 – The Call of Simon the Fisherman

• 6:24–26 – Four 'Woes' added after the Beatitudes

• 7:11–17 – The Raising of the Widow's Son at Nain

• 8:1–3 – Galilean Women Follow Jesus

• Much of 9:51—18:14, where Jesus and His Disciples Journey to Jerusalem (including Rejection by Samaritan Villagers, Mission of the Seventy, Parable of the Good Samaritan, Martha and Mary, Parable of a Friend at Midnight, Warning against Avarice, Parable of the Rich Fool, Parable of the Barren Fig Tree, Healing a Crippled Woman, Healing a Man with Dropsy, Teachings for Guests and Hosts, Cost of Discipleship, Parable of the Lost Coin, Parable of the Lost/Prodigal Son, Parable of the Unjust Steward, Parable of the Rich Man and Lazarus, Unprofitable Servants, Cleansing of Ten Lepers, Parable of the Widow and Judge; Prayers of the Pharisee and Publican)

•19:1–10 – Zacchaeus the Tax Collector

•19:41–44 – Jesus Laments over Jerusalem

•22:15–17, 31–32, 35–38 – Some of Jesus' Words at the Last Supper

•23:2–16 – Jesus appears before Pilate and before Herod

•23:27–31 – On the Way of the Cross, Jesus Speaks to some Weeping Women

•23:34, 39–43, 46 – The Repentant Thief, and some Details of the Crucifixion

•24:13–35, 36–49 – Jesus Appears to Disciples on the Road to Emmaus, and in Jerusalem

•24:50–53 – The Ascension of Jesus

Material common to other Gospels, but rendered in a significantly different manner in Luke, is also to be considered:

•3:1–2 – The Preaching of John the Baptist

•3:23–38 – The Genealogy of Jesus

•6:20–26 – The Beatitudes (at the beginning of the Sermon on the Plain)

•7:36–50 – The Pardon of the Sinful Woman

•9:18–22 – Peter's Confession about Jesus

•11:1–8 – The Lord's Prayer and Further Teachings on Prayer

•14:16–24 – The Parable of the Great Feast

•19:12–27 – The Parable of the Ten Gold Coins

•21:34–38 – The Exhortation to be Vigilant

• 22:15–38 – Jesus' Discourses at the Last Supper (including The Betrayal Foretold, The Role of the Disciples, Peter's Denial Foretold, and Instructions for the Time of Crisis)

• 24:1–12 – The Empty Tomb Story

The similarities between Matthew, Mark and Luke are thus so numerous and so close, not just in the order of the material presented but also in the exact wording of long stretches of text, that it is not sufficient to explain these similarities on the basis of common oral tradition. Rather, some type of literary dependence must be assumed. That is, someone copied from someone else; some of the evangelists made use of one or more previous Gospels as sources for their own compositions. But the question remains, who copied from whom? The vast majority of New Testament scholars believe that Matthew and Luke used Mark as a source. In other words, they used Mark's narrative in constructing their own gospels, sometimes staying very close to Mark's text, and other times altering the text somewhat more freely. However, what about those passages, absent from Mark, on which Matthew and Luke agree? How do we account for those? The most popular solution has been to assume that Matthew and Luke had another source that we don't have any longer. Scholars call this document 'Q', which comes from the German word *Quelle*, meaning 'source.' If there actually was a Q document, it was probably a collection of sayings that were attributed to Jesus. There was probably very little narrative material in this document. There seems to be an eschatological emphasis in Q (in other words, an emphasis on the return of Jesus and the end of this world). There is also a strong moral emphasis in which readers are exhorted to adhere to the law.

There are then five principal reasons for concluding a literary dependence among the Synoptic Gospels. First the verbatim agreement. It is rare for two independent reporters of the same event to share more than a few words in common, but the synoptic gospels often feature a substantial number of agreements in their exact words. For example, in one passage about John the Baptist, Matthew and Luke agree for 61 out of 63 Greek words of a presumably Aramaic speech. Generally, the verbatim agreement between Matthew, Mark, and Luke runs about 50% of the words, but, by contrast, their agreement with John in parallel episodes falls to about 10%. Next, there is extensive agreement in order, especially in which the arrangement of material is not strictly chronological but topical or exhibiting some other creativity in presentation. In these cases, it is difficult to attribute the non–chronological but topical narration to independent reporting. For example, Matthew and Mark relate the death of John the Baptist as a non–chronological flashback in the same place in their narrative. As another example, the Synoptics agree in the order in which certain parables and miracles are related in an arrangement that is probably intended to be topical. Third, we find substantially similar selection of material, when that selection features some amount of creative, editorial choice. Jesus did and said many things, so any account of his ministry must involve some editorial judgment in what to include and what to omit. The synoptic gospels, for instance, relate many of the same miracles, but these miracles hardly overlap with the ones related by John. Fourth, we note the presence of editorial comments and other redactional material in the Synoptics that are not necessitated by a mere telling of historical fact. For example, both Matthew and Mark feature an identical aside to the reader ('let the reader understand') in the synoptic apocalypse. Finally, there is a consistent literary pattern between the three documents that establishes Mark as the 'middle term' connecting Matthew and Luke. Specifically, agreements between Matthew and Luke against Mark are consistently much less prevalent than agreements against Matthew or

Luke in arrangement and wording. We would expect for independently composed documents to exhibit no such pattern.

The 'Q' Source or 'Q' Document, probably used by both Matthew and Luke, would have contained the material laid out in the following table.

Figure 8: Possible composition of 'Q'

Passage in Luke	Passage in Matthew	Theme
Luke 3:7-9, 16-17	Matt 3:7b-12	Preaching of John the Baptist
Luke 4:1-13a	Matt 4:1-11a	Temptation of Jesus
Luke 6:20b-23	Matt 5:3, 6, 4, 11-12	Beatitudes
Luke 6:27-33, 35b-36	Matt 5:44, 39b-40, 42; 7:12; 5:46-47, 45, 48	Love of Enemies
Luke 6:37a, 38c, 39-42	Matt 7:1-2; 15:14; 10:24-25a; 7:3-5	On Judging Others
Luke 6:43-45	Matt 7:16-20 and 12:33-35	On Bearing Fruit
Luke 6:46-49	Matt 7:21, 24-27	House Built on Rock
Luke 7:1-2, 6b-10	Matt 8:5-10, 13	Healing a Centurion's Servant
Luke 7:18-23	Matt 11:2-6	John the Baptist's Questions
Luke 7:24-28, 31-35	Matt 11:7-11, 16-19	Jesus Speaks about John
Luke 9:57-60	Matt 8:19-22	On Following Jesus
Luke 10:2-12	Matt 9:37-38; 10:7-16	Mission of the Seventy
Luke 10:13-16	Matt 11:21-23; 10:40	Woes against Galilean Cities

Passage in Luke	Passage in Matthew	Theme
Luke 10:21-24	Matt 11:25-27; 13:16-17	Thanksgiving to the Father
Luke 11:2-4	Matt 6:9-13	Lord's Prayer
Luke 11:9-13	Matt 7:7-11	Asking and Receiving
Luke 11:14-15, 17-23	Matt 12:22-30	Beelzebul Controversy
Luke 11:24-26	Matt 12:43-45	Return of the Evil Spirit
Luke 11:29-32	Matt 12:38-42	Sign of Jonah
Luke 11:33-35	Matt 5:15; 6:22-23	On Light and Seeing
Luke 11:39-44, 46-52	Matt 23:25-26, 23, 6-7a, 27, 4, 29-31, 34-36, 13	Woes against Pharisees
Luke 12:2-9	Matt 10:26-33; 12:32	Fearing Humans and God
Luke 12:10-12	Matt 12:32; 10:19	Role of the Holy Spirit
Luke 12:22-31, 33-34	Matt 6:25-33, 19-21	Anxiety; Treasure in Heaven
Luke 12:39-40, 42-46	Matt 24:43-51	Watch and Be Ready
Luke 12:51-53	Matt 10:34-36	Divisions in Families
Luke 12:54-56	Matt 16:2-3	Signs of the Times
Luke 12:58-59	Matt 5:25-26	Settling out of Court
Luke 13:18-21	Matt 13:31-33	Mustard Seed and Leaven
Luke 12:23-30	Matt 7:13-14, 22-23; 8:11-12; 20:16	Exclusion from the Kingdom
Luke 13:34-35	Matt 23:37-39	Lament over Jerusalem
Luke 14:16-24	Matt 22:1-10	Parable of the Banquet

Passage in Luke	Passage in Matthew	Theme
Luke 14:26-27	Matt 10:37-38	Carrying the Cross
Luke 14:34-35	Matt 5:13	Parable of Salt
Luke 15:4-7	Matt 18:12-14	Parable of the Lost Sheep
Luke 16:13	Matt 6:24	On Serving Two Masters
Luke 16:16-18	Matt 11:12-13; 5:18, 32	On the Law and Divorce
Luke 17:1, 3b-4	Matt 18:7, 15, 21-22	On Sin and Forgiveness
Luke 17:6	Matt 17:20	Faith Like a Mustard Seed
Luke 17:23-24, 26-27, 30, 33-35, 37	Matt 24:26-27, 37-39; 10:39; 24:40-41, 28	Coming of the Son of Man
Luke 19:12-27	Matt 25:14-30	Parable of the Talents
Luke 22:30	Matt 19:28	Disciples Will Judge Israel

Until last century, there were no documents like 'Q', but in the 1940's, at a place in upper Egypt called Nag Hammadi, a large jar was found with a number of ancient documents inside. One of these documents was the Gospel of Thomas, which is a sayings collection much like Q is thought to have been. Some scholars have created hypothetical reconstructions of the Q document based on material that is found in Matthew and Luke. However, Q may have contained material that was found in neither of these gospels. So, when Matthew and Luke have common material that is not in Mark, we call this 'double tradition' material, and we attribute it to Q. (On the other hand, 'triple tradition' material is that which is common to all three Synoptic Gospels.) Matthew and Luke do not present the Q material in the same order. However, some important scholars question the existence and the importance of Q.[7] Now we turn to some solutions to the Synoptic problem.

Some scholars find the solution in the oral tradition of the Church (Oral–Tradition theory). Here, the early Apostolic teaching took a fixed form and the life and teaching of our Lord came eventually to be told in practically the same particular way; the Synoptic writers, independently of each other, simply wrote down this particular oral Gospel. This theory is universally recognized to be insufficient. The Synoptics do not quite agree on some very important matters on which we would expect tradition to be unanimous, such as the words of the institution of the Eucharist, the Lord's Prayer, the narrative of Peter's confession. Others maintain that the three Synoptics were derived, with more or less modification, from one written source. This theory, however, fails to explain the omissions by St Mark and the differences in arrangement in the Synoptics. Again, why are all contemporaries and the Gospels themselves silent about this source?

The Traditional Theory (Augustinian Hypothesis)

The most traditional analysis of the external evidence is that of the Augustinian hypothesis, in which the chronological order of the Gospels is the same as the canonical order (Matthew, Mark, Luke).

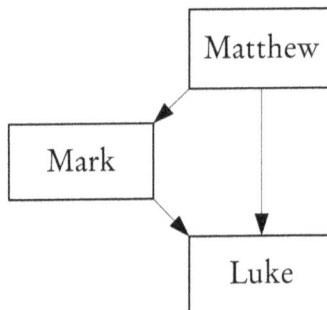

Figure 9: The Augustinian Hypothesis

The Griesbach Theory (Two–Gospel Hypothesis)

The Two Gospel Hypothesis, formerly known as the Gries-bach Hypothesis, presents a comprehensive solution to the Synoptic Problem. First given its name by Bernard Orchard, the Two Gospel Hypothesis proposes that the Gospel of Matthew was the earliest Gospel, that the author of the Gospel of Luke used the Gospel of Matthew as a source, and that the author of the Gospel of Mark wrote using both the Gospels of Matthew and Luke as sources.

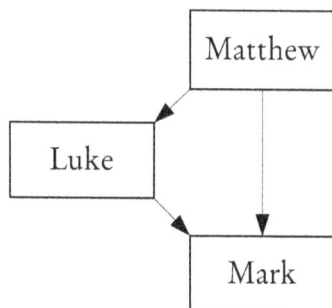

Figure 10: The Griesbach Theory

The Farrer/Goulder Theory (with Markan Priority)

The Farrer Theory adopts the Markan priority hypothesis for the triple tradition and the Lukan posteriority hypoth-esis for the double tradition. In other words, Mark was written first, adopted by Matthew, and then used by Luke. The double tradition is explained by Luke's further use of Matthew, thus dispensing with Q. The Farrer Theory is named for its seminal exponent A. M. Farrer (1955) and is currently the most serious contender to the Two–Source Theory in Britain and in North America. Michael D. Goul-der (1974) has recently been its most forceful advocate but other active proponents include Mark Goodacre (2002).[8]

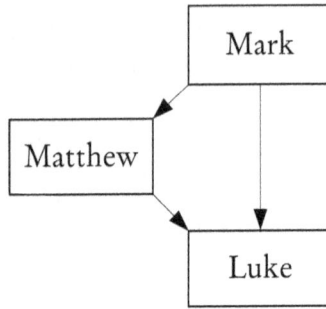

Figure 11: The Farrer/Goulder Theory

The Two–Source Hypothesis

The Two–Source Hypothesis has been the predominant source theory for the synoptic problem for over a century and a half. Originally conceived in Germany by C. H. Weisse in 1838, this idea came to dominate German Protestant scholarship after the fall of the Tübingen school with H. J. Holtzmann's endorsement of a related variant in 1863. In the latter part of the nineteenth century, the Oxford School brought the Two–Source Hypothesis to English scholarship, culminating in B. H. Streeter's 1924 treatment of the synoptic problem. Any viable solution to the synoptic problem has to account, at a minimum, for the two main textual features of the synoptic gospels, called the triple tradition and the double tradition. The triple tradition refers to the subject matter jointly related by Matthew, Mark, and Luke. Generally, the triple tradition is characterized by substantial agreements in arrangement and wording among all three gospels with frequent agreements between Mark and Matthew against Luke and between Mark and Luke against Matthew, but a near absence of agreements of Matthew and Luke against Mark. The double tradition, on the other hand, consists of the material that Matthew and Luke share outside of Mark and exhibits some of the most striking verbatim agreements in some passages and quite divergent versions in other passages. The Two–Source Hypothesis derives its name from its postulation of two distinct sources for the synoptic Gospels: a narrative source (Mark) for the triple tradition and a saying source (Q) for the double tradition. Sometimes, the Two–Source Hypothesis is more precisely called the two–document hypothesis to emphasize that the two sources are distinct documents or the Mark–Q hypothesis to identify those two documentary sources.

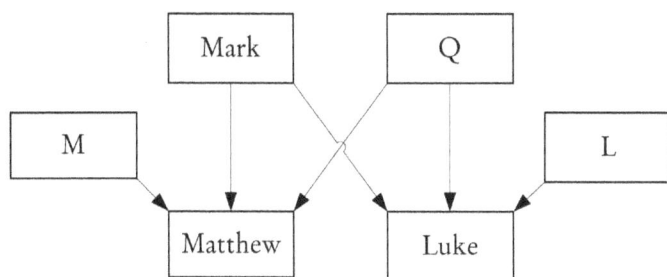

Figure 12: The Two–Source Hypothesis

Key:

Mark = the oldest written Gospel, which provided the narrative framework for both Matthew and Luke.
Q = 'Quelle' = a hypothetical written 'Source' of some sayings and teachings of Jesus (now lost).
M = various other materials (mostly oral, some maybe written) found only in Matthew.
L = various other materials (mostly oral, others probably written) found only in Luke.
Note: the arrows indicate direction of influence; older materials are above, later Gospels below.
Note: by definition, Q consists of materials found in Matthew and Luke, but not in Mark.

The Petrine origin hypothesis

The significance of Peter's mother–in–law is not incidental, but is rather tied to the whole Gospel message of Petrine primacy; it is very significant that at the beginning of the synoptic Gospels, Christ is associated with one of Peter's close relatives, and with his house. All three Synoptic Gospels include the account of the healing of Peter's mother–in–law, and this healing occurs towards the beginning of Jesus' ministry, right around the time He calls His first disciples. In Mark, Christ's healing ministry begins in Peter's house, and only afterwards does the healing ministry extend to the people. We are encountering here the first vestiges of Peter's pre–eminence. Indeed, most exegetes propose the special distinction given to Peter within the circle of the disciples as common to the entire ancient tradition behind the Synoptic Gospels.[9] This could also mean that the Synoptic teaching itself is based ultimately on Peter's preaching. The Petrine solution to the synoptic problem proposes that the Gospels written by traditional authors, who used both oral and written sources. Internal evidence looks like Mark is source for Matthew and Luke, but the order of writing does not corroborate this. We would suggest that Matthew and Luke depend on an oral form of Mark, namely the apostolic tradition transmitted by St Peter. St Peter's apostolic preaching formed the basis of an oral tradition behind St Mark's Gospel, but also underpinned a Hebrew version of St Matthew and his Greek version, as well as forming the basis of St Luke's sources which he researched with great clarity and precision. The diagram below outlines the possible relationship between the apostolic preaching of St Peter and the formation of the Synoptic Gospels.

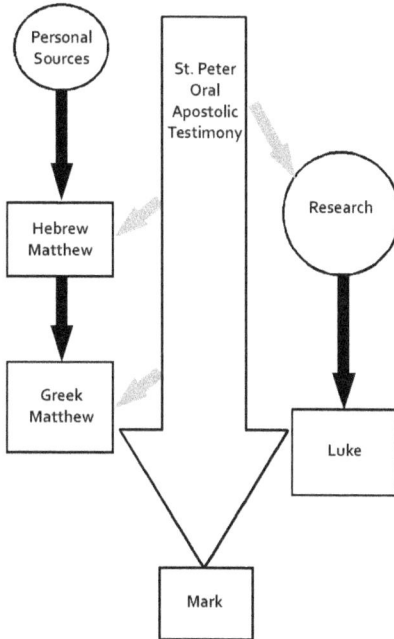

Figure 13: The Petrine origin Hypothesis

4.3 The Canon of the New Testament

As a prelude to discussing the important question of the Canon on the New Testament, we need to mention some ideas about the arrangement of the books. First, the twenty–seven books of the New Testament are not listed in chronological order, or the order in which they were written historically; several other principles were operative. In fact, the overall order begins with the life of Jesus (the four Gospels), then deals with the growth of the Christian Church (Acts, Letters, Epistles), and finally focuses on the

Eschaton (the end of time, as described symbolically in the Book of Revelation). In this way, a chronological and theological structure of past, present, and future can be discerned. The four Gospels are listed in what was traditionally regarded as their chronological order (namely Matthew was thought to be the oldest Gospel); most scholars today, however, believe that Mark was the first written Gospel (or at least the oldest of the four canonical Gospels in their full versions, as we know them today).

The Acts of the Apostles was originally the second volume of Luke's two–volume work; however, when the four Gospels were grouped together, Acts was placed after John. The letters written by Paul (or at least attributed to him) are divided into two sub–groups: those written to communities and those addressed to individuals; within each sub–group, the letters are arranged not in chronological order, but rather in decreasing order of length (more or less, although Galatians is slightly shorter than Ephesians). The anonymous Letter to the Hebrews comes immediately after the Pauline letters because some people attribute it to Paul. The Catholic or General Epistles are also listed in decreasing order of length, although letters attributed to the same apostle are grouped together. The Book of Revelation closes out the New Testament canon, since it concludes with a description of the end of time (New Heavens, New Earth, New Jerusalem, and so forth).

The word Canon comes from the Greek expression kanōn which is derived from a Semitic word (*qaneh* in Hebrew) meaning a reed. Classically it meant a measuring stick or metaphorically a rule or standard of excellence, a benchmark. In ecclesiastical usage it denoted a rule of faith. Most of us take it for granted to have a copy of Bible and do not ask how we received it. The question why the New Testament has twenty–seven books, not more and not less, hardly comes to our mind. While all of us are unlikely to think that they just simply dropped from the sky, we may not realize the long process which took place before those twenty–seven books were finally selected. The New Testament, as defined by the Council of Trent, does not differ, as regards the books contained, from that of all Christian bodies at present.

In the first place, Jesus wrote no book, and neither He nor His apostles (including Paul) directly gave us the list of the twenty–seven New Testament books. They neither used nor introduced the terms Old and New Testaments. Those terms were first used by Tertullian (around 170 AD). In fact Our Lord's and the later apostolic teachings were first transmitted and taught orally. One should bear in mind that the first Christians did not consider this oral transmission as inferior; the problem was simply that writing things down was time–consuming and costly. In Galatians 4:20, Paul wrote that he wished to be with the Galatians, so they could hear his tone. At that time, his personal presence was impossible and therefore a letter from him would be sufficient. On other occasions, Paul judged that a written communication would be more effective than anything he could say (2 Co 1:23–2:4). In short both oral and written forms were considered authoritative by the first Christians and are known to them as tradition (the Greek word translated as 'tradition' comes from the verb which means 'to deliver'). When Paul and others mentioned Scripture what they meant exactly is the Old Testament books. For example, the scripture known to Timothy (2 Tm 3:15) since his childhood definitely refers to Old Testament books. The first Christians did regard Jesus' unwritten words as authoritative as Scripture. Thus, in his First Letter to Timothy (1 Tm 5:18), Paul quoted as Scripture, both Deuteronomy 25:4 and Jesus' words, which are now recorded in Luke 10:7 (noting that the Gospel of Luke was probably written after Paul's epistles). In the same way, early Christian writers like Pope Clement of Rome (circa 96 AD), Ignatius, bishop of Antioch (circa 110 AD), Polycarp, bishop of Smyrna (circa 110–120 AD) considered Jesus' words as equal to those of Scriptures (Old Testament).

There are a number of surviving manuscripts of early New Testament books. The Codex Sinaiticus (4th Century) has all 27 books of our present New Testament, but also includes Epistle of Barnabas and Shepherd of Hermas. The Codex Vaticanus (4th century) was torn at the end, so does not reveal the whole list; the existing part consists of 21 books and part of Hebrews of our present New Testament. On the other hand Codex Alexandrinus (5th century) has the 27 books plus 1 and 2 Clement. Codex Claromontanus (6th century) has no Philippians, 1 and 2 Thessalonians and Hebrews but includes Epistle of Barnabas, Shepherd of Hermas, Acts of Paul and Revelation of Peter. Another fourth century list, now known as Cheltenham list has only 4 Gospels, 13 Pauline epistles (minus Hebrews), Acts, Revelation, 1 John and 1 Peter.

Like the Old Testament, the New has books whose canonicity was formerly a subject of some discussion in the Church. There was discussion about entire books: the Epistle to the Hebrews, that of James, the Second of St Peter, the Second and Third of John, Jude, and Apocalypse; giving seven in all as the number of the New Testament contested books. There was discussion about three disputed passages: the closing section of St Mark's Gospel, 16: 9–20 about the apparitions of Christ after the Resurrection; the verses in Luke about the bloody sweat of Jesus, 22:43, 44; the Pericope Adulteræ, or narrative of the woman taken in adultery, St John, 7:53 to 8:11. Since the Council of Trent it is not permitted for a Catholic to question the inspiration of these passages.

4.3.1 The formation of the New Testament Canon

The idea of a complete and clear–cut canon of the New Testament existing from the beginning, that is from Apostolic times, has no foundation in history. The Canon of the New Testament, like that of the Old, is the result of a development, of a process at once stimulated by disputes with doubters, both within and without the Church, and retarded by certain obscurities and natural hesitations, and which did not reach its final term until the dogmatic definition of the Council of Trent.

4.3.1.1 The early period (AD 100–220)

Those writings which possessed the unmistakable stamp and guarantee of Apostolic origin must from the very first have been specially prized and venerated, and their copies eagerly sought by local Churches and individual Christians of means, in preference to the narratives and Logia, or Sayings of Christ, coming from less authorized sources. Already in the New Testament itself there is some evidence of a certain diffusion of canonical books: 2 Peter 3:15–16, supposes its readers to be acquainted with some of St Paul's Epistles; St John's Gospel implicitly presupposes the existence of the Synoptics (Matthew, Mark, and Luke).

We may well presume that each of the leading Churches–Rome, Antioch, Thessalonica, Alexandria, Corinth, and others–would have possessed authoritative writings, although at this stage their lists may vary. Each community sought, by exchanging with other Christian communities, to add to its special treasure, and have publicly read in its religious assemblies all Apostolic writings which came under its knowledge. It was doubtless in this way that the collections grew, and reached completeness within certain limits, but a considerable number of years must have elapsed (counting from the composition of the latest book) before all the widely dispersed Churches of early Christendom possessed the new sacred literature in full. Since distribution was not easy, this meant that the Canon was not fixed very early, and this left room for variations which lasted a few centuries. However, evidence shows that from days touching on those of the last Apostles there were two well defined bodies of sacred writings of the New Testament, which constituted the firm, irreducible, universal minimum, and the nucleus of its complete Canon: these were the Four Gospels, as the Church now has them, and thirteen Letters of St Paul, and these two collections were known as the *Evangelium* and the *Apostolicum*. For example, Pope St Clement of Rome, writing to the Corinthians just before 100 AD stated: 'Take into your hands the epistle of Blessed Paul the Apostle. What did he write to you when the Gospel was first preached? Truly, under divine inspiration he wrote to you concerning himself, and Cephas, and Apollo, because even then you had formed factions among yourselves.'[10] Around the year 110 AD, St Ignatius of Antioch remarked to the Ephesians that St Paul mentioned them in 'every letter', an expression which implies a collection of Pauline letters of acknowledged authority.[11] Indeed, the word Gospel seems to have been first used by the same St Ignatius, in his letter to the Smyrnaeans.[12] Papias, bishop of Hierapolis (around 125 AD) was known to have identified at least two Gospels (Matthew and Mark). A generation after Papias, St Justin Martyr mentioned the memoirs of Peter (possible the Gospel of Mark) and memoirs of the apostles, both of which he called Gospels: 'For the Apostles, in the memoirs composed by them, which are called Gospels, have handed down to us what Jesus had thus enjoined upon them.'[13] His disciple, Tatian, introduced the Diatessaron, which are the four Gospels combined into one in a chronological order with the Gospel of John as a framework.

One early collection of New Testament books was made by the heretic Marcion (around 150 AD). His 'canon' consisted of the Gospel of Luke and ten of Paul's epistles which he referred to as Gospel and Apostle. However, he mutilated many of them to suit his error, in which he declared that the God of the Old Testament was different from the One whom Jesus spoke about. For this reason he rejected all Old Testament books. He broke away from Rome and established his own sect. The error of Marcion and other heretics was an occasion for the Church to define what belonged to written apostolic teaching, in terms of the collection of New Testament books.

By the end of the second century, all of the New Testament books were generally known, and the divine character of most of them was generally admitted. At that time, St Irenaeus, who was familiar with the traditions of many regions, and connected through his teachers with the close of the Apostolic era, explicitly names and accepts the four canonical Gospels, quotes twelve letters of St Paul as Scripture, mentions the letter to the Hebrews, and accepts the Apocalypse as Johannine.[14] Thus, Irenaeus testified to the existence of a Tetramorph, or Quadriform Gospel, given by the Word and unified by one Spirit. It seems clear, from Patristic testimonies, that an inviolable fourfold Gospel existed in the closing years of the Apostolic Era. Just how the Tetramorph was welded into unity and given to the Church, is a matter of conjecture.

Another known collection of New Testament books is the second century Muratorian canon, named after L.A. Muratori who published the list, copied from a seventh century codex, discovered in the Ambrosian Library in Milan in 1740. The manuscript is mutilated at the beginning, but we can conclude that it has four Gospels, Acts, thirteen of St Paul's epistles, the letter of Jude, two of St John's letters, the Apocalypse of John (Revelation) and of Peter, and the Wisdom of Solomon. The Apocalypse of Peter does not belong to our New Testament, while the Wisdom of Solomon is now part of (Catholic) Old Testament. The compiler of this Canon mentioned the Shepherd of Hermas which could be read, but was not to be published for the people. He also included Paul's epistle to the Laodiceans.

Parallel to the chain of evidence we have traced for the canonical standing of the Gospels, a similar chain exists for the thirteen Epistles of St Paul, forming the other half of the irreducible kernel of the complete New Testament canon. All the authorities cited for the Gospel Canon show acquaintance with, and recognize, the sacred quality of these letters. St Irenaeus employs all the Pauline writings, except the short Philemon, as sacred and canonical. In this formative period, the Letter to the Hebrews did not obtain a firm footing in the Canon of the Universal Church. At Rome it was not yet recognized as canonical, as shown by the Muratorian catalogue of Roman origin; Irenaeus cited it, but makes no reference to a Pauline origin. Yet it was known at Rome as early as St Clement, as the latter's epistle attests. The Alexandrian Church admitted it as the work of St Paul, and canonical.

The question of the principle that dominated the practical canonization of the New Testament Scriptures is significant. The faithful must have had from the beginning some realization that in the writings of the Apostles and Evangelists they had acquired a new body of Divine Scriptures, a New written Testament destined to stand side by side with the Old. That the Gospel and Epistles were the written Word of God, was fully realized as soon as the fixed collections were formed; but to seize the relation of this new treasure to the old was possible only when the faithful acquired a better knowledge of the faith. For Tertullian (circa 200) the body of the New Scripture is an *instrumentum* on at least an equal footing and in the same specific class as the *instrumentum* formed by the Law and the Prophets.

4.3.1.2 The period of discussion (AD 220–367)

In this stage of the historical development of the Canon of the New Testament we encounter for the first time a consciousness reflected in certain ecclesiastical writers, of the differences between the sacred collections in various sections of Christendom. This variation is witnessed to, and the discussion stimulated by, two of the most learned men of Christian antiquity, Origen, and Eusebius of Cæsarea, the ecclesiastical historian. Origen's travels gave him special opportunities to know the traditions of widely separated portions of the Church and made him very conversant with the discrepant attitudes toward certain parts of the New Testament He divided books with Biblical claims into three classes. First, those universally received, namely the four

Gospels, the thirteen Pauline Epistles, Acts, Apocalypse, 1 Peter, and 1 John. Then, he listed those works whose Apostolicity was questioned, and these comprised Hebrews, 2 Peter, 2 and 3 John, James, Jude, Barnabas, the Shepherd of Hermas, the Didache, and probably the Gospel of the Hebrews. Personally, Origen accepted all of these as divinely inspired, though he tolerated contrary opinions. Origen's authority seems to have given to Hebrews and the disputed Catholic Epistles a firm place in the Alexandrian Canon. Finally, Origen listed some apocryphal works. Eusebius, Bishop of Cæsarea in Palestine, was one of Origen's most eminent disciples, a man of great learning. In emulation of his master, he also divided religious literature into three classes. However, Eusebius diverged from Origen in personally rejecting Apocalypse as an non–Biblical, though he was compelled to acknowledge its almost universal acceptance.

During this period, there was discussion about the Canon in the African, or Carthaginian Church. St Cyprian, whose Scriptural Canon certainly reflects the contents of the first Latin Bible, received all the books of the New Testament except Hebrews, 2 Peter, James, and Jude; however, there was already a strong inclination in his environment to admit 2 Peter as authentic.

4.3.1.3 The period of fixation (AD 367–405)

Around the year 363 AD, the Council of Laodicea published a list of 26 New Testament books, in which the book of Revelation was not included. The same list of 26 books was given by St Cyril of Jerusalem (died 386 AD) and by St Gregory of Nazianzen. The influence of St Athanasius on the Canon of the New Testament was most constructive. In 367, Athanasius, bishop of Alexandria gave the list of 27 New Testament books, for the first time without making any distinction between them and which now becomes our New Testament.[15]

4.3.1.4 Subsequent history

A. In the West to the Middle Ages

The last trace of any Western contradiction within the Church to the Canon of the New Testament reveals a curious transplantation of Oriental doubts concerning the Apocalypse. An act of the Synod of Toledo, held in 633, states that many contest the authority of that book, and orders it to be read in the churches under pain of excommunication. The opposition in all probability came from the Visigoths, who had recently been converted from Arianism. The Gothic Bible had been made under Oriental auspices at a time when there was still much hostility to Apocalypse in the East.

During the Middle Ages the Church in the West received the Latin New Testament from the Vulgate, and the subject of the canon was seldom discussed. However, we still find a certain elasticity in the boundaries of the New Testament. There was no widespread contestation of any book, but here and there attempts by individuals to add something to the received collection. The most notable addition in some manuscripts is the Epistle to the Laodiceans. It was not until the Council of Florence (1439–43) that the See of Rome delivered for the first time a categorical opinion on the Scriptural Canon. In consequence of the efforts of this Council to bring about reunion with the Eastern Orthodox Church, which sought support from the West against the Turks, who were nearing Constantinople, Pope Eugenius IV published a bull setting forth the doctrines of the unity of the Old and New Testament, the inspiration of the Scriptures, and a statement of their extent. In the list of 27 books of the New Testament there are 14 Pauline Epistles, that to the Hebrews being last, with the book of Acts coming immediately before the Revelation of John. The Epistle to the Laodiceans is not even mentioned.

B. The New Testament and the Council of Trent (1546)

This ecumenical Council had to defend the integrity of the New Testament as well as the Old against the attacks of the Reformers. Luther, basing his action on his own particular angle of exegesis, had discarded Hebrews, James, Jude, and Apocalypse as altogether non–canonical. Zwingli could not see in Apocalypse a Biblical book. Oecolampadius placed James, Jude, 2 Peter, 2 and 3 John in an inferior rank. Even a few Catholic scholars of the Renaissance type, notably Erasmus and Cajetan, had thrown some doubts on the canonicity of these books. As to whole books, the Protestant doubts were the only ones the Fathers of Trent took cognizance of; there was not the slightest hesitation regarding the authority of any entire document. However, the deuterocanonical parts gave the council some concern, namely, the last twelve verses of Mark, the passage about the Bloody Sweat in Luke, and the *Pericope Adulteræ* in John. Cardinal Cajetan had approvingly quoted an unfavourable comment of St Jerome regarding Mark 16: 9–20; Erasmus had rejected the section on the Adulterous Woman as unauthentic. Still, even concerning these no doubt of authenticity was expressed at Trent; the only question was as to the manner of their reception. In the end, these portions were received, like the deuterocanonical books, without the slightest distinction. The clause 'cum omnibus suis partibus' regards especially these portions.

The Tridentine decree defining the Canon affirms the authenticity of the books to which proper names are attached, without however including this in the definition. The order of books follows that of the Bull of Eugenius IV (Council of Florence), except that Acts was moved from a place before Apocalypse to its present position, and Hebrews put at the end of St Paul's Epistles. The Tridentine order has been retained in the official Vulgate and vernacular Catholic Bibles. The same is to be said of the titles, which as a rule are traditional ones, taken from the Canons of Florence and Carthage. On April 8 1546, by a vote of 24 to 15 with 16 abstentions, a decree (*De Canonicis Scripturis*) was issued in which, for the first time in the history of the Church, the question of the contents of the Bible was made an absolute article of faith and confirmed by anathema. In translation this decree reads:

> The holy ecumenical and general Council of Trent, ... following the example of the orthodox Fathers receives and venerates all the books of the Old and New Testament ... and also the traditions pertaining to faith and conduct ... with an equal sense of devotion and reverence (*pari pietatis affectu ac reverentia*) ... If, however, anyone does not receive these books in their entirety, with all their parts (*cum omnibus suis partibus*), as they are accustomed to be read in the Catholic Church and are contained in the ancient Latin Vulgate edition as sacred and canonical, and knowingly and deliberately rejects the aforesaid traditions, let him be anathema.[16]

C. The New Testament Canon outside the Catholic Church

The Russian Orthodox and other branches of the Eastern Orthodox Church have a New Testament identical with that of the Catholic Church. In Syria the Nestorians possess a Canon almost identical with the final one of the ancient East Syrians; they exclude the four smaller Catholic Epistles and Apocalypse. The Monophysites receive all the books. The Armenians have one apocryphal letter to the Corinthians and two from the same. The Coptic–Arabic Church include with the canonical Scriptures the Apostolic Constitutions and the Clementine Epistles. The Ethiopic New Testament also contains the so–called 'Apostolic Constitutions'.

Among subsequent confessions of faith drawn up by Protestants, several identify by name the 27 books of the New Testament canon, including the French Confession of Faith (1559), the Belgic Confession (1561), and The Westminster Confession of Faith (1647). The Thirty–Nine

Articles, issued by the Church of England in 1563, names the books of the Old Testament, but not the New Testament. None of the Confessional statements issued by any Lutheran church includes an explicit list of canonical books.

Thus, as for Protestantism, the Anglicans and Calvinists always kept the entire New Testament. However, for over a century the followers of Luther excluded Hebrews, James, Jude, and Apocalypse, and even went further than their master by rejecting the three remaining deuterocanonicals, 2 Peter, 2 and 3 John. The trend of the seventeenth century Lutheran theologians was to class all these writings as of doubtful, or at least inferior, authority. However, gradually the German Protestants familiarized themselves with the idea that the difference between the contested books of the New Testament and the rest was one of degree of certainty as to origin rather than of intrinsic character. The full recognition of these books by the Calvinists and Anglicans made it much more difficult for the Lutherans to exclude the New Testament deuterocanonicals than those of the Old Testament. One of their writers of the seventeenth century allowed only a theoretic difference between the two classes, and in 1700 Bossuet could say that all Catholics and Protestants agreed on the New Testament Canon. The only trace of opposition now remaining in German Protestant Bibles is in the order: Hebrews, comes with James, Jude, and Apocalypse at the end; Hebrews not being included with the Pauline writings, while James and Jude are not ranked with the Catholic Epistles.

4.3.2 The Criteria for Canonicity

In the light of the definition of the Canon of the New Testament by the Church, we may wish to summarize the conditions for acceptance into this Canon. The first criterion is Apostolic authority, in other words that the book was written by an apostle or under his influence: the writers were direct or indirect eyewitnesses of Christ. Second, the book must be within orthodoxy, that is its contents held to the rule of faith and did not contain heresy. The book fits into the tradition of faith, and is mutually complementary and related to other accepted Christian writings. The third condition is catholicity, or universal acceptance as canonical within the Greek, Latin, and Eastern churches by the end of the fourth century. The fourth criterion is antiquity, namely that the book must have been written between birth of Christ and the death of the last apostle. A fifth condition is that of inspiration, which is the internal witness of the Holy Spirit in the text to the Church's authority defining the book as canonical and inspired. Finally, the liturgical use, or its acceptance as a reading in public liturgical worship, bears witness to its canonicity.

By itself, none of New Testament books can prove its canonicity and if we rely on the testimony of the Christians in the first and second century, they too may have different opinions on a particular book. As mentioned earlier, some (7 books) were accepted as canonical after some dispute. Thus we need other and final criteria, the authority of the Church which has the final say regarding which book belongs to our Old and New Testaments. Catholics have no problem to accept this criteria, which is a historical fact and is even supported by a testimony of Paul himself, recorded in 1 Timothy 3:15 which says: the Church is the foundation and pillar of truth. It was by the apostolic Tradition that the Church discerned which writings are to be included in the list of the sacred books.[17]

Even those Catholic theologians who defend Apostolicity as a test for the inspiration of the New Testament admit that it is not exclusive of another criterion, namely Catholic tradition as manifested in the universal reception of compositions as Divinely inspired, or the ordinary teaching of the Church, or the infallible pronouncements of ecumenical councils. This external guarantee is the sufficient, universal, and ordinary proof of inspiration. The unique quality of the Sacred Books is a revealed dogma. Moreover, by its very nature inspiration eludes human observation and is not self–evident, being essentially superphysical and supernatural. Its sole absolute criterion, therefore, is the Holy inspiring Spirit, witnessing decisively to Himself, not in the subjective experience of individual souls, as Calvin maintained, neither in the doctrinal and spiritual tenor of Holy Writ itself, according to Luther, but through the constituted organ and custodian of His revelations, the Church. All other evidences fall short of the certainty and finality necessary to evoke the absolute assent of faith.

4.3.3 Examples of non–canonical books

Our example is the Epistle to the Laodiceans, estimated to have been written at the close of the 3rd century AD. How it came to be held in high regard can be seen from the end of St Paul's Letter to the Colossians, where this request is made of its recipients: 'When this epistle has been read among you, have it read also in the church of the Laodiceans; and see that you read the epistle from Laodicea' (Col 4:16). This tantalizing reference, though somewhat ambiguous as to who wrote whom, offered a tempting invitation to some unknown author to provide the text of an Epistle of Paul to the Laodiceans, who were the neighbours of the congregation at Colossae. By the fourth century, St Jerome reported that 'some read the Epistle to the Laodiceans, but it is rejected by everyone.'[18] It commanded a certain respect in the Western Church for period of 1000 years. Comprising only 20 verses, the epistle is a collection of phrases and sentences taken from the genuine Pauline Epistles, particularly Philippians. After the author has expressed his joy at the faith and virtue of the Laodiceans, he warns them against heretics, and exhorts them to remain faithful to Christian doctrines and the Christian pattern of life. The epistle purports to have been written from prison.

There is no evidence of a Greek text. The epistle appears in more than 100 manuscripts of the Latin Vulgate (including the oldest, the celebrated Codex Fuldensis, 546 AD), as well as in manuscripts of early Albigensian, Bohemian,

English, and Flemish versions. At the close of the 10th century Aelfric, a monk in Dorset, wrote a treatise in Anglo–Saxon on the Old and New Testaments, in which he stated that the apostle Paul wrote 15 Epistles. In his enumeration of them he placed Laodiceans after Philemon. About 1165 AD, John of Salisbury, writing about the Canon of Scripture to Henry, Count of Champagne, acknowledges that 'it is the common, indeed almost universal, opinion that there are only 14 Epistles of Paul ... But the 15th is that which is written to the church of the Laodiceans.'[19] The Epistle to the Laodiceans is included in all 18 German Bibles printed prior to Luther's translation, beginning with the first German Bible, issued by Johann Mental at Strasburg in 1488. In these the Pauline Epistles, with the Epistle to the Hebrews, immediately follow the Gospels, with Laodiceans standing between Galatians and Ephesians. In the first Czech (Bohemian) Bible, published at Prague in 1488 and reprinted several times in the 16th and 17th centuries, Laodiceans follows Colossians and precedes I Thessalonians. Thus, as Bishop Lightfoot phrased it: 'for more than nine centuries this forged epistle hovered about the doors of the sacred Canon, without either finding admission or being peremptorily excluded.'[20] It was not until the Council of Florence (1439–43) that the See of Rome delivered for the first time a categorical opinion on the Scriptural canon. In the list of 27 books of the New Testament there are 14 Pauline Epistles, that to the Hebrews being last, with the book of Acts coming immediately before the Revelation of John. The Epistle to the Laodiceans is not even mentioned. It is clear that the reason for the exclusion of this book is that it is too late, namely not Apostolic. We furnish here the text of the Epistle to the Laodiceans:

> Paul, an apostle not of men and not through man, but through Jesus Christ, to the brethren who are in Laodicea: 2. Grace to you and peace from God the Father and the Lord Jesus Christ. 3. I thank Christ in all my prayer that you are steadfast in him and

persevering in his works, in expectation of the promise for the day of judgment. 4. And may you not be deceived by the vain talk of some people who tell (you) tales that they may lead you away from the truth of the gospel which is proclaimed by me. 5. And now may God grant that those who come from me for the furtherance of the truth of the gospel (...) may be able to serve and to do good works for the well–being of eternal life. 6. And now my bonds are manifest, which I suffer in Christ, on account of which I am glad and rejoice. 7. This ministers to me unto eternal salvation, which (itself) is effected through your prayers and by the help of the Holy Spirit, whether it be through life or through death. 8. For my life is in Christ and to die is joy (to me). 9. And this will his mercy work in you, that you may have the same love and be of one mind. 10. Therefore, beloved, as you have heard my presence, so hold fast and do in the fear of God, and eternal life will be your portion. 11. For it is God who works in you. 12. And do without hesitation what you do. 13. And for the rest, beloved, rejoice in Christ and beware of those who are out for sordid gain. 14. May all your requests be manifest before God, and be steadfast in the mind of Christ. 15. And what is pure, true, proper, just and lovely, do. 16. And what you have heard and received, hold in your heart and peace will be with you. 17. Salute all the brethren with the holy kiss. 18. The Saints salute you. 19. The grace of the Lord Jesus Christ be with your spirit. 20. And see that this epistle is read to the Colossians and that of the Colossians among you.[21]

A further example of a non–canonical book is the so–called *Gospel of Judas*. While the Epistle to the Laodiceans is excluded from the Canon of the New Testament because it was probably composed outside the Apostolic era, the Gospel of Judas is plainly a heretical work. The National Geographic Society has published an English translation of this text. The 31–page manuscript, written in Coptic, purportedly surfaced in Geneva in 1983 and has only now been translated. Though the manuscript still must be authenticated, it quite likely represents a fourth– or fifth–century text, and is a copy of an earlier document produced by a Gnostic sect called the Cainites. The document paints Judas Iscariot in a positive light, and describes him as obeying a divine ordinance in handing over Jesus to the authorities for the salvation of the world. It may well be a copy of the 'Gospel of Judas' referred to by St Irenaeus of Lyons in his work *Against the Heresies*, written around A.D. 180.

Indeed, Gnosticism is responsible for a number of non–canonical writings. The roots of Gnosticism are an esoteric collection of Eastern religious philosophies which are parasitic and dualistic in nature. Gnosticism, derived from the Greek word *gnosis* (knowledge) claimed a superior secret understanding of things. It was a system based on an elitist human striving for philosophical knowledge rather than on faith; in Gnosticism, the distinction between the eternal uncreated Supreme Being and all other beings was blurred or erased. In its widely various mythological forms, Gnosticism espouses a pantheon of divine beings anywhere from two to thirty. The production of matter was conceived of in terms of a downward emanation from God. Its basic myth attributes the creation of the material world to a lesser, evil god or demiurge while Jesus' heavenly father is the good god beyond all knowledge. Matter, on this account, is evil, and along with it, the human body as well. In man's creation a 'spark of divinity' got trapped in some human bodies. Salvation consists in liberating this divine spark from its material prison, and the only path to salvation is secret knowledge of the Gnostic myth imparted to an elect. In this system Jesus could not have really become man because such an incarnation would imply that a good divine being mixed with evil matter. Therefore, he only appeared to be human. The ancients called this theological approach to Christ *doceticism*, meaning a question simply of appearance, not reality. The canonical Scriptures portray a very human Jesus who hungers, thirsts, suffers temptation and weeps. The Gnostic gospels, on the other hand, depict a phantom–like Jesus that is, when they depict the life of Jesus at all. The Gnostic writings generally lack historical narrative, and are often simply a compilation of abstract sayings. It is little wonder that they appeal to the adherents of contemporary New Age philosophies. Gnosticism invaded other religious systems and exploited their symbols to its own end. So, even though a Gnostic might speak of Jesus, he would use the historical figure of Christ to convey his own mythological agenda.

It is out of these false sources that fantasy like *The Da Vinci Code* is concocted.[22] This blasphemous book is an attack on the basic beliefs of Christianity as remains clear from Dan Brown's statement: '...almost everything our fathers taught us about Christ is false.'[23] The *Da Vinci Code* presents a mistaken theory that Christianity is a lie, that Christian rituals are taken from pagan religions and that the New Testament of the Bible is a forgery. The *Da Vinci Code* denies the authority and veracity of the Gospels: 'More than eighty gospels were considered for the New Testament, and yet only a relative few were chosen for inclusion...The Bible as we know it today was collated by the pagan Roman Emperor Constantine the Great....From this sprang the most profound moment in Christian history. Constantine commissioned and financed a new Bible, which omitted those gospels that spoke of Christ's human traits and embellished those gospels that made him godlike. The other gospels were outlawed, gathered up, and burned.'[24]

Instead, there are four New Testament Gospels, which are named Matthew, Mark, Luke and John. Bible scholars believe that these were written during the first century in which Jesus lived. On the other hand, the Gnostic writings are generally believed to have been written later – about 100 to 300 years later. These Gnostic texts borrowed some elements from Christianity, including the names of Jesus and His apostles, but these writings are not Christian. In response to these new, false writings the regional churches drew up lists of the authentic books that had been handed down from the apostles. There were relatively very few 'gospels' and other documents with any confirmed link to apostolic times, not 80 gospels as claimed by Dan Brown. By the middle of the second century, Christian writers regularly cited only the gospels of Matthew, Mark, Luke and John, as well as Paul's letters, as the most reliable sources of information about Jesus' life and the faith of the apostles. On the question of 'mass burning of texts deemed heretical,' there is no evidence to support that claim. Books rejected by the Church simply disappeared because people stopped using them, and nobody bothered to make new copies in that age, long before the invention of the printing press.

The process by which the Bible formed was one that took time as we have described above. Constantine did not have anything to do with this process, either before or after he converted to Christianity. The process by which the canon of Scripture was formed was largely complete by the time of Constantine which was the early fourth century. The *Da Vinci Code* also asserts that the canon of Scripture was altered at the order of Constantine to support his 'new' doctrine of the divinity of Christ.[25] Brown asserts this myth in order to deny the evidence that exists against his position. He cannot back up this claim, for there is no evidence for it whatsoever. No Scripture scholar supports this position. On the contrary, the writings of the Church Fathers (and even non–Christian historians) before the time of Constantine show that Christians regarded Jesus as God.

According to Dan Brown, in the most dramatic cover–up in history, the official church suppressed the truth about Mary's relationship with Jesus and did its best to discredit Mary Magdalene. *The Da Vinci Code* makes the utterly false claim Jesus was married to Mary Magdalene. The novelist misuses Leonardo Da Vinci's painting of the Last Supper to support his false thesis. The reason that Brown and a handful of mainly New Age authors have tried to identify Mary Magdalene as the wife of Jesus is obvious. She is one of the few women disciplines of Christ who is prominent, whose name we know. Other female disciples of Jesus are known to be married to others (for example, Joanna the wife of Chuza in Luke 8:3) or are too insignificant ('the other Mary' in Matthew 28:1) or we don't know their names (the Syro–Phoenecian woman in Matthew 15:28). If one wants to force Jesus into the role of being married, Mary Magdalene is one of the few prominent and (seemingly) available women to be pushed into that role. There is nothing whatever in the New Testament that states or implies that Jesus was married to Mary Magdalene. According to the New Testament, Mary of Magdala was a devout follower of Christ and one of the first witnesses of His Resurrection (cf. Mt 28:1), but not His wife. There is no evidence in the writings of the Church Fathers that she was married to Jesus. Jesus also made affirmations that indicated that He wasn't married to anyone. He explained that some voluntarily refrain from marrying in order to be fully consecrated to God. He says that there are some disciples who 'have made themselves eunuchs for the kingdom of heaven's sake' (Mt 19:12). He portrays voluntary abstention from marriage as the highest form of consecration, and as the Founder of the Church, it would be strange for Him to hold up such a standard if He Himself did not meet it.

Jesus' celibacy is a historical fact with important theological ramifications. His celibacy is connected with His divine nature in a like manner that the perpetual virginity of Our Lady points to Christ's divinity. The fact that Jesus has no blood descendants is also important theologically since it means that a relationship to Him can only be by adoption; in the Gospels, in fact, He says: 'Whoever does the will of My Father in heaven is My brother and sister and mother' (Mt 12:50). This is to steer people away from the blood relationship to Him and towards the adoptive relationship. Moreover, the early Church was unanimous in regarding Jesus as unmarried. This is not a later doctrine of the Church Fathers but something found in the New Testament itself. The authors of the New Testament regularly depict the Church as 'the bride of Christ' (2 Co 11:2; Ep 5:21–33; cf. Rev 21:9–10). This metaphor would never have developed if a flesh–and–blood wife existed. Only if Christ was celibate would the Church have come to be depicted metaphorically as His bride.

4.4 Tradition, Scripture and the Magisterium

Divine revelation, given once and for all to the Church by Christ, is handed down in the same Church through Scripture and Tradition. The Scriptures constitute foundational Revelation, other later definitions are dependent Revelation. The Church in its faith and theology does not derive the fullness of the content of revelation and the certainty concerning this deposit of faith from Scripture alone, but also from all that is contained within the tradition of the Church. The idea of Tradition is already contained in Scripture:

> Now I make known to you, brethren, the gospel which I preached to you, which also you received, in which also you stand, by which also you are saved, if you hold fast the word which I preached to you, unless you believed in vain. For I delivered to you as of first importance what I also received, that Christ died for our sins according to the Scriptures, and that He was buried, and that He was raised on the third day according to the Scriptures(1 Co 15:1–4).

An example from the theology of creation lies in the fact that although the doctrine of creation out of nothing is indicated in the Scriptures (2 Maccabees 7:28 and Romans 4:17),

the complete doctrine and its certainty is contained in Tradition as taught by the Church's teaching office or
Magisterium.[26] The guidance of the Papal Magisterium or
teaching office, on creation and other topics is especially
important in this rapidly–changing global and scientific
age. St Peter's successor as 'the perpetual and visible source
and foundation of unity both of the bishops and of the
whole company of the faithful'[27] is not merely a static focus
of unity, but one which leads to still greater unity. Despite
the ebb and flow in the tide of the Church's fortunes in
history, there is nevertheless a prophetic direction in the
rôle of Peter's successor. The work of each Pope is woven
into the tapestry of salvation history as a whole, since the
Holy Spirit is guiding the Church into all truth (cf. Jn 16:13).
The organic relationship of the Pope within the Church is
beautifully illustrated by Bernini's 'Glory' in St Peter's basilica in Rome. From above, the Holy Spirit shines upon the
Chair (*Cathedra*) of Saint Peter, divinely guiding each of his
successors in their Magisterium. From below, the chair is
supported by four saints, who are also bishops and theologians: St Ambrose and St Augustine (of the Latin Church)
and St Athanasius and St John Chrysostom (of the Greek
Church). This illustrates in a marvellous way how St Peter's
successor, infallibly guided by the Spirit, acquires his theological formulations with the help of the bishops and the
faithful and is in close touch with the sense of faith (*sensus
fidei*)[28] of the entire People of God.

Each of the various layers of meaning in the Scriptures
needs to be uncovered by the Church so as to illustrate the
treasures contained therein. However, when Scripture has
been separated from its vital matrix of Tradition and the
teaching office of the Church, exegetes have not always
been able to avoid those possible pitfalls known as
concordism, fundamentalism and *liberalism*.

Concordism relates to the efforts whereby 'numerous
commentators of Genesis 1 tried to establish its concordance with cosmogonies taken for the last word in

science'.[29] The danger of this stance is clear, for when a
scientific position changes, as it necessarily must for science
is in continual development, faith in the word of God as
revealed in Scripture may be jeopardized. It is all too easy
to be amused by the concordist exegesis of Archbishop
Ussher which, in a seventeenth–century attempt to recon-
cile the six–day creation account with Newtonian physics,
fixed the time of creation in the year 4004 BC on Sunday
23rd October at 9 o'clock in the morning! Nevertheless,
concordism is still a possible trap for the Christian today
who attempts to read into the book of Genesis too close a
connection with the Big–Bang theory. The fundamentalist
approach 'starts from the principle that the Bible, being the
word of God, inspired and free from error, should be read
and interpreted literally in all its details. But by «literal
interpretation» it understands a naively literalist interpretation,..., which excludes every effort at understanding the
Bible that takes account of its historical origins and development. It is opposed, therefore, to the use of the
historico–critical method, as indeed to the use of any other
scientific method for the interpretation of Scripture'.[30] While
the fundamentalist approach is right to uphold the divine
inspiration of Scripture and the inerrancy of the Word of
God, it fails to see the full consequences of the Incarnation,
ignoring the historical, cultural and human aspects of biblical revelation. It often goes hand in hand with the
'Scripture alone' approach to theology, which was one of
the characteristics of the Protestant reformation.

On the other hand, the liberal or modernist approach to
Scriptural interpretation exaggerates the rôle of human
techniques in the formation of the Bible and in its exegesis.
In a rationalist way it seeks to reduce to merely symbolic or
mythological meanings that which in fact Scripture teaches
as true at the deepest level. Both Catholic and Protestant
theologies have at various times suffered the ravages of
modernist reductionism. The Church, on the other hand
has made it clear, in a realist key, that the Scriptures portray

and communicate Christ. From the Scriptures we can 'learn the surpassing knowledge of Jesus Christ, by frequent reading of the divine Scriptures. Ignorance of the Scriptures is ignorance of Christ.'[31]

Another important topic is that of the difference between the inspired texts of the Sacred Scriptures and the texts of other religions. On the one hand, there are some elements in these texts which may be *de facto* instruments by which countless people throughout the centuries have been and still are able today to nourish and maintain their life–relationship with God.[32] The Second Vatican Council, in considering the customs, precepts, and teachings of the other religions, teaches that 'although differing in many ways from her own teaching, these nevertheless often reflect a ray of that truth which enlightens all men.'[33] It pointed out that there are elements of good present 'in the particular customs and cultures of peoples.'[34] These elements of good and of truth present among non–Christians can be considered a preparation for the reception of the Gospel.[35] The Church's tradition, however, reserves the designation of inspired texts to the canonical books of the Old and New Testaments, since these are inspired by the Holy Spirit.[36] Taking up this tradition, the Dogmatic Constitution on Divine Revelation of the Second Vatican Council states: 'For Holy Mother Church, relying on the faith of the apostolic age, accepts as sacred and canonical the books of the Old and New Testaments, whole and entire, with all their parts, on the grounds that, written under the inspiration of the Holy Spirit (cf. Jn 20:31; 2 Tm 3:16; 2 Pet 1:19–21; 3:15–16), they have God as their author, and have been handed on as such to the Church herself.'[37] These books 'firmly, faithfully, and without error, teach that truth which God, for the sake of our salvation, wished to see confided to the Sacred Scriptures.'[38]

God, who desires to call all peoples to Himself in Christ and to communicate to them the fullness of His revelation and love, 'does not fail to make Himself present in many ways, not only to individuals, but also to entire peoples through their spiritual riches, of which their religions are the main and essential expression even when they contain 'gaps, insufficiencies and errors.'[39] Therefore, the sacred books of other religions, which in actual fact direct and nourish the existence of their followers, receive from the mystery of Christ the elements of goodness and grace which they contain. Technically, we would only describe the texts of the Scriptures as inspired, whereas the texts of other religions are imperfect, they are attempts to find God 'which need to be enlightened and healed; even though, through the kindly workings of Divine Providence, they may sometimes serve as leading strings toward God, or as a preparation for the Gospel.'[40] It is clear that not everything in these texts can possibly be true because they contradict themselves, as well as contradicting the truth revealed by Christ.

Notes

1. Compare Acts 13:16–41 with Acts 17:22–31.
2. Cf. St John Chrysostom, *Hom. in Matth.* 1, 3 in *PG* 57, 16–17; St Augustine, *De consensu Evangelistarum* 2, 12, 28 in *CSEL* 43, 127–29.
3. St Augustine, *De consensu Evangelistarum* 2, 21, 51–52 in *CSEL* 43, 153.
4. Vatican II, *Dei Verbum*, 19. Cf. Acts 1:1–2.
5. *Ibid.*.
6. *Ibid.*.
7. See M. Goodacre, *The Case Against Q*; see also M. D. Goulder, 'Is Q a Juggernaut?' in *Journal of Biblical Literature* 115 (1996), pp. 667–681.
8. See M. Goodacre, *The Case Against Q* (Harrisburg, Pa.: Trinity, 2002). The standard solution to the Synoptic Problem supposes that Matthew and Luke made independent use not only of Mark but also of another source, now lost, called 'Q'. But in *The Case Against Q*, Mark Goodacre combines a strong affirmation of Markan Priority with a careful and detailed

critique of the Q hypothesis, giving fresh perspectives on the evidence drawn not only from traditional methods but also from contemporary scholarly approaches. In an invigorating and imaginative approach to one of the most important issues in New Testament scholarship, Goodacre paints a plausible picture of Synoptic interrelationships in a bid to renew discussions about Christian origins.

9. See G. O'Collins, 'Peter as Easter Witness' in *The Heythrop Journal* 22/1 (1981), pp. 1–18.
10. Pope St Clement I, *Letter to the Corinthians*, 47, 1 in *PG* 1, 305.
11. St Ignatius of Antioch, *Letter to the Ephesians*, 12,2 in *SC* 10 (Paris: Cerf, 1945), pp.58–59.
12. Idem, *Letter to the Smyrnaeans*, 5,1 and 7,2 in *SC* 10, pp. 124–127.
13. St Justin Martyr, *First Apology*, 1, 66 in *PG* 6, 429.
14. St Irenaeus, *Against the heresies*, 3, 11 in *PG* 7, 885.
15. See St Athanasius, *Letter* 39 in *PG* 26, 1438.
16. Council of Trent, Fourth Session, *Decree concerning the Canonical Scriptures* in DS 1501, 1504.
17. Cf. Vatican II, *Dei Verbum*, 8.
18. St Jerome, *De viris illustribus*, 5.
19. John of Salisbury, *Epistle 209*.
20. J. B. Lightfoot, *Saint Paul's Epistles to the Colossians and to Philemon* (London: 1890[9]), p. 297.
21. Text from W. Schneemelcher (ed.), *New Testament Apocrypha* (Louisville: Westminster/John Knox Press, 1989[6]), Volume 2, pp.43–44. The Latin text runs as follows:
1:1 Paulus apostolus non ab hominibus neque per hominem sed per Iesum Christum, fratribus qui sunt Laodiciae. 1:2 gratia vobis et pax a Deo Patre et Domino Iesu Christo. 1:3 gratias ago Christo per omnem orationem meam, quod permanentes estis in eo et perseverantes in operibus eius, promissum expectantes in diem iudicii. 1:4 neque destituant vos quorundam vaniloquia insinuantium, ut vos evertant a veritate evangelii quod a me praedicatur. 1:5 et nunc faciet Deus, ut qui sunt ex me ad profectum veritatis evangelii deservientes et facientes benignitatem operum quae salutis vitae aeternae 1:6 et nunc palam sunt vincula mea quae patior in Christo; quibus laetor et gaudeo. 1:7 et hoc mihi est ad

salutem perpetuam; quod ipsum factum orationibus vestris et administrantem Spiritum Sanctum, sive per vitam sive per mortem. 1:8 est enim mihi vere vita in Christo et mori gaudium. 1:9 et in ipsum in vobis faciet misericordiam suam, ut eandem dilectionem habeatis et sitis unianimes. 1:10 ergo, dilectissimi, ut audistis praesentia mei, ita retinete et facite in timore Dei, et erit vobis vita in aeternum; 1:11 est enim Deus qui operatur in vos. 1:12 et facite sine retractu quaecumque facitis. 1:13 et quod est, dilectissimi, gaudete in Christo. et praecavete sordidos in lucro. 1:14 omnes sint petitiones vestrae palam apud Deum. et estote firmi in sensu Christi. 1:15 et quae integra et vera et pudica et iusta et amabilia facite. 1:16 et quae audistis et accepistis, in corde retinete, et erit vobis pax. 1:17 salutate omnes fratres in osculo sancto. 1:18 salutant vos sancti. 1:19 gratia Domini Iesu cum spiritu vestro. 1:20 et facite legi Colosensium vobis.

22. *The Da Vinci Code* is a novel by Dan Brown, a former English teacher and writer of three other books. This blasphemous and evil book is a piece of escapism, which produces a cocktail that mixes religion, conspiracy, sex, murder and mystery. In Brown's novel, the term *Da Vinci Code* refers to cryptic messages supposedly incorporated by Leonardo Da Vinci into his famous artwork, The Last Supper. According to the novel, Leonardo was a member of an ancient secret society called the 'Priory of Sion' dedicated to preserving the 'truths' that Jesus designated Mary Magdalene as his successor, that His message was about the celebration of the 'sacred feminine,' that Jesus and Mary Magdalene were married and they had a daughter, that the Holy Grail of legend and lore is really Mary Magdalene – the 'sacred feminine,' – the vessel who carried Jesus' blood or His child. A full refutation of *The Da Vinci Code* will not be undertaken here. There are many excellent books which have done this, like C.E. Olsen & S. Miesel, *The Da Vinci Hoax: Exposing the Errors in The Da Vinci Code* (San Francisco: Ignatius Press, 2004) and A. Welborn, *De–coding Da Vinci. The facts behind the fiction of The Da Vinci Code* (Huntington, IN: Our Sunday Visitor, 2004). Welborn also points out many blatant mistakes in Brown's art history concerning Leonardo da Vinci, on almost every aspect of the artist's life and work. Brown

presents himself as some sort of devotee and expert in art history. However, he also consistently refers to the artist in question as 'da Vinci,' as if this were his name. It's not. It's the indicator of his home town. The artist's name was 'Leonardo,' and that is the name by which he is called in any art book you might pick up. Anyone who claims to be an art expert and refers to the artist as 'da Vinci' is as credible as a person claiming to be a Church historian who refers to Jesus as 'of Nazareth.'

23. D. Brown, *The Da Vinci Code* (New York: Doubleday, 2003), p. 235.
24. *Ibid.*, pp. 231, 234.
25. See *ibid.*, p. 234.
26. See Lateran IV in DS 800.
27. Vatican II, *Lumen gentium*, 23.1.
28. Cf. *ibid.* 12.1.
29. S.L. Jaki, *Genesis 1 Through the Ages* (London: Thomas More Press, 1992), p.43.
30. Pontifical Biblical Commission, *The Interpretation of the Bible in the Church* (Vatican City: Libreria Editrice Vaticana, 1993), pp.69–70.
31. Vatican II, *Dei Verbum*, 25. Cf. Phil 3:8 and St Jerome, *Commentariorum in Isaiam libri xviii prol.* in *PL* 24, 17.
32. See Congregation for the Doctrine of the Faith, *Dominus Iesus*, 8. See Vatican II, Dei Verbum, 11.
33. Vatican II, *Nostra aetate*, 2.
34. Vatican II, *Ad gentes*, 9.
35. See Vatican II, *Lumen gentium*, 16
36. Cf. Council of Trent, *Decretum de libris sacris et de traditionibus recipiendis* in DS 1501; Vatican II, Dogmatic Constitution *Dei Filius*, chapter 2 in DS 3006.
37. Vatican II, *Dei Verbum*, 11.
38. *Ibid.*.
39. Pope John Paul II, Encyclical Letter *Redemptoris missio*, 55; cf. 56 and Pope Paul VI, Apostolic Exhortation *Evangelii nuntiandi*, 53.
40. Vatican II, *Ad gentes*, 3.

5

St Peter and St Paul

What fairer light is this than time itself doth own,
The golden day with beams more radiant brightening?
The princes of God's Church this feast day doth enthrone,
To sinners heavenward bound their burden lightening.
One taught mankind its creed, one guards the heavenly gate,
Founders of Rome, they bind the world in loyalty;
One by the sword achieved, one by the cross his fate;
With laurelled brows they hold eternal royalty.

Elpis, *Decora lux*

5.1 St Peter

After Jesus Christ, Peter is the figure best known and most frequently cited in the New Testament writings: he is mentioned 154 times with the special name of Pétros, 'rock', which is the Greek translation of the Aramaic name Jesus gave him directly: Kephas, attested to nine times, especially in St Paul's Letters. The frequently–occurring name Simon (75 times) is a hellenization of his original Hebrew name 'Symeon' (this occurs twice: in Ac 15: 14; and in 2 Pt 1: 1). He was the son of Jonah and was born in Bethsaida (Jn 1:42, 44), a little town to the east of the Sea of Galilee. The Apostle Andrew was his brother, and the Apostle Philip came from the same town. Simon pursued in Capernaum the profitable occupation of fisherman on Lake Gennesaret, possessing his own boat (Lk 5:3). Simon settled in Capernaum, where he was living with his mother–in–law in his own house (Mt 8:14; Lk 4:38) at the beginning of Christ's public ministry (around AD 26–28). Recent archaeological excavations have brought to light, beneath the octagonal mosaic paving of a small Byzantine church, the remains of a more ancient church built in that house, as the graffiti with invocations to Peter testify.[1] Simon was thus married, and, according to Clement of Alexandria, had children.[2] The same writer relates the tradition that Peter's wife suffered martyrdom.[3]

Like so many of his Jewish contemporaries, Simon was attracted by John the Baptist's preaching of penance and was, with his brother Andrew, among John's associates in Bethania on the eastern bank of the Jordan. John the Baptist pointed to Jesus who was passing, saying, 'Behold, the Lamb of God' (Jn 1:36), and Andrew and another disciple followed the Saviour to His residence and remained with Him that day. Later, meeting his brother, Simon, Andrew said 'We have found the Messiah', and brought him to Jesus, who, looking upon him, said: 'You are Simon the son of John; you will be called Kephas' (Jn 1:42). Already, at this first meeting, the Saviour foretold the change of Simon's name to Kephas, the Aramaic for rock, which is translated Pétros in Greek (in Latin Petrus) a proof that Christ had already special plans with regard to Simon. Later, probably at the time of his definitive call to the Apostolate with the eleven other Apostles, Jesus actually gave Simon the name of Kephas, after which he was usually called Peter, especially by Christ on the solemn occasion after Peter's profession of faith (Mt 16:18). The Evangelists often combine the two names, while St Paul uses the name Kephas.

After this first meeting, Peter with the other early disciples remained with Jesus for some time, accompanying Him to Galilee (for the Marriage at Cana), to Judaea, and to

Jerusalem, and through Samaria back to Galilee (Jn 2–4). Here Peter resumed his occupation of fisherman for a short time, but soon received the definitive call of the Saviour to become one of His permanent disciples. Peter and Andrew were engaged at their work when Jesus met and addressed them: 'Come after me, and I will make you fishers of men' (Mt 4:19). On the same occasion, the sons of Zebedee were called (Mt 4:18–22; Mk 1:16–20; Lk 5:1–11; it is here assumed that Luke refers to the same occasion as the other Evangelists). Thereafter, Peter remained always in the immediate neighbourhood of Our Lord. After preaching the Sermon on the Mount and curing the son of the centurion in Capernaum, Jesus came to Peter's house and cured his wife's mother, who was sick with a fever (Mt 8:14–15; Mk 1:29–31). A little later, Christ chose His Twelve Apostles as His constant associates in preaching the Kingdom of God.

The New Testament notes the growing prominence of Peter among the Twelve. Though of irresolute character, he clings with the greatest fidelity, firmness of faith, and inward love to the Saviour; rash alike in word and act, he is full of zeal and enthusiasm, though momentarily easily accessible to external influences and intimidated by difficulties. The more prominent the Apostles become in the Gospel narrative, the more conspicuous does Peter appear as the first among them. In the list of the Twelve on the occasion of their solemn call to the Apostolate, not only does Peter stand always at their head, but the name given him by Christ is especially emphasized. For example in the list of the Apostles we read: 'The names of the twelve apostles are these: first, Simon called Peter, and his brother Andrew; James, the son of Zebedee, and his brother John; Philip and Bartholomew, Thomas and Matthew the tax collector; James, the son of Alphaeus, and Thaddeus; Simon the Cananean, and Judas Iscariot who betrayed Him' (Mt 10:2–4).[4] On various occasions Peter speaks in the name of the other Apostles (Mt 15:15; 19:27; Lk 12:41). When Christ's words are addressed to all the Apostles, Peter answers in their name (see, for example Mt 16:16). Frequently the Saviour turns specially to Peter (Mt 26:40; Lk 22:31).

Very characteristic is the expression of true fidelity to Jesus, which Peter addressed to Him in the name of the other Apostles. Christ, after He had spoken of the mystery of the reception of His Body and Blood (Jn 6:22 ff.) and many of His disciples had left Him, asked the Twelve if they too would leave Him. Peter's answer comes immediately: 'Master, to whom shall we go? You have the words of eternal life.   We have come to believe and are convinced that you are the Holy One of God' (Jn 6:68–69).   Christ Himself unmistakably accords Peter a special precedence and the first place among the Apostles, and designates him as such on various occasions. Peter was one of the three Apostles (with James and John) who were with Christ on certain special occasions like the raising from the dead of the daughter of Jairus (Mk 5:37; Lk 8:51); the Transfiguration of the Lord (Mt 17:1; Mk 9:1; Lk 9:28), the Agony in the Garden of Gethsemane (Mt 26:37; Mk 14:33). On several occasions, also Christ favoured him above all the others.   For example, Jesus enters Peter's boat on Lake Gennesaret to preach to the multitude on the shore (Lk 5:3). When He was miraculously walking upon the waters, He called Peter to come to Him across the lake (Mt 14:28 ff). Moreover, Jesus sent him to the lake to catch the fish in whose mouth Peter found the stater coin to pay as tribute (Mt 17:24 ff.).

St Peter's profession of faith took place at Caesarea Philippi. This place was so named because it had been rebuilt by the tetrarch Philip in honour of Caesar Augustus. It was the summer before the Crucifixion, with Jesus filled with presentiments of His Death. Perhaps Jesus withdrew here because it is a pleasant place to escape in summertime the torrid heat of the Lake of Galilee. However, the area has other associations which make it a suitable site for this scene. Hermon is traditionally a holy mountain, a meeting place of God and man, a suitable background to this episode of revelation and solemn mission.

They walked a while up the mountain road to Mount Hermon. The Jordan had its source in these mysterious ravines; the spring of the Jordan is, in Jewish legend, the opening to hell.[5] The precipitous southern end of one of the foothills of Mount Hermon forms a wall of bare rock about 200 feet high and 500 feet wide, which formed the backdrop for Peter's profession of faith.[6] Here, Jesus asked His disciples: 'Who do people say that the Son of Man is?' (Mt 16:13). Some of them had heard that people took Him for the risen John the Baptist, others for Elijah or one of the prophets. 'But who do you say that I am?', continued Jesus. Quicker than any of the others, came Peter's confession of faith: 'You are the Christ, the Son of the living God' (Mt 16:16). Jesus responded with the words: 'Blessed are you, Simon son of Jonah. For flesh and blood has not revealed this to you, but my heavenly Father.' Then Jesus added 'And so I say to you, you are Peter, and upon this rock I will build my Church, and the gates of hell shall not prevail against it. I will give you the keys to the kingdom of heaven. Whatever you bind on earth shall be bound in heaven; and whatever you loose on earth shall be loosed in heaven' (Mt 16:18–19). These words of the Lord, written down in the latter half of the first century are inscribed in Latin, in golden letters, within the dome of St Peter's Basilica here in Rome.

In Hebrew thought, a person's name expresses the reality concerning that person. St Peter's new name encapsulates his mission as bedrock of the Church and foundation of its unity in Christ. By the word 'rock' the Saviour cannot have meant Himself, but only Peter, as is so much more apparent in Aramaic in which the same word (*Kipha*) is used for 'Peter' and 'rock'. His statement means that He wishes to make Peter the head of the whole community of those who believed in Him as the true Messiah; that through this foundation (Peter) the Kingdom of Christ would be unconquerable; that the guidance of the faithful was placed in the hands of Peter, as the special representative, or Vicar, of Christ. This meaning is also reinforced when one remembers that the words 'bind' and 'loose' are not merely metaphorical, but are concrete Jewish juridical terms. It is also clear that the position of Peter among the other Apostles and in the Christian community was the basis for the Kingdom of God on earth, that is, the Church of Christ. Peter was personally installed as Head of the Apostles by Christ Himself. This foundation created for the Church by its Founder could not disappear with the person of Peter, but was intended to continue and did in fact continue (as actual history shows) in the primacy of the Roman Church and its Popes.

In spite of his firm faith in Jesus, Peter had thus far no clear knowledge of the mission and work of the Saviour. The sufferings of Christ especially, transcended his worldly conception of the Messiah, and were inconceivable to him. Peter's incomplete conception occasionally elicited a sharp reproof from Jesus (Mt 16:21–23, Mk 8:31–33). During the Passion, Peter's weakness was manifested. The Saviour had already told him that Satan had desired to sift him as wheat. However, Christ had prayed for Peter that his faith may not fail, and, after being converted, he would confirm his brothers (Lk 22:31–32). Peter's assurance that he was ready to accompany his Master to prison and to death, elicited Christ's prediction that Peter would deny Him (Mt 26:30–35; Mk 14:26–31; Lk 22:31–34; Jn 13:33–38). When Christ proceeded to wash the feet of His disciples before the Last Supper, and came first to Peter, the latter at first protested, but, on Christ's declaring that otherwise he should have no part with Him, immediately said: 'Lord, not only my feet, but also my hands and my head' (Jn 13:1–10). In the Garden of Gethsemane, Peter had to submit to the Saviour's reproach that he had slept like the others, while his Master suffered deadly anguish (Mk 14:37). At the seizing of Jesus, Peter in an outburst of anger wished to defend his Master by force, but was forbidden to do so. At first he fled with the other Apostles (Jn 18:10–11; Mt 26:56); then turning he followed his captured Lord to the courtyard of the High Priest, and there denied Christ, asserting explicitly and swearing that he did not know Him (Mt 26:58–75; Mk 14:54–72; Lk 22:54–62; Jn 18:15–27). This denial did not constitute a lapse of interior faith in Christ, but was an expression of exterior fear and cowardice. His sorrow was thus so much the greater, when, after his Master had turned His gaze towards him, he clearly recognized what he had done.

In spite of this weakness, Peter's position as head of the Apostles was later confirmed by Jesus, and his precedence was at least as clear after the Resurrection as before. The women, who were the first to find Christ's tomb empty, received from the angel a special message for Peter (Mk 16:7). To him alone of the Apostles did Christ appear on the first day after the Resurrection (Lk 24:34; 1 Co 15:5). Moreover, most important of all, when He appeared at the Lake of Gennesaret, Christ renewed to Peter His special commission to feed and defend His flock, after Peter had thrice affirmed his special love for his Master (Jn 21:15–17). In conclusion, Christ foretold the violent death Peter would have to suffer, and thus invited him to follow Him in a special manner (Jn 21:20–23). In this manner, Peter was called and prepared to exercise the primacy of the Apostles, which he carried out with courage after Christ's Ascension into Heaven.

Among the crowd of Apostles and disciples who, after Christ's Ascension into Heaven from the Mount of Olives, returned to Jerusalem to await the fulfilment of His promise to send the Holy Spirit, Peter clearly stands out as the leader of all, and is henceforth constantly recognized as the head of the original Christian community in Jerusalem. He takes the initiative in the appointment to the Apostolic College of another witness of the life, death and resurrection of Christ to replace Judas (Ac 1:15–26). After the descent of the Holy Spirit on the first feast of Pentecost, Peter standing at the head of the Apostles delivers the first public sermon to proclaim the life, death, and resurrection of Jesus, and wins a large number of Jews as converts to the Christian community (Ac 2:14–41). As the first among the Apostles he worked a public miracle, when with John he went up into the temple and cured the lame man at the Beautiful Gate. To the people crowding in amazement about the two Apostles, he preaches a long sermon in the Porch of Solomon, and brings new members to the flock of believers (Ac 3:1–4:4).

In the subsequent examinations of the two Apostles before the Jewish High Council, Peter defends in courageous fashion the cause of Jesus and the obligation and liberty of the Apostles to preach the Gospel (Ac 4:5–21). When Ananias and Sapphira attempt to deceive the Apostles and the people, Peter appears as judge of their action, and God executes the sentence of punishment passed by the Apostle by causing the sudden death of the two guilty parties (Ac 5:1–11). By numerous miracles, God confirms the Apostolic activity of Christ's witnesses, and here also there is special mention of Peter, since it is recorded that the inhabitants of Jerusalem and neighbouring towns carried their sick in their beds into the streets so that the shadow of Peter might fall on them and they might thereby be healed (Ac 5:12–16). The ever–increasing number of the faithful caused the Sanhedrin to adopt new measures against the Apostles, but 'Peter and the Apostles' answer that they 'ought to obey God rather than men' (Ac 5:29 ff.). Not only in Jerusalem itself did Peter labour in fulfilling the mission entrusted to him by his Master. He also retained connection with the other Christian communities in Palestine, and preached the Gospel both there and in the lands situated farther north. When Philip the Deacon had won a large number of believers in Samaria, Peter and John were deputed to travel there from Jerusalem to organize the community and to invoke the Holy Spirit to descend upon the faithful. Peter appears a second time as judge, in the case of the magician Simon, who had wished to purchase from the Apostles the power that he also could invoke the Holy Spirit (Ac 8: 14–25). On their way back to Jerusalem, the two Apostles preached the joyous tidings of the Kingdom of God. Subsequently, after Paul's departure from Jerusalem and conversion on the road to Damascus, the Christian communities in Palestine were left in peace by the Jewish council.

Peter now undertook an extensive missionary tour, which brought him to the maritime cities, Lydda, Joppe, and Caesarea. In Lydda he cured the paralyzed Aeneas, in Joppe he raised Tabitha (Dorcas) from the dead; and at Caesarea, instructed by a vision which he had in Joppe, he baptized and received into the Church the first non–Jewish Christians, the centurion Cornelius and his kinsmen (Ac 9:32–10:48). On Peter's return to Jerusalem a little later, the strict Jewish Christians, who regarded the complete observance of the Jewish law as binding on all, asked him why he had entered and eaten in the house of the uncircumcised. Peter tells of his vision and defends his action, which was ratified by the Apostles and the faithful in Jerusalem (Ac 11:1–18).

A confirmation of the position accorded to Peter by Luke, in the Acts, is afforded by the testimony of St Paul (Gal 1:18–20). After his conversion and three years' residence in Arabia, Paul came to Jerusalem 'to see Peter'. Here the Apostle of the Gentiles clearly designates Peter as the authorized head of the Apostles and of the early Christian Church. Peter's long residence in Jerusalem and Palestine soon came to an end. Herod Agrippa I began (AD 42–44) a new persecution of the Church in Jerusalem; after the execution of James, the son of Zebedee, this ruler had Peter cast into prison, intending to have him also executed after the Jewish Passover was ended. Peter, however, was freed in a miraculous manner, and, proceeding to the house of the mother of John Mark, where many of the faithful were assembled for prayer, informed them of his liberation from the hands of Herod, commissioned them to communicate

New Testament Theology

the fact to James and the brethren, and then left Jerusalem to go to 'another place' (Ac 12:1–18). Concerning St Peter's subsequent activity we receive no further connected information from the Scriptural sources, although we possess short notices of certain individual episodes of his later life.

It is certain that St Peter remained for a time at Antioch; he may even have returned there several times. The Christian community of Antioch was founded by Christianized Jews who had been driven from Jerusalem by the persecution (Ac 11:19ff.). Peter's residence among them is proved by the episode concerning the observance of the Jewish ceremonial law even by Christianized pagans, related by St Paul (Gal 2:11–21). The chief Apostles in Jerusalem, the 'pillars', Peter, James, and John, had unreservedly approved St Paul's Apostolate to the Gentiles, while they themselves intended to labour principally among the Jews. While Paul was dwelling in Antioch (the date cannot be accurately determined), St Peter came there and mingled freely with the non–Jewish Christians of the community, frequenting their houses and sharing their meals. However, when the Christianized Jews arrived from Jerusalem, Peter, fearing lest these rigid observers of the Jewish ceremonial law should be scandalized, and his influence with the Jewish Christians be endangered, afterwards avoided eating with the uncircumcised. His conduct made a great impression on the other Jewish Christians at Antioch, so that even Barnabas, St Paul's companion, now avoided eating with the Christianized pagans. As this action was entirely opposed to the principles and practice of Paul, and might lead to confusion among the converted pagans, this Apostle addressed a public reproach to St Peter, because his conduct seemed to indicate a wish to compel the pagan converts to become Jews and accept circumcision and the Jewish law. The whole incident is another proof of the authoritative position of St Peter in the early Church, since his example and conduct was regarded as decisive. Tradition makes Peter the first bishop of Antioch, and thus its first Patriarch.

178

Some scholars interpret Paul's mention of Peter in 1 Corinthians 1:12 as evidence that Peter had also visited Corinth.

Peter returned occasionally to the original Christian Church of Jerusalem, the guidance of which was entrusted to St James, the relative of Jesus, after the departure of the Prince of the Apostles (AD 42–44). The last mention of St Peter in the Acts (15:1–29; see Gal 2:1–10) occurs in the report of the Council of the Apostles on the occasion of such a passing visit. Between Peter and Paul there was no dogmatic difference in their conception of salvation for Jewish and Gentile Christians. The recognition of Paul as the Apostle of the Gentiles (Gal 2:1–9) was entirely sincere, and excludes all question of a fundamental divergence of views. St Peter and the other Apostles recognized the converts from paganism as Christian brothers on an equal footing.

It is an established historical fact that St Peter laboured in Rome during the last portion of his life, and there ended his earthly course by martyrdom. As to the duration of his Apostolic activity in the Roman capital, the continuity or otherwise of his residence there, the details and success of his labours, and the chronology of his arrival and death, all these questions are uncertain, and can be solved only on more or less well–founded hypotheses. The essential fact is that Peter died at Rome, which is linked to the historical foundation of the claim of the Bishops of Rome to the Apostolic Primacy of Peter. The manner, and therefore the place of his death, must have been known in widely extended Christian circles at the end of the first century. This is clear from is clear from the remark in the Gospel of St John concerning Christ's prophecy that Peter would be led where he do not want to go, signifying by this the type of death with which he would glorify God (Jn 21:18–19).

St Peter's First Letter was written almost undoubtedly from Rome, since the salutation at the end reads: 'The chosen one at Babylon sends you greeting, as does Mark, my son.' (1 Pt 5:13). Babylon must here be identified with the Roman capital; since Babylon on the Euphrates, which lay in ruins, or New Babylon (Seleucia) on the Tigris, or the Egyptian Babylon near Memphis, or Jerusalem cannot be meant, the reference must be to Rome, the only city which is called Babylon elsewhere in ancient Christian literature (Rev 17:5; 18:10). From Bishop Papias of Hierapolis and Clement of Alexandria, who both appeal to the testimony of the old disciples of the Apostles, we learn that Mark wrote his Gospel in Rome at the request of the Roman Christians, who desired a written memorial of the doctrine preached to them by St Peter and his disciples, and this is confirmed by St Irenaeus.[7]

A testimony concerning the martyrdom of Peter and Paul is supplied by Pope Clement of Rome, around AD 95–97: 'Through zeal and cunning the greatest and most righteous supports of the Church have suffered persecution and been put to death. Let us place before our eyes the good Apostles, like St Peter, who in consequence of unjust zeal, suffered not one or two, but numerous miseries, and, having thus given testimony, has entered the merited place of glory.'[8] He then mentions Paul and a number of elect, who were assembled with the others and suffered martyrdom 'among us' (namely among the Romans). He is speaking undoubtedly of the persecution under Nero, and thus refers the martyrdom of Peter and Paul to that epoch.

St Irenaeus of Lyons, a native of Asia Minor and a disciple of Polycarp of Smyrna (himself a disciple of St John the Apostle), passed a considerable time in Rome shortly after the middle of the second century, and then proceeded to Lyons, where he became bishop in AD 177. Irenaeus described the Roman Church as the most prominent and chief preserver of the Apostolic tradition:

> However, since it would be too long to enumerate in such a volume as this the succession of all the churches, we shall confound all those who, in whatever manner, whether through self-satisfaction

or vainglory, or through blindness and wicked opinion, assemble other than where it is proper, by pointing out here the successions of the bishops of the greatest and most ancient church known to all, founded and organized at Rome by the two most glorious apostles, Peter and Paul, that church which has the tradition and the faith which comes down to us after having been announced to men by the apostles. With that church, because of its superior origin, all the churches must agree, that is, all the faithful in the whole world, and it is in her that the faithful everywhere have maintained the apostolic tradition.[9]

He thus cites the universally known and recognized fact of the Apostolic activity of Peter and Paul in Rome. Irenaeus also outlines the Papal succession:

The blessed apostles [Peter and Paul], having founded and built up the church [of Rome], then handed over the office of the episcopate to Linus. Paul makes mention of this Linus in the letter to Timothy. To him succeeded Anacletus, and after him, in the third place from the apostles, Clement was chosen for the episcopate. He had seen the blessed apostles and was acquainted with them. It might be said that he still heard the echoes of the preaching of the apostles and had their traditions before his eyes. And not only he, for there were many still remaining who had been instructed by the apostles... To this Clement, Evaristus succeeded... and now, in the twelfth place after the apostles, the lot of the episcopate [of Rome] has fallen to Eleutherus. In this order, and by the teaching of the apostles handed down in the Church, the preaching of the truth has come down to us.[10]

Eusebius records that Paul was beheaded in Rome itself, and Peter, likewise, was crucified, during the reign of the Emperor Nero: 'The account is confirmed by the names of Peter and Paul over the cemeteries there, which remain to the present time. And it is confirmed also by a stalwart man of the Church, Caius by name, who lived in the time of Zephyrinus, Bishop of Rome (198–217 AD). This Caius speaks of the places in which the remains of the aforementioned apostles were deposited: 'I can point out the trophies of the apostles. For if you are willing to go to the Vatican or to the Ostian Way, you will find the trophies of those who founded this Church'.'[11]

Around 210 AD, Tertullian provides a further testimony to the martyrdom of St Peter and St Paul and its importance for Rome: 'But if you are near Italy, you have Rome, where authority is at hand for us too. What a happy church that is, on which the apostles poured out their whole doctrine with their blood; where Peter had a passion like that of the Lord, where Paul was crowned with the death of John the Baptist, by being beheaded.'[12]

Tradition has it that St Peter suffered martyrdom under Nero in the year 67, having arrived in Rome under the Emperor Claudius (according to Jerome, in 42). He would thus have completed in Rome twenty–five years of Papacy. Eusebius also records the manner of St Peter's crucifixion, from a theologian named Origen (who wrote about AD 230): 'Peter appears to have preached through Pontus, Galatia, Bithynia, Cappadocia, and Asia, to the Jews that were scattered abroad; who also, finally coming to Rome, was crucified with his head downward, having himself requested to suffer in this way.'[13] These facts are borne out by St Jerome also:

> Simon Peter, the son of Jonah, from the village of Bethsaida in the province of Galilee, brother of Andrew the apostle, and himself chief of the apostles, after having been bishop of the church of Antioch and having preached to the Dispersion ... pushed on to Rome in the second year of Claudius to over–throw Simon Magus, and held the sacerdotal chair there for twenty–five years until the last, that is the fourteenth, year of Nero. At his hands, he

received the crown of martyrdom being nailed to the cross with his head towards the ground and his feet raised on high, asserting that he was unworthy to be crucified in the same manner as his Lord.[14]

In art, St Peter is featured with the keys, based on Christ giving to him the keys of the kingdom of heaven (Mt 16:19), these keys are of silver and gold, referring to the episode in Acts 3:6.

5.2 St Paul

St Paul was born in the city of Tarsus at the dawn of the Christian era. Tarsus was the capital of Cilicia, and was of Greek language, but Roman in its political persuasion, through the favour of Caesar. The city was distinguished for its commercial accomplishments and its literary achievements. Like most trading centres in the Graeco–Roman world, it had a Jewish colony into which the future Apostle was born. It appears that the boy was given two names after birth: Saul, an honored name in the tribe of Benjamin to which he belonged (Phil 3:5), and Paul, in token of the Roman citizenship which he inherited, for his father was a Roman citizen (Ac 22:26–28; cf. 16:37). The Latin word paulus also means small or little, an allusion perhaps to his small stature which is recorded in the apocrypha of the New Testament.

Paul himself admits that, at first, he persecuted Christians to the death (Phil 3:6), but later embraced the belief that he had fought against. In the Acts of the Apostles there are three accounts of the conversion of St Paul (Ac 9:1–19; 22:3–21; 26:9–23) presenting some slight differences, which can be harmonized and which do not affect the basis of the narrative, which is perfectly identical in substance. Acts 9:1–9 clearly describes the vision Paul had of Jesus on the road to Damascus, a vision that led him to turn to Christ. Further evidence for this vision is found when Paul wrote that Jesus appeared to him 'last of all, as to one untimely born' (1 Co 15:8), and frequently claimed that his authority as Apostle to the Gentiles came directly from God (Gal 1:13–16), and not from man. The only adequate explanation for Paul's conversion is found in this vision.

Following his stay in Damascus after conversion, Paul first went to live in the Nabataean kingdom (which he called 'Arabia') for an unknown period, then came back to Damascus, which by this time was under Nabataean rule. After three more years (Gal 1:17–18) he was forced to flee from that city under the cover of night (Ac 9:23; 25; 2 Co 11:32ff.) because of the explosive reaction of some of the strict Jews to his preaching. He went to Jerusalem to see Peter (Gal 1:18), but remained only fifteen days, for the snares of the Greeks threatened his life. He then left for Tarsus and is lost to sight for five or six years (Ac 9:29–30; Gal 1:21). Barnabas went in search of him and brought him to Antioch where for a year they worked together and their apostolate was most fruitful (Ac 11:25–26). Together also they were sent to Jerusalem to carry alms to the brethren on the occasion of the famine predicted by Agabus (Ac 11:27–30). They do not seem to have found the Apostles there; these had been scattered by the persecution of Herod.

The period of twelve years encompassing 45–57 was the most active and fruitful of St Paul's life. It comprises three great Apostolic expeditions of which Antioch was in each instance the starting–point and which invariably ended in a visit to Jerusalem. St Paul's first missionary journey is described in Acts 13:1–14:27, his second missionary journey in Acts 15:36–18:22 and his third in Acts 18:23–21:26. Then, falsely accused by the Jews of having brought Gentiles into the Temple, Paul was ill–treated by the populace and led in chains to the fortress Antonia by the tribune Lysias. The latter having learned that the Jews had conspired treacherously to slay the prisoner sent him under strong escort to Caesarea, which was the residence of the procurator Felix. Paul had little difficulty in confounding his accusers, but as he refused to purchase his liberty, Felix kept him in chains for two years and even left him in prison in order to please the Jews, until the arrival of his successor, Festus. The new governor wished to send the prisoner to Jerusalem there to be tried in the presence of his accusers; but Paul, who was acquainted with the snares of his enemies, appealed to Caesar. Thenceforth his cause could be tried only at Rome.

The journey of the captive Paul from Caesarea to Rome is described by St Luke with exactness and vividness. The centurion Julius had shipped Paul and his fellow–prisoners on a merchant vessel, taking also on board Luke and Aristarchus. As the season was advanced, the voyage was slow and difficult. They skirted the coasts of Syria, Cilicia, and Pamphylia. At Myra in Lycia the prisoners were transferred to an Alexandrian vessel bound for Italy, but with contrary winds they reached with difficulty a place in Crete called Fair Havens, near the city of Lasea (Ac 27:8). Paul advised that they should spend the winter there, but his advice was not followed, and the vessel driven by the tempest drifted aimlessly for fourteen whole days, being finally wrecked on the coast of Malta. The three months during which navigation was considered most dangerous were spent there, but with the first days of spring all haste was made to resume the voyage: 'We put in at Syracuse and stayed there three days, and from there we sailed round the coast and arrived at Rhegium. After a day, a south wind came up and in two days we reached Puteoli. There we found some brothers and were urged to stay with them for seven days. And thus we came to Rome. The brothers from there heard about us and came as far as the Forum of Appius and Three Taverns to meet us. On seeing them, Paul gave thanks to God and took courage' (Ac 28:12–15). Paul must have reached Rome some time in March. There, 'he remained for two full years in his lodgings. He received all who came to him, and with complete assurance and without hindrance he proclaimed the kingdom of God and taught about the Lord Jesus Christ' (Ac 28:30–31). With these words the Acts of the Apostles conclude.

The last period of St Paul's life is wrapped in deep obscurity since we have no guide save an often uncertain tradition and the brief references of the Pastoral epistles. Paul had long cherished the desire to go to Spain (Rom 15:24, 28) and there is no evidence that he was led to change his plan. When towards the end of his captivity he announces his coming to Philemon (Phm 22) and to the Philippians (Ph 2:23–24), he does not seem to regard this visit as immediate since he promises the Philippians to send them a messenger as soon as he learns the issue of his trial; he therefore plans another journey before his return to the East. Tradition renders probable Paul's journey to Spain. In any case he can not have remained there long, for he was in haste to revisit his Churches in the East. He may have returned from Spain through southern Gaul if it was there, as some Fathers have thought, and not to Galatia, that Crescens was sent later (2 Tm 4:10). We may readily believe that afterwards he kept the promise made to his friend Philemon and that on this occasion he visited the churches of the valley of Lycus, Laodicea, Colossus, and Hierapolis.

The itinerary now becomes very uncertain, but the following facts seem indicated by the Pastoral Letters: Paul remained in Crete exactly long enough to found there new churches, the care and organization of which he confided to his fellow–worker Titus (Tt 1:5). He then went to Ephesus, and besought Timothy, who was already there, to remain until his return while he proceeded to Macedonia (1 Tm 1:3). On this occasion he paid his promised visit to the Philippians (Phil 2:24), and naturally also saw the Thessalonians. The Letter to Titus and the First Letter to Timothy must date from this period; they seem to have been written about the same time and shortly after the departure from Ephesus. The question is whether they were sent from Macedonia or, which seems more probable, from Corinth. The Apostle instructs Titus to join him at Nicopolis of Epirus where he intends to spend the winter (Tt 3:12). In the following spring he must have carried out his plan to return to Asia (1 Tm 3:14–15). Here occurred the obscure episode of his arrest, which probably took place at Troas; this would explain his having left with Carpus a cloak and books which he needed (2 Tm 4:13). He was taken from there to Ephesus, capital of the Province of Asia, where he was deserted by all those on whom he thought he could rely (2 Tm 1:15). Being sent to Rome for trial, he left Trophimus sick at Miletus, and Erastus, another of his companions, remained at Corinth, for a reason which is unclear (2 Tm 4:20). When Paul wrote his Second Letter to Timothy from Rome he felt that all human hope was lost (2 Tm 4:6); he begs his disciple to rejoin him as quickly as possible, for he is alone with Luke. We do not know if Timothy was able to reach Rome before the death of the Apostle.

Ancient tradition makes it possible to establish the following points. First, Paul suffered martyrdom near Rome at a place called *Aquae Salviae* (now known as Tre Fontane), somewhat east of the Ostian Way, about two miles from the Basilica of St Paul's Outside the Walls (*San Paolo fuori le mura*), which marks his burial place. St Paul was beheaded, and where his head fell, three fountains sprang up miraculously. Second, the martyrdom took place towards the end of the reign of Nero, in the fourteenth year, according to St Jerome. Third, according to the most common opinion, Paul suffered in the same year (67 AD) and on the same day as Peter. Fourth, from time immemorial the solemnity of the Apostles Peter and Paul has been celebrated on 29 June, which is the anniversary either of their death or of the translation of their relics. Formerly the Pope, after having pontificated in the Basilica of St Peter, went with his attendants to that of St Paul, but the distance between the two basilicas (about five miles) rendered the double ceremony too exhausting, especially at that season of the year. Thus arose the custom of transferring to the next day (30 June) the Commemoration of St Paul. The feast of the Conversion of St Paul (25 January) is of comparatively recent origin. In

art, St Paul is represented with the sword, symbolizing the
Word of God (see Heb 4:12).

Notes

1. See pp.66–67 above.
2. Clement of Alexandria, *Stromata*, 3, 6.
3. Ibid., 7, 11.
4. See also the parallels in Mark 3:14–19, and Luke 6:13–16.
5. See *Revue Biblique* 62 (1955), p.405. See also Mt 16:18.
6. See S. L. Jaki, *And on this Rock. The Witness of One Land and Two Covenants* (Manassas, Va.: Trinity Communications, 1987^2), p. 16.
7. See Eusebius, *Ecclesiastical History*, 2, 15; 3, 40; 6, 14. See also St Irenaeus, *Adversus haereses*, 3, 1. Clement of Alexandria stated: 'After Peter had announced the Word of God in Rome and preached the Gospel in the spirit of God, the multitude of hearers requested Mark, who had long accompanied Peter on all his journeys, to write down what the Apostles had preached to them.' From Eusebius, *Ecclesiastical History*, 4, 14.
8. Pope Clement I, *Letter to the Corinthians*, 5.
9. See St Irenaeus, *Adversus haereses*, 3, 3, 2.
10. *Ibid.*, 3, 3, 3.
11. Eusebius, *Ecclesiastical History*, 2, 25. He quotes Caius, *Disputation with Proclus*.
12. Tertullian, *On the prescription of heretics*, 36.
13. Eusebius, *Ecclesiastical History*, 3,1.
14. St Jerome, *Lives of Illustrious Men*, 1.

6

Mary, Mother of God

The Gospels are the first fruits of all Scripture and the Gospel of
John is the first of the Gospels: no one can grasp its meaning
without having leaned his head on Jesus' breast and having
received Mary as Mother from Jesus.

Origen, Commentary on St. John's Gospel

6.1 Mary fulfils the Old Testament

At first sight, Holy Scripture seems to offer relatively little
detail about Mary. One reason for this may be the focus on
Jesus Christ, the Son of God. However, a deeper look at the
Scriptures reveals that beneath the surface, beyond the
purely literal sense of the Bible, a wealth of indications are
to be found concerning the Mother of God. Mary serves as
a link between the two Covenants not just through parallel
or prophetic verses but by embodying common themes. She
is a bridge between the Old and the New Testaments
because Scripture shows her representing both the people
of Israel and the Church begun by her Son:

> A very important insight of modern exegesis has
> brought to light that the mystery of Mary forms in
> some way the synthesis of all the former revelation
> about the people of God, and of all that God by his
> salvific action wishes to realise for his people. In

Mary are accomplished all the important aspects of the promises of the Old Testament to the Daughter of Zion, and in her real person there is an anticipation which will be realised for the new people of God, the Church. The history of revelation on the subject of the theme of the Woman Zion, realised in the person of Mary, and continued in the Church, constitutes a doctrinal bastion, an unshakeable structured ensemble for the comprehension of the history of salvation, from its origin up to its eschatology. A vision of the mystery of Mary, biblically founded, ecclesiologically integrated and structurally developed, gives then a complete image of the concrete realisation of the total mystery of the Covenant.[1]

Various different schemes from biblical theology, which attempt to organise the data contained in Scripture, can be applied to Mary as the fulfilment of the Old Testament. Negative (or apophatic) theology considers that, despite having revealed Himself to man, God remains a mystery. According to this approach, characteristic in some ways of Eastern Christendom, God is better understood in silence than in a discourse about him. Within this perspective, Mary appears at the climax of the time of promise, as the convergence of the fulfilment of God's ways. Because God remains hidden despite His revelation, also the way of Mary is shrouded in mystery; it reveals and yet veils God's revelation. Biblical theology can also be organised according to positive (or kataphatic) theology. One example of this direction is the thematic approach, characteristic of Western Christendom, where specific topics such as Covenant, the Kingdom of God, the Name of Yahweh, election, and redemption are considered. Our Lady is the woman of the Covenant who is the realisation of the prophecies concerning the Daughter of Sion, in view of the indissoluble union between God and man.

A further approach involves the narrative method. Here, the Old Testament describes an economy of salvation which is brought to fulfilment in the New. The Scriptures trace God's mode of action and discover the principles that guide this. First, the Christ–event is the fundamental principle of the Bible. According to the scheme promise–fulfilment, the Old Testament is intrinsically open to the future and Christ is the final cause of the whole of the Old Covenant. Here, the principle of election–substitution consists in the election of a minority for the redemption of the totality. The history of salvation consists in two movements. One proceeds from plurality to unity: Israel is elected for the salvation of the world; the faithful remnant replaces the people as a whole; this remnant is reduced to one Man, the servant of Yahweh or the Son of Man; Jesus fulfils this mission becoming the Centre of history. Mary stands alongside her Son as this faithful remnant. The second movement starts with Christ and proceeds from unity to plurality in the Church, applying the salvation which He has won. Here also, Mary collaborates in the distribution of the effects of Christ's salvation within the Church.[2]

A further scheme of biblical theology concerns the event of a dialogue. Biblical revelation is based not only upon concepts such as election, salvation, covenant, but above all upon actions. The theology of the Old Testament as fulfilled in the New, is based on the actions and words of God and man's response. The encounter with God takes the form of an experience of salvation (danger, invocation, God's listening, salvation, answer). The concepts of election and covenant are dependent on this relationship of dialogue, which is not however between two equal partners. The person who partakes of a dialogue with God in an eminent manner is Mary, the woman who experiences God's blessing and salvation. She is in a way, a 'microhistory of salvation', since God's ways converge in her, and again in her the exemplary response to God's economy of salvation can be found. This is seen, for example in her response to the Annunciation: 'You see before you the Lord's servant, let it happen to me as you have said' (Lk 1:38). The various

Old Testament categories which we have discussed are thus brought to fulfilment in the New, in Mary.

6.2 Mary in the Synoptic Gospels

6.2.1 The Gospel of Mark

There are three passages in St. Mark's Gospel which reveal certain questions for Mariology. These passages are Mark 3:20–21, Mark 3:31–35 and Mark 6:1–6 respectively.[3] The issues are first Jesus' relation with his family; second, the unusual title *Son of Mary*; and third the question of the brothers of Jesus. As regards this first question, Mark never says explicitly that Mary opposed Jesus, but rather just his fellow citizens, relatives, and family. The passage poses a distinction between the biological family of Jesus and his eschatological family, the Church. This would also imply that Mary always had a growing knowledge of Jesus' salvific mission, even if earlier on that knowledge was partial. Next, the title *Son of Mary* can be partially explained by St. Joseph's death. Nevertheless, its meaning is above all that Mark knew about the virginal conception and wanted to avoid any confusion which would arise by calling him the son of Joseph. Thus, Mark's expression draws specific attention to the Virginal conception and birth of Christ.[4] Third, as regards the question of the brothers of Jesus, these brothers are never called sons of Mary. Also, two of the four sons (James and Joset) are sons of another Mary as can be seen from a later passage of Mark's Gospel: 'There were some women watching from a distance. Among them were Mary of Magdala, Mary who was the mother of James the younger and Joset, and Salome' (Mk 15:40, see 15:47). Further, in Semitic languages, brother is the title used to refer to more distant relations like nephews or cousins.[5] Thus, these passages present no problem for the doctrine concerning Mary's virginity. Rather, they witness to her maternal care and her growth in faith, but not from incredulity to faith but rather from a Judaic faith to a faith in Christ.

6.2.2 *The Gospel according to Matthew*

Even through the first two chapters of St. Matthew's Gospel are written in a popular form of the time and not according to the criteria of modern history, their testimony belongs to a mature Christian faith and they transmit historical events. The text reveals a theological development in Judaeo–Christian circles. According to Matthew, Mary forms part of the salvific plan announced in the Old Covenant and fully realised in the New.

Matthew begins his Gospel with the genealogy of Jesus. He does this for three reasons. First, to focus on the identity of Jesus by showing that He belongs to the people of Israel as *Son of David* and *Son of Abraham*. Second, he wishes to stress the special status of Jesus as the awaited Davidic Messiah. Third, Matthew desires to present Jesus as the vertex and synthesis of history. This genealogy shows how God works in the history or economy of salvation. Matthew presents the Virginal conception and Birth under the scheme of prophecy–fulfilment:

> 'Joseph son of David, do not be afraid to take Mary home as your wife, because she has conceived what is in her by the Holy Spirit. She will give birth to a Son and you must name Him Jesus, because He is the one who is to save His people from their sins.' Now all this took place to fulfil what the Lord had spoken through the prophet: Look! the virgin is with child and will give birth to a son whom they will call Immanuel, a name which means 'God–is–with–us' (Mt 1:20–23).

In Matthew 1:25, it is stated that Joseph had not had marital relations with Mary when she gave birth to a Son, and named Him Jesus. Some English translations are closer to the Greek, saying that Joseph 'knew her not until she had

borne a son; and he called His name Jesus.' The word
'until', in biblical language, negates an action in the past,
but does not imply that it will occur in the future.[6] This
indicates that Matthew is concerned to emphasise that St.
Joseph had no part in the conception of Jesus.

In the episodes of the Magi and of the flight into Egypt,
St. Matthew repeatedly asserts that Christ is the Child of
Mary and not of Joseph, and represents Joseph as simply
the guardian and protector of them both. In the example of
the adoration of the Magi, we read: 'and going into the
house they saw the Child with His mother Mary, and falling
to their knees they did Him homage. Then, opening their
treasures, they offered Him gifts of gold and frankincense
and myrrh' (Mt 2:11). Later, we find that an angel appeared
to St. Joseph: 'After they had left, suddenly the angel of the
Lord appeared to Joseph in a dream and said, "Get up, take
the Child and His mother with you, and escape into Egypt,
and stay there until I tell you, because Herod intends to
search for the Child and do away with Him."' (Mt 2:13). St.
Joseph's response was that he 'got up and, taking the Child
and His mother with him, left that night for Egypt' (Mt
2:14). Later again, an angel encourages St. Joseph to return
from Egypt: 'Get up, take the Child and His mother with
you and go back to the land of Israel, for those who wanted
to kill the Child are dead' (Mt 2:20). It is noteworthy that in
all these passages the angel who addresses Joseph concerning our Lord, never refers to Him as 'your Child.' According
to Matthew, Mary is not only the 'Mother of God' but also
'the Virgin' who conceives in an extraordinary manner.
While the legal adoptive paternity of St. Joseph ensures
Jesus' Davidic descent, the virginity of Mary guarantees His
divine origin. Her virginity, therefore, has a Christological
function as it reveals Christ's true identity.

In St. Matthew's Gospel, several passages deal with
Jesus' relationship with His family, and by that token also
with His Mother. However, these passages stress above all
the intimate relationship with His new and larger family

constituted by His disciples, with ecclesiological connotations. These passages adopt a specific Semitic structure which appears to deny one reality in order to emphasise another one:

> He was still speaking to the crowds when suddenly His mother and His brothers were standing outside and were anxious to have a word with Him. But to the man who told Him this Jesus replied, 'Who is my mother? Who are my brothers?' And stretching out His hand towards His disciples He said, 'Here are my mother and my brothers. Anyone who does the will of my Father in heaven is my brother and sister and mother' (Mt 12: 46–50).

This passage does not therefore deny in any way that Jesus Christ is the only Son of Mary the Virgin, but rather seeks to extend His human family in an ecclesiological and eschatological sense, as is seen fulfilled when Jesus entrusts His Mother to John at the Crucifixion.

In the following chapter of St. Matthew's Gospel, there is a passage which has often been discussed in relation to Mary's virginity:

> When Jesus had finished these parables He left the district; and, coming to His home town, He taught the people in the synagogue in such a way that they were astonished and said, 'Where did the man get this wisdom and these miraculous powers? This is the carpenter's son, surely? Is not His mother the woman called Mary, and His brothers James and Joseph and Simon and Jude? His sisters, too, are they not all here with us? So where did the man get it all?' And they would not accept Him. But Jesus said to them, 'A prophet is despised only in his own country and in his own house,' and He did not work many miracles there because of their lack of faith (Mt 13:53–58).

The passage names the following as 'brothers' of Jesus: James, Joseph, Simon and Jude.[7] However, Matthew 27:56

indicates that Mary, the mother of James and Joseph, was at the foot of the Cross. On the other hand, Mark 15:40 states that Mary the mother of James the younger and Joset was there. So, although the proof is not conclusive, it seems that (unless we propose these were others with the same names), the first two, James and Joseph (Joset) had a mother other than the Mother of Jesus. Therefore, the term 'brother' was employed for those who were not sons of Mary the Mother of Jesus. So the same use of language could easily have been applied with the other two, Simon and Judas. Further, if Mary had given birth to other natural sons and daughters too at the time of the cross, it would be strange for Jesus to ask John to take care of her, rather than one of His hypothetical blood brothers. In particular, according to St. Paul's Letter to the Galatians (Ga 1:19), James the 'brother of the Lord' was alive in 49 AD. He should have taken care of Mary, if he were her son. This usage of the expression 'brother' or 'sister' to denote a close relative who is not a brother or sister according to modern terminology is common in ancient Semitic culture, as can be seen in the Old Testament. One example is Lot, who although the nephew of Abraham (cf. Gn 11:27–31) is called his brother (Gn 13:8 and 14:14–16). The Hebrew and Aramaic expression 'ah' was adopted for various types of relations.[8] Hebrew had no word for cousin. They could say 'ben–dod' which means son of a paternal uncle, but for other kinds of cousins they would need a complex phrase, such as 'the son of the brother of his mother' or, 'the son of the sister of his mother.'[9]

6.2.3 The Gospel according to Luke and Acts

Luke adopts the scheme 'promise–fulfilment' in his Gospel and presents Mary as part of the culmination of the economy of salvation. For Luke, John the Baptist fulfils the time of preparation and Jesus inaugurates the eschatological era.

The Annunciation in Luke 1:26–38 is one of the key Mariological high points of the New Testament, and has been much represented in art and literature.[10] Four different schemes of interpretation can be proposed for the wonder of the Annunciation. First, the consideration of a miraculous birth scheme. The Annunciation shares the same structure as the other miraculous birth scenes in the Old and New Testaments (Gn 18:1–15; Jg 13:3–22; Lk 1:5–25). The scheme runs in this fashion: apparition – perturbation – message – obedience – sign. The miraculous birth is due to the creative action of the Holy Spirit. The second scheme is that of vocation or calling. There are similarities between Mary's calling and that of Gideon (Jg 6:11–24). The structure of this scheme runs as follows: angel's greeting – doubt or perturbation – first message – difficulty – second message – sign – consent. Mary answers a divine call. A third possible scheme is that of apocalyptic whereby everything starts from God above, leading to a new beginning. Finally, the Covenant scheme is also helpful in illustrating the Annunciation. This scheme consists of a discourse concerning a mediator and an answer from the people. By proclaiming herself as the Lord's servant, Mary enters into the work of salvation with total availability. Her 'fiat' is a positive and immediate co–operation in the redemptive Incarnation. Without this, the Incarnation would not have taken place.

The salutation of the angel to Mary ('Rejoice, you who enjoy God's favour! The Lord is with you' Lk 1:28), recalls the expressions used of the Daughter of Sion in the Old Testament, who rejoices because the time of the Messiah is near. The angel Gabriel, addressing the Virgin of Nazareth uses the greeting *chaire* (Rejoice in Greek) and then calls her *kecharitomene* (full of grace). The words of the Greek text, *chaire* and *kecharitomene,* are essentially interconnected: Mary is invited to rejoice primarily because God loves her and has filled her with grace in view of her divine motherhood.[11] This fullness of grace indicates a condition or state of being, a gift signifying divine favour. It implies a divine choice or election in relation to the Covenant. The expressions 'Full of grace' and 'you who enjoy God's favour' are renderings of the Greek word *kecharitomene*, which is a passive participle. The verb utilised here by Luke (*charitoun*) is very rare in Greek. It is present only twice in the New Testament: in the text of Luke on the Annunciation (Lk 1:28). '*kecharitomene*,' and in the Epistle to the Ephesians (Ep 1:6) '*echaritosen*.' These verbs convey the idea of a change of something in the person or the thing affected. Thus, since the root of the verb 'charitoo' is 'charis' or grace, the idea which is expressed is that of a change brought about by grace. In addition the verb used by Luke is in the past participial form. '*Kecharitomene*' signifies then, in the person to whom the verb relates, that is, Mary, that the action of the grace of God has already brought about a change. It does not tell us how that came about. What is essential here is that it affirms that Mary has been transformed by the grace of God. The perfect passive participle is used by Luke to indicate that the transformation by grace has already taken place in Mary, well before the moment of the Annunciation.

In what then would this transformation of grace consist? According to the text of the Letter to the Ephesians, Christians have been transformed by grace in the sense that according to the richness of His grace, they find redemption by His blood, the remission of sins (cf. Ep 1:7). This grace, in reality, takes away sin. This sheds light on the case of Mary, who 'transformed by grace', because she has been sanctified by the grace of God. Mary has been transformed by the grace of God in view of the task which she awaits, that of becoming the Mother of the Son of God, while remaining a virgin. There is a double announcement from the angel: Mary as Mother brings to the world the Son of the Most High (v.33), but that will take place by the 'power of the Most High' (v.35), that is virginally. God had prepared Mary for this by inspiring in her the desire for virginity.[12]

Therefore to convey even more exactly the nuance of the

Greek word, one should not say merely 'full of grace', but 'made full of grace', or even 'filled with grace', which would clearly indicate that this was a gift given by God to the Blessed Virgin. This term, in the form of a perfect participle, enhances the image of a perfect and lasting grace which implies fullness. The same verb, in the sense of 'to bestow grace', is used in St. Paul's Letter to the Ephesians to indicate the abundance of grace granted to us by the Father in His beloved Son (Ep 1:6), and which Mary receives as the first fruits of Redemption.[13] The greeting 'the Lord is with you' used by the angel is customary in the context of accounts of callings in the Bible, and highlights Mary's special vocation in God's new covenant. The angel's invitation 'Mary, do not be afraid; you have won God's favour', provides reassurance that God is acting. It stresses that Mary is the recipient of a unique favour and privilege in the history of salvation, namely to give birth to the Son of God. The annunciation shows that God chooses the humble. The words of the angel, 'You are to conceive in your womb and bear a Son, and you must name Him Jesus' reflect the structure of the words of the promise in the book of Isaiah: 'the young woman is with child and will give birth to a son whom she will call Immanuel' (Is 7:14). Thus the prophetic promise and its fulfilment are intimately linked. Moreover, the expression of the angel to Mary, 'He will be great and will be called Son of the Most High' re–echo the prophecy of Nathan to David regarding the Davidic dynastic, and thus the phrase emphasises the fulfilment of the Messianic prophecy. Mary's words of concern 'But how can this come about, since I have no knowledge of man?' bear various possible interpretations. The most probable opinion is that she had made a vow of virginity, because when she received the angel's greeting she was already betrothed to Joseph, and therefore, in the ordinary course of events, would be expecting to conceive with him, unless she had already made a vow.[14]

The Annunciation parallels certain biblical accounts that

relate the communication of an extraordinary birth to a childless woman. Those cases concerned married women who were naturally sterile, to whom God gave the gift of a child through their typical conjugal life (1 S 1:19–20), in response to their anguished prayers (cf. Gn 15:2, 30:22–23, 1 S 1:10; Lk 1:13). Mary receives the angel's message in a different situation. She is not a married woman with problems of sterility; by a voluntary choice she intends to remain a virgin. Therefore her intention of virginity, the fruit of her love for the Lord, appears to be an obstacle to the motherhood announced to her. At first sight, Mary's words would seem merely to express only her present state of virginity: Mary would affirm that she does not 'know' man, that is, that she is a virgin. Nevertheless, the context in which the question is asked: 'How can this come about?', and the affirmation that follows: 'since I have no knowledge of man', emphasise both Mary's present virginity and her intention to remain a virgin. The expression she uses, with the verb in the present tense, reveals the permanence and continuity of her state.[15]

The angel answered: 'The Holy Spirit will come upon you, and the power of the Most High will cover you with its shadow. And so the child will be holy and will be called Son of God' (Lk 1:35). The expression which the angel adopted is characteristic of a consecration of the temple. Mary's response is one of totally free adherence as consecration to God's will: 'Behold the handmaid of the Lord; be it done to me according to your word' (Lk 1:38).

6.2.4 The Magnificat

The Visitation is rich in both Christological and Mariological perspectives. It follows the same structure as the narration of the transportation of the ark to Jerusalem (2 S 6:2–15). Both take place in the region of Judah and involve expressions of joy and acclamation. Blessings are received, religious fear is present and a period of three months is significant.[16] Through these parallelisms, Luke expressed the truth that Mary, the Mother of the Lord is God's dwelling place and the Ark of the New Covenant, bringing the old one to fulfilment and perfection. Also, Elisabeth's exclamation 'Most blessed are you among women, and blessed is the fruit of your womb' can be compared with two other significant passages, both from the Old Testament. The first is the blessing of Abram by Melchizedek: 'Blessed be Abram by God Most High, Creator of heaven and earth. And blessed be God Most High for putting your enemies into your clutches.' (Gn 14:19). The second passage reports the blessing imparted by Uzziah upon Judith: 'May you be blessed, my daughter, by God Most High, beyond all women on earth; and blessed be the Lord God, Creator of heaven and earth, who guided you to cut off the head of the leader of our enemies!' (Jdt 13:18). These parallels highlight the fact that the blessings imparted by God to Abram, to Judith and to Mary from part of an economy of salvation, in which the person who is blessed is to be a mediator of God's loving kindness. However, in the case of Mary, there is something different: Mary and her Son Jesus are together united in being blessed, which unites them in the culmination of God's economy.

Mary's greeting to Elizabeth causes John, filled with the Holy Spirit, to leap with joy. Elizabeth recognises who Mary is and greets her with three titles: Most blessed among women, the mother of my Lord, and 'blessed is she who believed'. Mary responds with a special song of thanksgiving. This Canticle, known as the *Magnificat* (Latin) or *Megalynei* (Byzantine), is the song both of the Mother of God and of the Church; the song of the Daughter of Sion and of the new People of God; the song of thanksgiving for the fullness of graces poured out in the economy of salvation and the song of the 'poor' or 'little ones' (*anawim*) whose hope is met by the fulfilment of the promises made to our ancestors, to Abraham and to his posterity for ever.[17]

Mary's Song of thanksgiving closely parallels the Song of Hannah, Samuel's mother, in 1 Samuel 2: 1–10, with some very specific similarity in detail. For example, Hannah proclaims: 'My heart exults in Yahweh, in my God is my strength lifted up' (1 S 2:1). This is very similar to Mary's formulation: 'my spirit rejoices in God my Saviour...he has routed the arrogant of heart' (Lk 1: 47, 51). Hannah portrays herself three times as the Lord's 'servant' (1 S 1:11, 16), which Mary does twice (Lk 1:38, 48). The mother of Samuel proclaims: 'Yahweh makes poor and rich, He humbles and also exalts. He raises the poor from the dust, He lifts the needy from the dunghill to give them a place with princes, to assign them a seat of honour' (1 S 2: 7–8). Mary exclaims: 'He has used the power of His arm, He has routed the arrogant of heart. He has pulled down princes from their thrones and raised high the lowly. He has filled the starving with good things, sent the rich away empty' (Lk 1: 51–53). Furthermore, the relation between Mary and Hannah continues from the Magnificat into Luke's second chapter. Hannah took her child, Samuel, into the temple of the Lord at Shiloh (1 S 1: 24). Similarly, Mary presents her child, Jesus, to the Lord in the temple in Jerusalem (Lk 2: 22, 27).

The Magnificat contains, in a sense, the most ancient Mariology. The first part refers to God's action in Mary and the second to God's action in human history. She praises God for having looked upon the humiliation of his servant. This refers to the spiritual attitude of the poor of Yahweh. The praise of Mary is based on both her humility and the great things the Almighty has done for her. The proclamation 'The Mighty One has done great things for me, and holy is his name' contains the expression 'great things' (*megala* in Greek) which is a technical term signifying all the magnificent actions the Lord has carried out for His people throughout the history of His chosen people, culminating in the coming of Christ through Mary. However, these great things can also include the wonders worked by God in His Church, right from the early moments of its life.

6.2.5 The Presentation of the Lord

When Our Lady fulfilled the demands of the Mosaic Law and presented Jesus in the Temple, Simeon proclaimed: 'Now, Master, You are letting your servant go in peace as You promised; for my eyes have seen the salvation which You have made ready in the sight of the nations; a light of revelation for the gentiles and glory for your people Israel' (Lk 2:29–32). Simeon also said to Mary His mother, 'Look, He is destined for the fall and for the rise of many in Israel, destined to be a sign that is opposed – and a sword will pierce your soul too – so that the secret thoughts of many may be laid bare' (Lk 2:34–35). Simeon's hymn reveals the universality of the redemption. Simeon also announces a prophecy with regards to Mary which complements the angel's message. The 'sword' has been interpreted variously the challenge to Mary's faith when faced with the scandal of the cross; the word of God which penetrates the soul; Jesus' passion which will have its impact upon Mary's soul and make her an intimate sharer in it, to the point of earning the palms of martyrdom at the foot of the Cross; the opposition against Jesus which Mary shares. [18]

6.2.6 The Finding in the Temple

In a sense, the 'sword' is already present, as a stimulus to a growth in faith for Our Lady, when Jesus goes to Jerusalem for the feast of the Passover, when He was twelve years old. Jesus stayed behind in Jerusalem without His parents knowing it. Three days later, they found Him in the Temple, sitting among the teachers, listening to them, and asking them questions; and all those who heard Him were astounded at His intelligence and His replies. It is certainly no accident that Mary and Joseph found Him three days later, because this episode foreshadows the Death of Christ and His Resurrection on the third day. When Jesus is lost to Mary and Joseph, this prefigures His death, and when He is found, it foreshadows His Resurrection. 'They were overcome when they saw Him, and His mother said to Him, "My child, why have you done this to us? See how worried your father and I have been, looking for you." He replied, "Why were you looking for me? Did you not know that I must be in my Father's house?" But they did not understand what He meant' (Lk 2:48–50). This moment marks a growth in faith for Mary and maybe also a sense of the sorrow, as well as the joy, which lie in the future.

During the ministry of Jesus, He makes an affirmation which does not undermine the importance of Mary's blood relationship to Him, but rather extends it. 'It happened that as He was speaking, a woman in the crowd raised her voice and said, "Blessed the womb that bore you and the breasts that fed you!" But He replied, "More blessed still are those who hear the word of God and keep it!"' (Lk 11:27–28). This passage highlights the fact that Mary is the first hearer and keeper of the Word of God, she has carried the eternal Word in her womb and kept Him, and she is also Christ's first and foremost disciple.[19]

6.2.7 Mary and the early Christian Community

St. Luke also recounts, in his Acts of the Apostles, that with one heart all the Apostles 'joined constantly in prayer, together with some women, including Mary the mother of Jesus, and with His brothers' (Ac 1:14). This passage shows that Mary had a special place in the Jewish–Christian community of Palestine due to her union with Christ as Mother. Moreover, she is part of the community and prays, believes and practices the faith with the others. She forms part of the new people of God which receives the Spirit and proclaims the risen Christ but in continuity with the traditions. Mary is called to enter into the divine plan with a special mission of her own. She responds to God's calling with exemplary faith. This faith is the most important aspect of her spiritual life.

6.3 Mary in the writings of St. John

There is a well–known passage of Origen on the presence of Mary and John on Calvary: 'The Gospels are the first fruits of all Scripture and the Gospel of John is the first of the Gospels: no one can grasp its meaning without having leaned his head on Jesus' breast and having received from Jesus Mary as Mother.'[20] It is most probable that in the years which Mary spent with St. John in the house traditionally held to be at Ephesus, Our Lady would have shared with the beloved disciple many of her most profound insights regarding Jesus Christ her Son. In the quiet and humble way that characterised Mary's life on earth, therefore, John's Gospel should be regarded also as a profoundly Marian Gospel. One of the keys to understanding St. John's Gospel is the use of the expression 'woman', by which Jesus addresses His Mother. Far from being a way of distancing Himself from His blessed Mother, the expression is a term of intimacy and great respect and love all at the same time. 'Here,' writes de la Potterie, 'the Old Testament texts of the 'Daughter of Zion' are applied to a definite woman.... This is precisely the reason why, in the Fourth Gospel, both at Cana and at the Cross, Jesus addresses Mary calling her Woman.'[21] In this context, the relation between the Wedding Feast at Cana, Mary at the foot of the Cross and the Woman of the Apocalypse is of capital importance.

As regards the wedding at Cana in Galilee, it is highly significant that it takes place on the third day, like the Resurrection. There are links between this passage and the texts dealing with the establishment of the Covenant at Sinai (Ex 19:3–8; 24:3.7). Using the scheme of the Covenant, John shows that Cana is the new Sinai. Jesus takes Yahweh's place and Mary that of Moses. In the Old Testament, the chosen people were often represented by the figure of a woman. The wedding is thus inscribed in a series of theophanic mysteries, which reveal the divinity of Christ and His economy of salvation, of whom the key player next to

Christ is His blessed Mother (Jn 2:1–11). The key figures are therefore Christ and His Mother, rather than the couple who had just married. The enormous quantity of wine which Jesus offered, changed from the water in the six stone water jars, each holding twenty or thirty gallons, indicates the divine generosity. The fact that the best wine was kept till last indicates the fulfilment of God's economy in the New Covenant, in which Mary plays a singular part. It is curious also that the servants are not referred to as *douloi*, but *diakonoi*, indicating a liturgical role, rather than a merely functional one. This is all the more interesting given the fact that this miracle also prefigures the far greater wonder in which wine will be changed into His Precious Blood. The miracle of the multiplication of the loaves (Jn 6:1–13) is also a New Testament prefiguration of the Eucharist.[22] At the wedding feast at Cana, water is changed into wine; at the Last Supper, in which wine is changed into Christ's Blood, we have a kind of wedding feast in which the marriage of Christ to His Church is celebrated. This is supported by Christ's own words at the Last Supper 'From now on, I tell you, I shall not drink wine until the day I drink the new wine with you in the kingdom of my Father' (Mt 26:29). Jesus' words indicate that the Eucharist is a participation in the definitive Wedding Feast of the Lamb.

Closely linked with the miracle of Cana is the scene of Mary is standing at the foot of Christ's Cross. 'Near the cross of Jesus stood His mother and His mother's sister, Mary the wife of Clopas, and Mary of Magdala. Seeing His mother and the disciple whom He loved standing near her, Jesus said to His mother, "Woman, this is your son." Then to the disciple He said, "This is your mother." And from that hour the disciple took her into his home' (Jn 19:25–27). This scene is linked to Cana. Both use the term 'woman' and talk about Jesus' 'hour'. Mary becomes the mother of the beloved disciple. She has a role to fulfil in the history of salvation as mother of Jesus' disciples. Mary is the Daughter of Sion, who generates a messianic people. The standing at the foot of the Cross is not merely physical, but also in the context of St. John's Gospel refers to the co–operation of Mary in Christ's work of Redemption.[23] The parallelism 'this is your son' and 'this is your mother' highlights the fact that here we are seeing not only an historical fact, but a spiritual motherhood of Mary within the Church.[24]

Finally, the two passages just considered are linked with a third Mariological passage in St. John's Apocalypse. The expression *woman*[25], as found in the Wedding at Cana and as addressed by Jesus to Mary at the Foot of the Cross, is also employed in chapter twelve of the book of Revelation, and sheds light on the Mariological import of that chapter. The book of Revelation never mentions Mary by name, and does not speak explicitly of her. The perspective offered is essentially ecclesiological; however the figure of the *Woman* in chapter twelve, although a personification of the new people of God, cannot be adequately explained unless full account be taken of the historical role of the Mother of Jesus.[26] 'Now a great sign appeared in heaven: a woman, robed with the sun, standing on the moon, and on her head a crown of twelve stars. She was pregnant, and in labour, crying aloud in the pangs of childbirth' (Rv 12:1–2). The Woman represents first of all the messianic people who become the Church. However, she also represents Mary, the mother of Jesus and figure of the Church. In Mary, the maternal function of the New Testament community is inaugurated. The figure of the woman is symbolic, but in a polyvalent sense, referring to both Mariological and ecclesiological realities. It would therefore be incorrect to detach this symbol from its concrete historical point of reference, namely Mary. Therefore it is completely one–sided and incomplete to stress solely the ecclesiological interpretation of this passage from the Book of the Apocalypse at the expense of the Mariological one. In St. John's writings, Mary is progressively Mother of Jesus, the woman at the service of the faith of the Apostles, and finally mother of the beloved disciple, and Mother in turn of all those 'who obey

God's commandments and have in themselves the witness of Jesus' (Rv 12:17). It is most likely that St. John would have therefore based his ecclesiological symbolism on a Mariological foundation.

One difficulty which could be raised is how the Woman in Revelation could refer to Mary if she suffered the pains of childbirth. This difficulty can be eliminated by the following consideration. In Revelation 5:6, Christ appears in heaven in the form of an *immolated* lamb (cf. Jn 19:36). The sufferings of the woman who also appears in heaven (Rv 12:2), stands in relation to the *immolation* of the celestial Lamb (Rv 12:11). Thus, in the twelfth chapter of Apocalypse, the reference is not to the childbirth at Bethlehem, but to the birth pangs of the Redemption, echoed in the words of Christ upon the Cross: 'Son, behold your Mother' (Jn 19:27). Thus, here John is speaking about a different type of suffering, which is also found in other parts of the New Testament. For example, speaking to the Galatians, Paul went through the pain of giving birth until Christ was formed within his readers (see Ga 4:19). Also, the Letter to the Romans states: 'We are well aware that the whole creation, until this time, has been groaning in labour pains' (Rm 8:22). What is being described is the spiritual motherhood of Mary and the compassion with which the Mother of Jesus shares in the sufferings of the immolated Lamb. The woman of the Crucifixion and the woman of the Apocalypse are closely tied together. In each passage, Mary's motherhood *in relation to the disciples* entails a context of suffering.[27]

6.4 The writings of St. Paul

Paul's writings present God's great economy of salvation, in which He offers to all, Jews and Gentiles alike, the gift of eternal life, in Jesus who has died and is risen from the dead. The Christian participates in this gift of salvation, by being united to Christ by faith, dying in Him to sin, and sharing in the power of His Resurrection. This salvation is still being completed in His Body the Church, until He comes again in glory (see Col 1:24). Paul presents Christ's death and resurrection as a expiatory sacrifice, bringing the Jewish sacrifices to fulfilment (Rm 3:24–25; 1 Co 15:3; 2 Co 5:21). Christians participate in this mystery through baptism and the Eucharist. In this context, one finds the only reference to Mary given by Paul but it is very important because of its antiquity and its relation to the history of salvation. Even if the person of Mary remains anonymous, her function is indispensable for the kenotic and salvific incarnation of the Son of God: 'When the completion of the time came, God sent His Son, born of a woman, born a subject of the Law, to redeem the subjects of the Law, so that we could receive adoption as sons' (Ga 4:4–5). In this only direct reference to Mary, Paul refers to her as 'woman'. Thus, Mary is again referred to as 'woman', even outside a Johannine context. This phraseology of 'a woman' being tied to Mary has evidently been passed on to Paul, who hands it on to his readers. Here he indicates implicitly the fact of the virginal conception of Jesus. This is highlighted by the expression 'born of a woman' in a Semitic society where the usual expression would be 'born of Jesse' or whoever the father was. Pointing to Jesus as born of a 'woman' instead of a man indicates the uniqueness of Virginal Conception and therefore of the Incarnation.

6.5 Conclusions

Although the citations in Scripture referring to Mary may seem be few in number, they are nevertheless of great importance. Passages which at first seem rather terse convey a rich tradition. What is important is not the quantity but the quality and depth of the texts. This richness may not be apparent upon a cursory and superficial reading, but becomes clear through a profound analysis which reveals that Mary is present and plays an important part in the decisive moments of the history of salvation.

Scripture presents a series of harmonic images of Mary. There is perhaps a development in the portrayal of Mary in the New Testament. First, an historical presentation of Mary features in Matthew and Luke, which speak of her fullness of grace, her virginal maternity and her relationship with Jesus as a disciple. John proposes a mature theological reflection on Mary in which she recognises the messianic transcendence of her Son and receives from Him her maternal mission. Scripture always presents Mary in union to the mystery of Christ. The history of salvation is the context of this presentation in all its stages. Mary appears in the prophecies and prefigurations in the Old Testament, and is then united with Christ in the mysteries of His infancy. She is present at the beginning of the public ministry of her Son. She participates in the Paschal mystery and is attendant at the beginning of the Church. Mary cannot be separated from this economy of salvation and this economy cannot be understood apart from Mary.

Notes

1. I. de la Potterie, *Mary in the Mystery of the Covenant* (New York: Alba House, 1992), p. 262.
2. For the collaboration of Mary with Christ's act of Redemption and then with the distribution of the effects of this act, see P. Haffner, *The Mystery of Mary* (Leominster/Chicago: Gracewing/Liturgy Training Publications, 2004), chapter 7, pp.187–201 and chapter 9, pp.254–266 respectively.
3. For the convenience of the reader, we set out the three passages here.
   1) 'He went home again, and once more such a crowd collected that they could not even have a meal. When His relations heard of this, they set out to take charge of Him; they said, "He is out of His mind"' (Mk 3:20–21).
   2) 'Now His mother and His brothers arrived and, standing

outside, sent in a message asking for Him. A crowd was sitting round Him at the time the message was passed to Him, "Look, your mother and brothers and sisters are outside asking for you." He replied, "Who are my mother and my brothers?" And looking at those sitting in a circle round Him, He said, "Here are my mother and my brothers. Anyone who does the will of God, that person is my brother and sister and mother"' (Mk 3:31–35).

3) 'Leaving that district, He went to His home town, and His disciples accompanied Him. With the coming of the Sabbath He began teaching in the synagogue, and most of them were astonished when they heard Him. They said, "Where did the man get all of this? What is this wisdom that has been granted Him, and these miracles that are worked through Him? This is the carpenter, surely, the son of Mary, the brother of James and Joset and Jude and Simon? His sisters, too, are they not here with us" And they would not accept Him. And Jesus said to them, "A prophet is despised only in his own country, among his own relations and in his own house"; and He could work no miracle there, except that He cured a few sick people by laying His hands on them. He was amazed at their lack of faith' (Mk 6:1–6).

4. See R. Laurentin, *La Vergine Maria* (Roma: Edizioni Paoline, 1983³), p. 22, note 4.

5. See Haffner, *The Mystery of Mary*, pp. 159–166.

6. The Greek expression is ἕως. To confirm this usage see Ps 110:1 and 2 S 6:23.

7. The manuscripts vary on the spelling of at least one of these, namely Joseph, who in Mark 6:3 is put as Joset: 'This is the carpenter, surely, the son of Mary, the brother of James and Joset and Jude and Simon? His sisters, too, are they not here with us?' And they would not accept Him.'

8. Cf. M. Sokoloff, *A Dictionary of Jewish Palestinian Aramaic of the Byzantine period* (Ramat–Gan, Israel: Bar Ilan University Press, 1990), p. 45.

9. See *ibid.*, p. 111 and 139.

10. Among the famous artists who have painted the Annunciation are Leonardo da Vinci, Carolo Crivelli, Fra Angelico and Sandro Botticelli. Paul Claudel wrote *L'annonce faite a Marie* (Paris: Gallimard, 1950). The passage in question runs: 'In the sixth month the angel Gabriel was sent by God

to a town in Galilee called Nazareth, to a virgin betrothed to a man named Joseph, of the House of David; and the virgin's name was Mary. He went in and said to her, "Rejoice, you who enjoy God's favour! The Lord is with you." She was deeply disturbed by these words and asked herself what this greeting could mean, but the angel said to her, "Mary, do not be afraid; you have won God's favour. Look! You are to conceive in your womb and bear a son, and you must name Him Jesus. He will be great and will be called Son of the Most High. The Lord God will give Him the throne of His ancestor David; He will rule over the House of Jacob for ever and His reign will have no end." Mary said to the angel, "But how can this come about, since I have no knowledge of man?" The angel answered, "The Holy Spirit will come upon you, and the power of the Most High will cover you with its shadow. And so the child will be holy and will be called the Son of God. And I tell you this too: your cousin Elizabeth also, in her old age, has conceived a son, and she whom people called barren is now in her sixth month, for nothing is impossible to God." Mary said, "You see before you the Lord's servant, let it happen to me as you have said." And the angel left her' (Lk 1:38).

11. See Pope John Paul II, *Discourse at General Audience* (8 January 1986), 1.

12. See I. de la Potterie, *Mary in the Mystery of the Covenant* (New York: Alba House, 1992), pp. 17–20.

13. See Pope John Paul II, *Discourse at General Audience* (8 January 1986), 2

14. See St. Augustine, *De sancta virginitate*, I, 4, in *PL* 40, 398: 'Her virginity also itself was on this account more pleasing and accepted, in that it was not that Christ being conceived in her, rescued it beforehand from a husband who would violate it, so as to preserve it Himself; but, before He was conceived, chose it, already dedicated to God, as that from which to be born. This is shown by the words which Mary spoke in answer to the Angel announcing her conception. She said: "But how can this come about, since I have no knowledge of man?" Which assuredly she would not say, unless she had before vowed herself unto God as a virgin. But, because the habits of the Israelites as yet refused this, she was espoused to a just man, who would not take from her by violence, but

rather guard against violent persons, what she had already vowed.'

15. See Pope John Paul II, *Discourse at General Audience* (24 July 1996), 1.
16. See Haffner, *The Mystery of Mary*, pp. 30–31, where these parallels are dealt with in detail.
17. See *CCC* 2619.
18. See P. Benoit, 'Et toi–même, un glaive te transpercera l'âme' in *Catholic Biblical Quarterly* 25(1963), pp. 251–261.
19. For a development of the various aspects of Mary's discipleship, see Haffner, *The Mystery of Mary*, chapter 7.
20. Origen, *Commentary on St John's Gospel* I, 6 in *PG* 14, 31. See Saint Ambrose, *Exposition on the Gospel* according to St Luke, X, 129–131 in *CSEL* 32/4, 504f.
21. I. de la Potterie, *Mary in the Mystery of the Covenant* (New York: Alba House, 1992), p. 48.
22. See P. Haffner, *The Sacramental Mystery* (Leominster: Gracewing, 2007²), pp. 91-92.
23. See Haffner, *The Mystery of Mary*, pp. 187–201.
24. For the theme of the spiritual motherhood of Mary within the Church, see Haffner, *The Mystery of Mary*, chapter 9.
25. In Greek the expression used is γυνή.
26. A. Valentini, 'Il grande segno di Apocalisse 12. Una Chiesa ad immagine della Madre di Gesù' in *Marianum* 59 (1997), p.62.
27. See Jn 19:25 and Rv 12:2 and also S. Manelli, *All Generations Shall Call Me Blessed* (New Bedford, Massachusetts: Academy of the Immaculate, 1995), pp. 359–360.

7

Faith and Reason

The preaching of Christ crucified and risen is the reef upon which the link between faith and philosophy can break up, but it is also the reef beyond which the two can set forth upon the boundless ocean of truth. Here we see not only the border between reason and faith, but also the space where the two may meet.

Pope John Paul II, *Fides et ratio, 23*

Human beings have always looked for God in various ways, often as a result of asking questions dealing with ultimate realities, like the origin of the world, the origin of mankind, the meaning of life, of suffering, of love and of death. In many and varied ways, throughout history down to the present day, people have expressed their quest for God in their religious beliefs and behaviour: in their prayers, sacrifices, rituals, meditations, as well as in philosophical reasoning about God. These forms of religious expression, despite the ambiguities they often brought with them, are so universal that one may well call man a 'religious being' as well as a thinking being.[1]

According to the Scriptures and Christian tradition, 'God, the source and end of all things, can be known with certainty from the things that were created.'[2] Nevertheless, in practice, outside the Judaeo–Christian tradition, the rational side of religion has not been very keenly felt. This could be due to the irrationality of belief in most religions outside of Christianity and Judaism.[3] To some extent Islam respects human reason. For example, in the Koran expressions of a rational and ordered cosmos are found: 'O men, adore your Lord who has created you and those who were before you, and fear God, who has made the earth a carpet for you and of the sky a castle, and has made water come down from the sky with which to extract from the earth those fruits that are your daily food.'[4] Islam however contains many elements which militate against a rational approach to faith. One is that three of the 99 names of Allah imply that there is no resemblance at all between Him and His creatures which effectively means that the way of analogy is closed off.[5] Moreover, some passages of the Koran smack of voluntarism, or the tendency to stress strongly the divine Will at the expense of divine Rationality. This is expressed by the very frequent use in the Koran of the phrase 'Allah does what He pleases.' For example 'He chastises whom He pleases; and forgives whom He pleases.'[6] Furthermore, the following verse of the Koran also carries a voluntarist touch: 'Allah makes whom He pleases err and He guides whom He pleases.'[7] for Muslim teaching, God is absolutely transcendent. His will is not bound up with any of our categories, even that of rationality.[8]

It is important to defend the capacity of human reason to know God, since from this capacity flows the possibility of speaking about Him to all peoples and cultures, and therefore of discourse with other people of other religions, of discussions involving philosophers and scientists, as well as with agnostics and unbelievers.[9] Now and again outside the Judaeo–Christian tradition, valid attempts have been made to read the book of nature in order to arrive at an affirmation of the Creator of the universe. Of all the ancient philosophers, Aristotle drew closest to the affirmation of God through human reason: 'For the most divine science is also most honourable; and this science alone must be, in two ways, most divine. For the science which it would be most meet for God to have is a divine science, and so is any science that deals with divine objects; and this science alone has both these qualities; for (1) God is thought to be among the causes of all things and to be a first principle, and (2) such a science either God alone can have, or God above all others.'[10] Aristotle arrived at the point where his idea of God compelled wonder: 'If, then, God is always in that good state in which we sometimes are, this compels our wonder; and if in a better this compels it yet more. And God is in a better state. And life also belongs to God; for the actuality of thought is life, and God is that actuality; and God's self–dependent actuality is life most good and eternal. We say therefore that God is a living being, eternal, most good, so that life and duration continuous and eternal belong to God; for this is God.'[11] Nevertheless, it is in the Old and New Testaments that we find the most penetrating insights into the relationship between faith and reason in the search for God.

7.1 Old Testament preparation

The book of Genesis recounts how God made man and woman in His own image and likeness, and made them for communion with Himself, a communion of grace and faith. 'God created man in the image of Himself, in the image of God He created him, male and female He created them.' (Gn 1:27) This threefold expression of the creation of the human person signifies that God is responsible for the creation of man's body, of man's soul and also for the differentiation between man and woman. It further signifies that God's image is found in man's body, man's soul and equally in man and in woman. However, this creation in the image of God reflects the supreme rationality of God and so also implies the human powers of reason. In order to be masters of creation (Gn 1:28–30), man and woman were endowed with sufficient reason to know what they were doing. Nevertheless, God also imposed a limit on the knowledge that Adam and Eve were allowed to access: 'But of the tree of the knowledge of good and evil you are not to eat; for, the day you eat of that, you are doomed to die' (Gn 2:17). This symbol indicates that man and woman were unable of themselves to discern and decide for themselves what was good and what was evil, but required guidance from a higher source. Instead of obeying God's command, they gave way to the temptations of the devil and were deceived into considering themselves sovereign and autonomous, and into imagining that they could ignore the knowledge which comes from God. The devil tempted our first parents to commit a sin similar to his own. In the theology of some of the Eastern Churches, the first sin, rather than being simply of pride and disobedience, consists rather in the lowering of man from the divine and the eternal to the human and the temporal spheres. The divine plan was that man should know the earthly realities only after having known the heavenly and divine mysteries. However man gave way to the devil's temptation and preferred first to know the things of earth represented by eating of the tree of the knowledge of good and evil. All men and women were caught up in this primal disobedience, which wounded reason so that thereafter its path to full truth would be strewn with obstacles.[12] St Thomas indicated that, as a result of the Fall, the will suffered a greater wound than the intellect.[13] This clouding of the intellect and weakening of the will represent only a *relative* and not an *absolute* deterioration of human nature, and one which is *extrinsic* to the human faculties.[14] The human person can still know natural truths (including religious ones) through reason, and can perform morally good actions.

However it is effectively in the Wisdom literature that the intimate relationship between the knowledge of God conferred by faith and the knowledge of Him conferred by reason becomes apparent.[15] The author of the book of Ecclesiasticus, Jesus Ben Sirach, expresses a theme common to all the wisdom literature, namely the figure of the wise man who loves the truth and seeks it:

> Happy the man who meditates on wisdom, and
> reasons with good sense, who studies her ways in
> his heart, and ponders her secrets. He pursues her
> like a hunter, and lies in wait by her path; he peeps
> in at her windows, and listens at her doors; he
> lodges close to her house, and fixes his peg in her
> walls; he pitches his tent at her side, and lodges in an
> excellent lodging; he sets his children in her shade,
> and camps beneath her branches; he is sheltered by
> her from the heat, and in her glory he makes his
> home (Si 14:20–27).

The Israelite mind did not traditionally proceed to knowledge by way of abstraction, but approached life in the
concrete reality. The Semitic concept of knowledge is one
which is global and concrete, in complementarity with the
Greek idea which is more abstract. As time went on, contact
with the Egyptian and Greek cultures stimulated the
Hebrew mind to approach reality also from the abstract
viewpoint. However, any interchange with other cultures
was purified of those elements which would have
corrupted the faith of the Chosen People. Moreover, the
Hebrew world of the Old Testament has its own distinctive
offering to ways of knowing. What is specific to the biblical
text is the conviction that there is a profound and indissoluble unity between the knowledge of reason and the
knowledge of faith. The world and all that happens within
it, including history and the fate of peoples, are realities to
be observed, analysed and assessed with all the resources of
reason, but always in the context of faith in God the Creator
and Guarantor of the Covenant. God has created the
cosmos in wisdom and has impressed upon this cosmos
rationality and coherence: 'In wisdom, the Lord laid the
earth's foundations, in understanding He spread out the
heavens. Through His knowledge the depths were cleft
open, and the clouds distil the dew' (Pr 3:19–20). Thus the
world and the events of history cannot be understood in

depth without professing faith in the God who is at work in them. Faith sharpens the inner eye, opening the mind to discover the treasure of the workings of Providence within the flotsam and jetsam of daily events. This is to say that with the light of reason human beings can know which path to take, but they can follow that path to its end, quickly and unhindered, only if with a rightly tuned spirit they search for it within the horizon of faith. This message is echoed in the Book of Proverbs: 'The human heart may plan a course, but it is the Lord who makes the steps secure' (Pr 16:9). Therefore, reason and faith cannot be separated without diminishing the capacity of men and women to know themselves, the world and God in an appropriate way.[16]

In the Old Testament, there is no opposition between faith and reason. Nevertheless, there was an awareness of the difference and relatedness of these two realms of human experience. The Book of Proverbs underlines this difference: 'To conceal a matter, this is the glory of God, to sift it thoroughly, the glory of kings' (Pr 25:2). Through the Revelation received from God, the people of Israel understood that, if reason were to be fully true to itself, and not be damaged or deformed then it must respect certain basic rules:

> The first of these is that reason must realise that human knowledge is a journey which allows no rest; the second stems from the awareness that such a path is not for the proud who think that everything is the fruit of personal conquest; a third rule is grounded in the 'fear of God' whose transcendent sovereignty and provident love in the governance of the world reason must recognise.[17]

When these rules are abandoned, the human person perverts reason and becomes 'the fool.' For the Bible, in this foolishness there lies a threat to life. The fool thinks that he knows many things, but really he is incapable of fixing his gaze on the things that truly matter. Therefore he can neither order his mind (Pr 1:7) nor assume a correct attitude to himself or to the world around him. Thus when he claims that 'God does not exist' (cf. Ps 14:1), he shows with conclusive clarity just how deficient his knowledge is and just how far he is from the full truth of things, their origin and their destiny.

The relation of reason with Revelation gives to reason a clearer picture of its own value. The results of the process of human reasoning acquire a deeper meaning when they are set within the larger horizon of faith, as is seen in the book of Proverbs: 'The Lord guides the steps of the powerful: but who can comprehend human ways?' (Pr 20:24). What God bestows by His grace is itself a stimulus for knowledge: 'The fear of Yahweh is the beginning of knowledge' (Pr 1:7; cf. Si 1:14). The wisdom which comes from God transcends man, so that he will always return to a fountain of knowledge to drink further (cf. Si 24:21–22).

God has created the human person as a searcher on the pilgrimage towards knowledge and wisdom: 'The first principle of wisdom is: acquire wisdom; at the cost of all you have, acquire understanding! Hold her close, and she will make you great; embrace her, and she will be your pride' (Pr 4:7–8). This is demanding and tiring, indicating that man must search patiently among the folds of reality for the truth. 'Wisely I have applied myself to investigation and exploration of everything that happens under heaven. What a wearisome task God has given humanity to keep us busy!' (Qo 1:13). The process of acquiring knowledge and wisdom is almost endless, likened to the great quantity of the drops of rain or sand in the sea:

> All wisdom comes from the Lord, she is with him for ever. The sands of the sea, the drops of rain, the days of eternity — who can count them? The height of the sky, the breadth of the earth, the depth of the abyss — who can explore them? Wisdom was created before everything, prudent understanding subsists from remotest ages. For whom has the root of wisdom ever been uncovered? Her resourceful

ways, who knows them?' (Si 1:1–6).

Qoheleth introduced some interesting nuances regarding faith and reason. He pointed out the difficulty and, it seems, even the futility of human knowledge: 'I have applied myself to understanding philosophy and science, stupidity and folly, and I now realise that all this too is chasing after the wind. Much wisdom, much grief; the more knowledge, the more sorrow' (Qo 1:17–18). At the same time, he avoided agnosticism, or a denial that we can have valid knowledge about God and creation, by his praise of wisdom: 'Wisdom is as good as a legacy, profitable to those who enjoy the light of the sun. For as money protects, so does wisdom, and the advantage of knowledge is this: that wisdom bestows life on those who possess her' (Qo 7:11–12). The limits of human knowledge even in the natural order are always stressed: 'You do not understand how the wind blows, or how the embryo grows in a woman's womb: no more can you understand the work of God, the Creator of all' (Qo 11:5).

In the Psalms, an indication is to be found of how the mystery of reason penetrates the mystery of creation, the cosmos and above all the creation of the human person. Nevertheless, the Psalmist shows that God's work cannot be comprehended by reason alone:

> You created my inmost self,
> knit me together in my mother's womb.
> For so many marvels I thank you;
> a wonder am I, and all your works are wonders.
> You knew me through and through,
> my being held no secrets from you,
> when I was being formed in secret,
> textured in the depths of the earth.
> Your eyes could see my embryo.
> In your book all my days were inscribed,
> every one that was fixed is there.
> How hard for me to grasp your thoughts,
> how many, God, there are!

If I count them, they are more than the grains of sand;
if I come to an end, I am still with you (Ps 139: 13–18).

The book of Job also portrays an interesting perspective on the human capacity for knowing God. It makes clear that we do have valid knowledge of God, for example through a consideration of His work of creation. Nevertheless this knowledge is limited and incomplete:

> Yes, the greatness of God exceeds our knowledge, the number of His years is past counting. It is He who makes the raindrops small and pulverises the rain into mist. And the clouds then pour this out, sending it streaming down on the human race. And who can fathom how He spreads the clouds, or why such crashes thunder from His tent? He spreads a mist before Him and covers the tops of the mountains. By these means, He sustains the peoples, giving them plenty to eat. He gathers up the lightning in His hands, assigning it the mark where to strike (Job 36: 26–32).

Moreover, in the face of suffering and its origin and purpose, knowledge of God is challenged, so that Job, through his process of purification arrives at a realisation of the inadequacy of his former knowledge and passes from a notional to a real assent of God. 'Before, I knew you only by hearsay but now, having seen you with my own eyes, I retract what I have said, and repent in dust and ashes' (Jb 42:5–6).

A search for God bestows benefits also on human understanding, 'for those who seek the Lord understand everything' (Pr 28:5), and 'those who trust in Him will understand the truth' (Ws 3:9). In a sense, God offers a share in His own infinite knowledge and understanding when he confers the gift of wisdom: 'But the One who knows all discovers her, He has grasped her with his own intellect, He has set the earth firm for evermore and filled it with four–footed beasts, He sends the light — and it goes, He recalls it — and trembling it obeys; the stars shine joyfully at their posts; when He calls them, they answer, 'Here we are'; they shine to delight their Creator. It is He who is our God, no other can compare with Him' (Ba 3:32–36).

In the book of Wisdom, knowledge as the fruits of reason involves a painstaking investigation of the world, the human being and history, in a manner open to what is received from Revelation. Indeed, even in seeking the fruits of rational endeavour, people sought the help of God, avoiding any exaggerated autonomy between two spheres of activity:

> May God grant me to speak as He would wish and conceive thoughts worthy of the gifts I have received, since He is both guide to Wisdom and director of sages; for we are in his hand, yes, ourselves and our sayings, and all intellectual and all practical knowledge. He it was who gave me sure knowledge of what exists, to understand the structure of the world and the action of the elements, the beginning, end and middle of the times, the alternation of the solstices and the succession of the seasons, the cycles of the year and the position of the stars, the natures of animals and the instincts of wild beasts, the powers of spirits and human mental processes, the varieties of plants and the medical properties of roots. And now I understand everything, hidden or visible, for Wisdom, the designer of all things, has instructed me (Wis 7:15–21).

In the book of Wisdom is to be found a vision which affirms a rationally ordered universe, a world picture in stark contrast to that of the pagan neighbours of Israel like Egypt and Babylon where a magical and superstitious view of the cosmos dominated the understanding: 'You, however, ordered all things by measure, number and weight' (Ws 11:20). The truly realist world picture of ancient Israel, as described in the book of Wisdom paved the way of reason so that it was to become a sure road towards the affirmation of God:

Yes, naturally stupid are all who are unaware of God, and who, from good things seen, have not been able to discover Him–who–is, or, by studying the works, have not recognised the Artificer. Fire, however, or wind, or the swift air, the sphere of the stars, impetuous water, heaven's lamps, are what they have held to be the gods who govern the world. If, charmed by their beauty, they have taken these for gods, let them know how much the Master of these excels them, since He was the very source of beauty that created them. And if they have been impressed by their power and energy, let them deduce from these how much mightier is He that has formed them, since through the grandeur and beauty of the creatures we may, by analogy, contemplate their Author. Small blame, however, attaches to them, for perhaps they go astray only in their search for God and their eagerness to find Him; familiar with his works, they investigate them and fall victim to appearances, seeing so much beauty. But even so, they have no excuse: if they are capable of acquiring enough knowledge to be able to investigate the world, how have they been so slow to find its Master? (Ws 13:1–9).

The idea of 'analogy' is thus present in the book of Wisdom at this point, as a fundamental basis of human knowing of God. This is the only point in the Old Testament where the expression is to be found.[18]

The 'book of nature' thus represents a first stage of divine Revelation. If the cosmos is read with the proper tools of human reason within a realist perspective it can be a stepping stone to knowledge of the Creator. If human beings with their intelligence fail to recognise God as Creator of all, it is not because they lack the means to do so, but because a disordered will and clouded intellect place an impediment in the way.[19] In some of the prophetic literature also, there is an indication of the stupidity of ignoring the Creator's hand at work in His creation. For example, the prophet Isaiah points out 'What perversity this is! Is the potter no better than the clay? Can something that was made say of its maker, 'He did not make me'? Or a pot say of the potter, 'He does not know his job'?' (Is 29:16).

In the Old Testament context, faith liberated reason in such a way that reason is enabled to attain rightly what it seeks to know and to place it within the ultimate order of things, in which everything acquires true meaning. In brief, human beings attain truth by way of reason because, enlightened by faith, they discover the deeper meaning of all things and most especially of their own existence.[20]

7.2 The problem of evil

The problem of evil is often framed in the following terms: 'If God the Father almighty, the Creator of the ordered and good world, cares for all His creatures, why does evil exist?' This question is urgent, as many ask it, and is thus unavoidable. It is painful as it challenges both faith and reason. Finally it is mysterious, and no quick answer will suffice to answer the problem of evil.[21] A further formulation could be: 'Why did God not create a world so perfect that no evil could exist in it?' One answer is that with infinite power God could always create something better.[22]

Among erroneous answers to the problem of evil is monism, or the notion that good and evil are simply twin aspects of the same ultimate reality. Other false views like Zoroastrianism and Manichaeism, on the other hand, explicitly posit an ultimate dualism in the universe. Good and evil have existed both co–eternally and independently, in the form of finite deities. Neither has so far destroyed the other. This accounts for the mixture of good and evil in our world. Another insufficient approach is that of Leibniz who contended that God was morally bound to create the best of all possible worlds:

> One may say that as soon as God has decreed to create something there is a struggle between all the

possibles, all of them laying claim to existence, and that those which, being united, produce most reality, most perfection, most significance carry the day. It is true that all this struggle can only be ideal, that is to say, it can only be a conflict of reasons in the most perfect understanding, which cannot fail to act in the most perfect way, and consequently to choose the best. Yet God is bound by a moral necessity, to make things in such a manner that there can be nothing better: otherwise not only would others have cause to criticize what he makes, but, more than that, he would not himself be satisfied with his work, he would blame himself for its imperfection; and that conflicts with the supreme felicity of the divine nature.[23]

Leibniz speaks of God's moral responsibility to create the best out of a number of possible worlds, each of which is more or less good. This is an inversion of reality: God did not choose this world because it is best; rather, it is best because God chose it. God's choices are not determined by anything or anyone outside Himself. Leibniz's view also tends to eliminate man's responsibility for sin by representing sin as little more than a misfortune that has befallen him.

The Christian picture proposes instead that, with infinite wisdom and goodness, God freely willed to create a world 'in pilgrimage' towards its ultimate perfection. In God's plan, this process of becoming involves the appearance of certain beings and the disappearance of others, the existence of the more perfect alongside the less perfect, both constructive and destructive forces of nature. This allows the possibility that alongside physical good there exists also *physical evil* as long as creation has not reached perfection.[24] Even worse than physical evil is the *moral evil* which arises from the sins of rational creatures. God is in no way, directly or indirectly, the cause of moral evil.[25] God permits it, however, because He respects the freedom of His creatures and, mysteriously, knows how to derive good from it.

Almighty God, because He is supremely good, would never allow any evil whatsoever to exist in His works if He were not so all–powerful and good as to cause good to emerge from evil itself.[26] It is possible that physical evil, such as earthquakes and other natural disasters, could, as has been argued elsewhere could also be a secondary consequence of original sin.[27] Diabolical action against on God's creation is also not to be excluded. Thus the irrationality of sin may even lie behind apparent physical evil.

Now evil is a privation of good; 'there is no such thing as a nature of evil, because all nature, as nature is good.'[28] St Augustine was one of the first Christian thinkers to stress this fundamental point, that evil is the privation of good:

> In this universe, even what is called evil, when it is rightly ordered and kept in its place, commends the good more eminently, since good things yield greater pleasure and praise when compared to the bad things. For the Omnipotent God, whom even the heathen acknowledge as the Supreme Power over all, would not allow any evil in his works, unless in his omnipotence and goodness, as the Supreme Good, he is able to bring forth good out of evil. What, after all, is anything we call evil except the privation of good? In animal bodies, for instance, sickness and wounds are nothing but the privation of health. When a cure is effected, the evils which were present (namely the sickness and the wounds) do not retreat and go elsewhere. Rather, they simply do not exist any more. For such evil is not a substance; the wound or the disease is a defect of the bodily substance which, as a substance, is good. Evil, then, is an accident, namely a privation of that good which is called health. Thus, whatever defects there are in a soul are privations of a natural good.[29]

Evil therefore has its origin, not in nature, but in the will. Sin is an action which is against the right use of reason. An accumulation of sins, which leads to great evils cause great difficulties as regards affirmation of God. The existence of evil therefore is sometimes used against proofs of God's existence. Nevertheless, evil is connected with free choices of rational creatures, and without freedom it is impossible to love. Sometimes, to counter the argument of those who maintain that evil represents an obstacle to the affirmation of God, the reply could be that what we see is only part of the mosaic, and that within the whole picture God can bring a final good out of evil, the supreme example being the crucifixion of His Son as the source of human salvation. From the greatest moral evil ever committed, the rejection and murder of God's only Son, caused by the sins of all men, God, by His grace that 'abounded all the more'(Rm 5:20), brought the greatest of goods: the glorification of Christ and our redemption. Nevertheless, evil is not simply imaginary nor does it ever become a good.[30] The very human capacity of being able rationally to identify evil for what it is, to reject it, and to perceive its incongruity in a good world created by God, is in itself a pointer towards God. As Josef Pieper pointed out: 'The incomprehensibility of evil in the world becomes fully apparent only against the background of the indestructible happiness of God.'[31] Thus very fact that all evil is to some degree shocking and remarkable triggers an argument for God's real existence.[32] Or, in other words, if the universe were chaotic and absurd, we would not be able to identify evil as evil.

A world in which earthquakes, tsunamis and hurricanes occur is not the world that God originally made. We see a world filled with natural disasters and death, but that is not the original order of things. Originally God created a very good world. Originally, man lived in perfect communion with God. Originally all creation was unified with its components functioning in symbiotic balance. There was no death, no violent natural upheavals by a world out of balance, a world convulsing harmfully against itself. For God saw all that He had made, and behold, it was very good (Gn 1:31). The earth itself was also affected as a consequence of Adam's sin. Death enveloped creation. The components of the perfectly balanced creation became separated, disjointed, and imbalanced. The earth was cursed and man's body would return to the dust in physical death (Gn 3:17–19). The world that previously sustained life would continue to do so, but as a cursed earth. Fallen man is consigned to live in a cursed earth in which both he and the world are visited by death. The state of the earth continues to be integrally bound up with the state of man's relationship to God. This is a good world that has been brought, by man's sin, into a bad state. When we experience death and the tragedies of things like tsunamis, we are experiencing the repercussions of the Fall. We are experiencing life in a world enveloped by death, a world essentially separated from God, a world in need of deliverance – for we are a people in need of deliverance.

Once we view suffering and death in the context of Creation and the Fall, we are then able to perceive how it is that God is at work redemptively in the world. Suffering, for the Christian, is not meaningless, but is to be viewed in the context of God's redemptive purpose for this fallen world. The apostle Paul writes:

> For I consider that the sufferings of this present time are not worthy to be compared with the glory that is to be revealed to us. For the anxious longing of the creation waits eagerly for the revealing of the sons of God. For the creation was subjected to futility, not of its own will, but because of Him who subjected it, in hope that the creation itself also will be set free from its slavery to corruption into the freedom of the glory of the children of God. For we know that the whole creation groans and suffers the pains of childbirth together until now. And not only this, but also we ourselves, having the first fruits of the Spirit, even we ourselves groan within ourselves, waiting eagerly for our adoption as sons, the redemption of our body. (Rom 8:18–23)

The problem of evil also has an eschatological sense. History, according to the Bible, is linear: it has a beginning and an end and moves like a straight line. History is not a revolving circle, an endless repetition whose beginning and ultimate purpose is unknown. History began at Creation and is moving to Final Judgment. As the line of history progresses, the world will experience more frequent and more intense eschatological 'birth pains'. In teaching about the end of the world, Jesus employs the metaphor of a woman in childbirth: 'And you will be hearing of wars and rumors of wars; see that you are not frightened, for those things must take place, but that is not yet the end. For nation will rise against nation, and kingdom against kingdom, and in various places there will be famines and earthquakes. But all these things are merely the beginning of birth pangs' (Mt 24:6–8).[33]

However one must also explain how natural disasters signify divine judgment. The world has seen many horrific catastrophes and will continue to do so until the end of history. Those who are suffering in present catastrophes are not worse sinners than all others and are not being visited by a specific judgment of God because of specific sin. In Jesus' day, violence and tragedy were headline news too. There were some present who reported to Him about the Galileans, whose blood Pilate had mingled with their sacrifices. And He answered and said to them, 'Do you suppose that these Galileans were greater sinners than all other Galileans, because they suffered this fate? I tell you, no, but unless you repent, you will all likewise perish. Or do you suppose that those eighteen on whom the tower in Siloam fell and killed them, were worse culprits than all the men who live in Jerusalem? I tell you, no, but unless you repent, you will all likewise perish' (Lk 13:2–5). There is also a sense in which God does punish sin: 'He wants you to keep away from sexual immorality, and each one of you to know how to control his body in a way that is holy and honourable, not giving way to selfish lust like the nations who do not acknowledge God. He wants nobody at all ever to sin by taking advantage of a brother in these matters; the Lord always pays back sins of that sort, as we told you before emphatically' (1 Th 4:3–6). The further question arises: Is the punishment connatural to the sin, like when overeats and is ill as a result. Or is the punishment a positive action which God applies to punish specific sins, like that of Sodom and Gomorrah (Gn 19:24–29). Jesus also warned the man he had cured: 'Now you are well again, do not sin any more, or something worse may happen to you' (Jn 5:14). It is important also to remember that God is not responsible for evil (God cannot be tempted by evil – Jm 1:13). Moreover, 'all things work together for the good, for those who love God, and are called according to His purposes.' (Rm 8:28)

The problem of evil is one area where reason can only offer a partial answer to the question. Only Christian faith as a whole furnishes an answer to this question: the goodness of creation, the drama of sin and the patient love of God who comes to meet man by His covenants, the redemptive Incarnation of His Son, His gift of the Holy Spirit, His institution of the Church, the power of the sacraments and His call to a blessed life to which free creatures are invited to consent in advance, but from which, they can also turn away.[34]

7.3 New Testament fulfilment

Pontius Pilate's question when faced with Jesus Christ was 'What is truth?' (Jn 18:38). This question has been repeated down the centuries by searchers and sceptics alike. However, Christ Himself is the final and definitive answer to the question for He is 'the Way, the Truth and the Life'(Jn 14:6). In the New Testament, Christ uses various images for Himself which are based on the use of analogy. For example in the parable of the Vine and the branches: 'I am the vine, you are the branches. Whoever remains in me, with me in him, bears fruit in plenty; for cut off from me you can

do nothing' (Jn 15:5). This image is a very powerful indication of communion within the Church, and at the same time
a eucharistic allusion.

The episode of the miraculous catch of fish recounted by
St Luke can be taken as a powerful image for the relationship between faith as personal commitment and reason.

> Jesus said to Simon Peter, 'Put out into deep water
> and pay out your nets for a catch.' Simon replied,
> 'Master, we worked hard all night long and caught
> nothing, but if You say so, I will pay out the nets.'
> And when they had done this they netted such a
> huge number of fish that their nets began to tear, so
> they signalled to their companions in the other boat
> to come and help them; when these came, they filled
> both boats to sinking point. When Simon Peter saw
> this he fell at the knees of Jesus saying, 'Leave me,
> Lord; I am a sinful man'' (Lk 5:4–8).

In this image of the intellectual search for God, the net of the
mind must go into deep waters, since God is not to be
found in superficialities. St Peter trusts the words of Christ,
even though, humanly speaking, they seem to be unrea-
sonable, because they had worked all night and caught
nothing. The key is this: 'If You say so, I will pay out the
nets.' Afterwards St Peter felt ashamed that he had not
trusted Christ fully, and expressed the sentiment that he
was a sinful man. By analogy, casting out into the depths of
God with the intellect brings about, by the grace of Christ,
a process of conversion of the intellect. A further example of
an episode of coming to faith in a process of interaction
with empirical reason, was Christ's appearance to doubting
Thomas. This apostle missed the earlier appearance of
Christ, and did not believe the others but required empirical evidence that the Lord was indeed risen: 'Unless I can
see the holes that the nails made in His hands and can put
my finger into the holes they made, and unless I can put
my hand into His side, I refuse to believe' (Jn 20:25). When
Thomas did see the Lord and was invited, to his embar-

rassment, to put his hand into the Risen Christ's wounded
side, he arrived at faith and Jesus said to him: 'You believe
because you can see me. Blessed are those who have not
seen and yet believe' (Jn 20:29).

In St Paul's letters, the very specific nature of Christian
wisdom is outlined. In this context emerges in a poignant
manner the contrast between 'the wisdom of this world'
and the wisdom of God revealed in Jesus Christ. The depth
of revealed wisdom disrupts the cycle of our habitual
patterns of thought, which are in no way able to express
that wisdom in its fullness. The crucified Son of God is the
historic event upon which every attempt of the mind to
construct an adequate explanation of the meaning of existence upon merely human argumentation comes to grief.
The true key–point, which challenges every philosophy, is
Jesus Christ's death on the Cross. It is here that every
attempt to reduce the Father's saving plan to purely human
logic is doomed to failure. St Paul emphasised that Christ
sent him to preach the Gospel 'not by means of wisdom of
language, wise words which would make the cross of
Christ pointless' (1 Co 1:17). The Apostle paraphrases a
passage in the book of the prophet Isaiah, and exclaims: 'As
scripture says: I am going to destroy the wisdom of the wise
and bring to nothing the understanding of any who understand'(1 Co 1:19; See Is 29:14). When St Paul stated that
'God has shown up human wisdom as folly' (1 Co 1:20), this
does no mean that it is without value, rather that God
wished to save believers through the 'folly of the Gospel' (1
Co 1:21). The content of this Gospel is the crucified Christ,
'to the Jews an obstacle they cannot get over, to the gentiles
foolishness, but to those who have been called, whether
they are Jews or Greeks, a Christ who is both the power of
God and the wisdom of God' (1 Co 1:23–24). This shows
that 'God's folly is wiser than human wisdom' (1 Co 1:25).
Here is portrayed the approach of the negative way, namely
that God's Wisdom so transcends human wisdom, that the
one seems almost totally dissimilar from the other. At the

same time, St Paul's adoption of the human categories of wisdom and folly to describe the disparity between human wisdom and Divine Wisdom implies some kind of analogy, so that there is a positive way as well, a resemblance between the two orders of knowledge.[35] At the same time, 'it is not the wisdom of words, but the Word of Wisdom which Saint Paul offers as the criterion of both truth and salvation.'[36] The wisdom of the Cross, therefore is a challenge to reason which does not destroy human thinking but rather purifies elevates and transforms it, heals it and redeems it, so that it can rise higher. This is a very specific aspect of Christian understanding of faith and reason, in contrast to other approaches where reason is regarded as irrelevant, unhelpful or an obstacle in the search for divine realities.

When St Paul visited Athens on one of his missionary journeys, he used one of the religious monuments as a convenient starting-point to establish a common base for his preaching of the Truth. He exclaimed:

> Men of Athens, I have seen for myself how extremely scrupulous you are in all religious matters, because, as I strolled round looking at your sacred monuments, I noticed among other things an altar inscribed: To An Unknown God. In fact, the unknown God you revere is the one I proclaim to you. Since the God who made the world and everything in it is Himself Lord of heaven and earth, He does not make his home in shrines made by human hands. Nor is He in need of anything, that He should be served by human hands; on the contrary, it is He who gives everything – including life and breath – to everyone. From one single principle He not only created the whole human race so that they could occupy the entire earth, but He decreed the times and limits of their habitation. And He did this so that they might seek the deity and, by feeling their way towards Him, succeed in finding Him; and indeed He is not far from any of us, since it is in Him

that we live, and move, and exist, as indeed some of
your own writers have said: 'We are all his children.'
(Ac 17:23–28)

The truth that God is 'not far from any of us' is an expression of His immanence within His creation, the theological basis for searching for God through His creation, and at the same time the foundation for using human categories to express divine truths. A well–known and classic passage from St Paul's letter to the Romans deals with this fundamental capacity of human reason to search for God. The passage recalls the flavour of a similar passage from the book of Wisdom (Ws 13:1–9) cited above:

> The retribution of God from heaven is being revealed against the ungodliness and injustice of human beings who in their injustice hold back the truth. For what can be known about God is perfectly plain to them, since God has made it plain to them: ever since the creation of the world, the invisible existence of God and His everlasting power have been clearly seen by the mind's understanding of created things. And so these people have no excuse: they knew God and yet they did not honour Him as God or give thanks to Him, but their arguments became futile and their uncomprehending minds were darkened. While they claimed to be wise, in fact they were growing so stupid that they exchanged the glory of the immortal God for an imitation, for the image of a mortal human being, or of birds, or animals, or crawling things. That is why God abandoned them in their inmost cravings to filthy practices of dishonouring their own bodies–because they exchanged God's truth for a lie and have worshipped and served the creature instead of the Creator, who is blessed for ever. Amen (Rm 1:18–25).

Through the mediation of His creation, God arouses in reason an intuition of His power and His divinity. Elsewhere in the New Testament, an idea of the Creator responsible for His creation is presupposed as in the Letter to the Hebrews: 'Every house is built by someone, of course; but God built everything that exists' (Heb 3:4). The process of reasoning starts from the human experience that every house has been built by someone, therefore the cosmos must have been created by God. This seems to endow human reason with a capacity which overcomes its natural limitations. The concept is not limited to sensory knowledge, but goes on from the data provided by the senses to reach the cause lying at the origin of all perceptible reality. St Paul effectively affirms that this passage from creation to Creator should have been very straightforward had the Fall not occurred. However, because of the disobedience by which man and woman chose to bypass their relation to the One who had created them, this easy access to God through their reasoning power diminished. As a result of the desire to exercise reason without reference to God, the eyes of the mind were no longer able to see clearly: reason became more and more enslaved to its own confusion.[37] Along with the incapacity to know God with ease, the fallen state of man brought a difficulty in arriving at moral truths, which reason should be able to see as connected with man's nature. Thus anarchy gave way to tyranny. The coming of Christ was to redeem and heal reason from this weakness, setting it free from the bondage in which it had been held captive. As Jesus said: 'If you make my word your home you will indeed be my disciples; you will come to know the truth, and the truth will set you free' (Jn 8:31–32).

Faith, although primarily connected with eternal life has a real effect on the here and now, and on the human capacity of reason in the present context. This vision has its basis in the passage where Christ says to His followers that setting their hearts first on God's Kingdom will have beneficial effects not only in heaven, but also here upon earth: 'Set your hearts on His Kingdom first, and on His righteousness and all these other things will be yours as well.' (Mt 6:33) The followers of Christ are promised something of a reward in this life (despite persecutions) as well as a reward in the life to come: 'And everyone who has left houses, brothers, sisters, father, mother, children or land for the sake of My name will be repaid a hundred times over and also inherit eternal life' (Mt 19:29).[38] This healing of the powers of reason is one of the blessings which the Gospel is bringing as it spreads throughout the world (cf. Col 1:6). In this way, 'God works with those who love Him, those who have been called in accordance with His purpose, and turns everything to their good' (Rom 8:28).

St Paul elucidated how the validity of the Mystery of Christ does not depend upon 'brilliance of oratory or wise argument' (1 Co 2:1), and he did not wish to convince his hearers using philosophical argument (1 Co 2:4). Rather it is the power of the Holy Spirit which supplies conviction to the Christian message. In this way, Christian faith does not depend 'on human wisdom but on the power of God' (1 Co 2:5). Nevertheless a knowledge and a wisdom are involved in St Paul's proclamation, a knowledge of Christ crucified and 'the mysterious wisdom of God that we talk, the wisdom that was hidden, which God predestined to be for our glory before the ages began' (1 Co 2:7). This knowledge and wisdom are not accessible to the mind which is locked in its own natural categories, to the mind which has not recognised the power of the crucified Christ. St Paul made clear that there is an order of knowledge which transcends reason, namely the gift of revelation, 'God has given revelation through the Spirit, for the Spirit explores the depths of everything, even the depths of God' (1 Co 2:10). St Paul uses a human analogy to indicate that only the Spirit of God knows the depths of God. Just as a human individual knows himself through his own spirit, within him; 'in the same way, nobody knows the qualities of God except the Spirit of God' (1 Co 2:11). Human reason is surpassed when it comes to framing categories for what God has revealed. Christ blessed His Father for 'for hiding these things from the learned and the clever and revealing them to little children' (Lk 10:21; see also Mt 11:25).

Revelation cannot therefore be simply expressed 'in the terms learnt from human philosophy, but in terms learnt from the Spirit, fitting spiritual language to spiritual things' (1 Co 2:13). Human language is not incapable of expressing divine revelation, but rather revelation itself must reshape this human language into a new wineskin in order to enable it to contain the new wine of divine truths (see Mt 9:17). Here is implied that revelation brings about a conversion of the intellect, a real change which does not destroy the power of reason, but enables the Christian to put on 'the mind of Christ' (1 Co 2:16). The mind must be renewed by a spiritual revolution, so that the Christian 'could put on the New Man that has been created on God's principles, in the uprightness and holiness of the truth' (Ep 4:23). This spiritual revolution enables one to live by the truth and in love (Ep 4:15). The gift of the Holy Spirit enables the believer to understand and appreciate the gifts of God, and to 'assess the value of everything' (1 Co 2:15). This revelation is a wisdom, but one which is not recognised by the intellectual authorities of this present passing world. It is a wisdom which also looks forward to a completion in the glory of heaven where God has prepared for those who love Him, 'What no eye has seen and no ear has heard, what the mind of man cannot visualise' (1 Co 2:9). This type of expression had already been used by the prophet Isaiah in the Old Testament to express the coming of Christ: 'Never has anyone heard, no ear has heard, no eye has seen any god but you act like this for the sake of those who trust him' (Is 64:3).

The Apostle also taught that reason is perfected by love, and that reason without love remains sterile:

> Though I command languages both human and angelic – if I speak without love, I am no more than a gong booming or a cymbal clashing. And though I have the power of prophecy, to penetrate all mysteries and knowledge, and though I have all the faith necessary to move mountains – if I am without

love, I am nothing (1 Co 13:1–2).

Love is however based on truth in which it rejoices. St Paul seems to imply that while imperfect knowledge will be done away with, 'love never comes to an end' (1 Co 13:8). He adopts the two famous analogies of the growth of a child and the reflection in the mirror to express the pilgrimage towards heavenly perfection:

> When I was a child, I used to talk like a child, and think like a child, and think like a child, and argue like a child, but now that I am an adult, all childish ways are put behind me. Now we are seeing a dim reflection in a mirror; but then we shall be seeing face to face. The knowledge that I have now is imperfect; but then I shall know just as fully as I am myself known (1 Co 13:11–12).

This latter analogy of the mirror implies that there will be a heavenly form of knowledge, one which is perfect. St John also illustrates the way of love which starts from the brother whom we can see, proceeding from the visible creation towards God, a process which tellingly also lies at the basis of rational proofs for the existence of God: 'Anyone who says 'I love God' and hates his brother, is a liar, since whoever does not love the brother whom he can see cannot love God whom he has not seen.' (1 Jn 4:20).

St Paul illustrates how the problem of non–belief can come about when the Gospel appears veiled or hidden in its meaning to the unbelievers whose minds have been blinded by the god of this world, so that they cannot see shining the light of the gospel of the glory of Christ, who is the image of God. (2 Co 4:4). Once again, this text implies that a conversion of intellect is required in order that reason may approach the threshold of faith. This process of conversion is not without a struggle in which the Apostle employs powerful military imagery: 'The weapons with which we do battle are not those of human nature, but they have the power, in God's cause, to demolish fortresses. It is ideas that we demolish, every presumptuous notion that is set up against the knowledge of God, and we bring every thought into captivity and obedience to Christ' (2 Co 10:4–5). The Apostle exhorts the presiding elders, the forerunners of the bishops,[39] to have a firm grasp of the unchanging message of the tradition, so that they can be counted on both for giving encouragement in sound doctrine and for refuting those who argue against it (Tt 1:9). This capacity for encouraging sound doctrine and refuting error necessarily involved the use of reason and elementary philosophy, in order to enable his hearers to grasp his points in ways they could understand. The reason for this struggle (see Col 2:1) lies in the fact that the word of God transcends merely human thought; it is not the word of any human being, but God's word, a power that is working among believers (see 1 Th 2:13). Nevertheless there is a real and valid knowledge involved in understanding the mystery of God, and here are hid 'all the jewels of wisdom and knowledge' (Col 2:3). When the Christian is filled with knowledge of the mystery of Christ, their mind is 'filled with everything that is true, everything that is honourable, everything that is upright and pure, everything that we love and admire – with whatever is good and praiseworthy.' (Ph 4:8). Here the light of Christ scatters the shadows of doubt from the mind of the believer. Moreover he or she is protected against deceptive and specious arguments (Col 2:4), and cannot be imprisoned by the 'empty lure of a 'philosophy' of the kind that human beings hand on, based on the principles of this world and not on Christ.' (Col 2:8).

St Paul also speaks of a 'reasonable service'[40] which the Christian is expected to offer to God: 'I urge you, then, brothers, remembering the mercies of God, to offer your bodies as a living sacrifice, dedicated and acceptable to God; that is the kind of worship for you, as sensible people' (Rm 12:1). This implies a worship of God which involves both the mind and the heart, therefore the power of reason cannot be left out of the relationship with God. For the knowledge of the truth that leads true religion (Tt 1:1), and his knowledge of Christ spreads like a pleasant fragrance (2 Co 2:14). This knowledge is based on love which enables the Christian in union with all God's holy people to acquire the strength to grasp the breadth and the length, the height and the depth; so that, knowing the love of Christ, which is beyond knowledge, he or she may be filled with the utter fullness of God (Eph 3: 18–19). Knowledge and love of Christ are therefore correlative and one needs the other; knowledge without love is sterile and a love without knowledge could be misguided.[41] This knowledge of the Mystery of Christ also has an eschatological dimension, which leads to the final revelation of the Lord when He comes in glory at the end of the ages. This knowledge and complete understanding foster a growth towards true discernment, so that the Christian will be innocent and free of any trace of guilt when the Day of Christ comes (Ph 1:9–10).

In apostolic times there existed a sect of spirituals (*pneumatikoi*), who regarded as inferior those who were not completely liberated from matter; they rejected marriage because of its connection with matter (see 1 Tm 4:3). The spirituals preceded the Gnostics of the second century.[42] St Paul warned Timothy of the dangers of this type of system: 'My dear Timothy, take great care of all that has been entrusted to you. Turn away from godless philosophical discussions and the contradictions of the 'knowledge' which is not knowledge at all; by adopting this, some have missed the goal of faith.' (1 Tm 6:20–21). Perhaps in the same context, St Paul also warns about avoiding 'godless philosophical discussions' which 'only lead further and further away from true religion.' (2 Tm 2:16).

St Peter encouraged a reasoned hope as well as a reasoned faith, so indicating that Christian hope, like faith, is not irrational but can be proclaimed in rational categories, though the mystery of hope is beyond reason: 'Simply reverence the Lord Christ in your hearts, and always have your answer ready for people who ask you the reason for the hope that you all have.' (1 Pt 3:15). St Peter uses the Greek word λόγος for 'reason', and this expression has various shades of meaning in the New Testament, including a word of speech spoken by a living voice embodying a conception or idea, a matter under discussion, the power of reason, the mental faculty of thinking. The meaning becomes especially powerful in St John's writings, where it refers to the Word of God, the Second Person of the Blessed Trinity, who to win man's salvation assumed human nature as Jesus the Christ. St James indicates that true wisdom comes from God, and this gift is given when it is asked for 'with faith, and no trace of doubt, because a person who has doubts is like the waves thrown up in the sea by the buffeting of the wind' (Jm 1:6). Both gifts of faith and reason come down from above, from the Father of all light; with Him there is no such thing as alteration, no shadow caused by change (Jm 1:17).

Notes

1. CCC 28
2. Vatican I, *Dei Filius* Chapter II in ND 113. See also Canon 1 in ND 115. See also P. Haffner, *The Mystery of Reason* (Leominster: Gracewing, 2001), chapter 7, where we deal with proofs of the existence of God.
3. For more about the irrational element in religion, see Haffner, *The Mystery of Reason*, pp.240–247.
4. The Koran, Sura 2, verses 21–23.
5. The names in question are Name 10 'Al–Mutakabbir–The One who is clear from the attributes of the creatures and from resembling them.' Name 36 'Al–'Ali–The One who is clear from the attributes of the creatures.' Name 78 'Al–Muta'ali–The One who is clear from the attributes of the creation.'
6. The Koran, Sura 5, verse 40.
7. *Ibid.*, Sura 14, verse 4; see Sura 35, verse 8. See also R. Scruton, *The West and the Rest. Globalization and the Terrorist Threat*

(Continuum, London 2002), in which the author illustrates the consequences of the irrationalism of Islam at the socio–political level.

8. See Pope Benedict XVI, Lecture at Regensburg University, *Faith, Reason and the University. Memories and Reflections* (12 September 2006).

9. See *CCC* 39.

10. Aristotle, *Metaphysics*, Book 1, 2.

11. *Ibid.*, Book 12, 7.

12. See Pope John Paul II, *Fides et ratio*, 22. See also P. Haffner, *Mystery of Creation* (Leominster: Gracewing, 1995), p.119.

13. See St Thomas Aquinas, *Summa Theologiae* I–II°, q.83, aa.3–4.

14. See Pope John Paul II, *Discourse at General Audience* (8 October 1986), 7 in *IG* 9/2 (1986, p.972. There is discussion as to whether the wound to human nature consists simply of the loss of preternatural gifts or of an intrinsic but accidental weakening. The Thomist approach considers that a person born in original sin compares to the human being in the state of pure nature as a person stripped of his clothes is to a naked person. Those who admit some intrinsic weakening use the analogy between the healthy man (before the Fall) and the sick person (in original sin).

15. Pope John Paul II, *Fides et ratio*, 16.

16. *Ibid.*.

17. *Ibid.*, 18.

18. In the Greek text, the word is ἀναλόγως, which literally means 'proportionally.' See Haffner, *The Mystery of Reason*, pp.19–22 for a presentation of analogy.

19. See Pope John Paul II, *Fides et ratio*, 19.

20. Cf. *Ibid.*, 20

21. See *CCC* 309.

22. Cf. St Thomas Aquinas, *Summa Theologiae* I, q.25, a.6. See also See my *Mystery of Creation* (Leominster: Gracewing, 1995), p.57.

23. G. W. Leibniz, *Theodicy. Essays on the Goodness of God, the Freedom of Man and the Origin of Evil*, 201.

24. Cf. St Thomas Aquinas, *Summa Contra Gentiles* III, 71.

25. Cf. St Augustine, *De libero arbitrio*, Book 1, chapter 1, n.1 in *PL* 32, 1221–1223; St Thomas Aquinas, *Summa Theologiae* I–II,

q.79, a.1.

26. See St Augustine, *Enchiridion*, chapter 11 in *PL* 40, 236.

27. See Haffner, *Mystery of Creation*, p.191.

28. Council of Florence, *Decree for the Copts* in DS 1333. See also St Thomas Aquinas, *Summa Theologiae* I, q.48, a.1.

29. St Augustine, *Enchiridion*, chapter 11 in *PL* 40, 236.

30. See *CCC* 312.

31. J. Pieper, *Happiness and Contemplation*, translated by R. and C. Winston (New York: Pantheon Books, 1958), p. 31.

32. See St Thomas Aquinas, *Summa Contra Gentiles* III, chapter 71: 'A certain philosopher ... asks: 'If God exists, whence comes evil?' But it could be argued to the contrary: 'If evil exists, God exists.' For, there would be no evil if the order of good were taken away, since its privation is evil. But this order would not exist if there were no God.'

33. These eschatological birth pangs are also referred to in St Luke's Gospel: 'And there will be signs in sun and moon and stars, and upon the earth dismay among nations, in perplexity at the roaring of the sea and the waves, men fainting from fear and the expectation of the things which are coming upon the world; for the powers of the heavens will be shaken. And then they will see the Son of Man coming in a cloud with power and great glory. But when these things begin to take place, straighten up and lift up your heads, because your redemption is drawing near' (Lk 21:25–28).

34. See *CCC* 309.

35. See Haffner, *The Mystery of Reason*, pp.21–22, for a description of the positive and negative ways.

36. Pope John Paul II, *Fides et ratio*, 23

37. See *ibid.*, 22.

38. Cf. Mk 10:29–30; Lk 18:29–30; 1 Tm 4:8. See also Vatican II, *Gaudium et spes*, 38.2: 'Constituted Lord by His resurrection and given all authority in heaven and on earth, Christ is now at work in the hearts of all men by the power of His Spirit; not only does He arouse in them a desire for the world to come but He quickens, purifies and strengthens the generous aspirations of mankind to make life more humane and conquer the earth for this purpose.'

39. For a development of sacred orders in the primitive Church,

see my work, *The Sacramental Mystery* (Leominster: Gracewing, ²2007), pp.201–204.

40. The Greek expression is λογικη λατρεία which literally means reasonable worship. Cardinal Ratzinger indicates the importance of this expression as that which distinguishes Christian worship, with Christ the Logos at the centre, from ancient pagan cults. See J. Ratzinger, *Introduzione allo spirito della liturgia* (Cinisello Balsamo: Edizioni San Paolo, 2001), pp.42–47. See also Pope Benedict XVI, Lecture at Regensburg University, *Faith, Reason and the University. Memories and Reflections* (12 September 2006), where he affirmed: 'Christian worship is, again to quote Paul – λογικη λατρεία – worship in harmony with the eternal Word and with our reason.' Cfr. Pope Benedict XVI, Apostolic Exhortation *Sacramentum Caritatis*, 70. Cf. also S.L. Jaki, «Creation and Monastic Creativity» in *Monastic Studies* (Toronto) 16 (Christmas 1985), p.84.

41. See Haffner, *The Mystery of Reason*, chapter 9, for further discussion of this theme.

42. See pp.156–158 above for the definition of Gnosticism.

Bibliography

Magisterial Teachings

Primary Sources:

Pope Leo XIII, *Providentissimus Deus* (Encyclical on the Study of Sacred Scripture, 1893).

Pope Benedict XV, *Spiritus Paraclitus* (Encyclical on the Fifteenth Centenary of the Death of St. Jerome, 1920).

Pope Pius XII, *Divino Afflante Spiritu* (Encyclical on the Promotion of Biblical Studies, 1943).

Vatican II, *Dei Verbum* (Dogmatic Constitution on Divine Revelation, 1965).

Pope John Paul II, Encyclical Letter *Fides et Ratio* (Encyclical on Faith and Reason, 1998).

Pope Benedict XVI, Encyclical Letter *Deus caritas est* (2006).

Joseph Ratzinger – Pope Benedict XVI, *Jesus of Nazareth.* New York: Doubleday, 2007.

Pontifical Biblical Commission, *The Historicity of the Gospels.* Boston: Daughters of St. Paul, 1964.

Pontifical Biblical Commission, *The Interpretation of the Bible in the Church.* Boston: Daughters of St. Paul, 1993.

The Bishops of England, Wales and Scotland, *The Gift of Scripture*. London: CTS, 2005.

Secondary Sources:

Bea, Cardinal A., *The Study of the Synoptic Gospels* (New York: Harper & Row, 1965).

Bea, Cardinal A., *The Word of God and Mankind* (Chicago: Franciscan Herald Press, 1967).

Cano, M., *De locis theologicis*. First edition from 1563. In Melchioris Cani Opera Theologica [3 vols.] (Rome, Libraria Editrice ella Vera Roman di E. Filiziana, 1900).

Harrison, B. W., *The Teaching of Pope Paul VI on Sacred Scripture*. Rome: Pontificium Athenaeum Sanctae Crucis, 1997.

Louis, C. (ed.), *Rome and the Study of Scripture: A Collection of Papal Enactments on the Study of Holy Scripture Together with the Decisions of the Biblical Commission* (7th ed.). St. Meinrad, IN: Abbey Press, 1964.

Lubac, H. de, *Sources of Revelation* (New York: Herder and Herder, 1968).

Megivern, J. J., ed., *Official Catholic Teachings: Bible Interpretation* (Wilmington, NC: McGrath, 1978).

Myers, E., *What Does the Church Really Say About the Bible?* (St. Paul, MN: Wanderer Press, 1979).

Pope, H., *The Catholic Church and the Bible* (New York: Macmillan, 1928).

Williamson, P. S., *Catholic Principles for Interpreting Scripture A study of the Pontifical Biblical Commission's The Interpretation of the Bible in the Church* (1993) (Editrice Pontificio Istituto Biblico, Rome, 2001. Subsidia biblica–22)

Commentaries

Brown, R. E., Fitzmeyer, J. A., Murphy, R. E., *The New Jerome Biblical Commentary*. Englewood Cliffs, N.J.: Prentice–Hall, 2000³.

Casciaro, J. M. (ed.), *The Navarre Bible* (New Testament – 12 vols.). Dublin: Four Courts Press, 1989–92.

Fuller, R.C., Johnston, L., Kearns, C., *A New Catholic Commentary on Holy Scripture*. London: Nelson, 1969.

Hartman, L. (ed.), *A Commentary on the New Testament*. Kansas City: Catholic Biblical Association, 1942.

Leon–Dufour, X. (ed.), *Dictionary of Biblical Theology* (revised edition). New York: Seabury, 1973.

Orchard, B. et al. (eds.), *A Catholic Commentary on Holy Scripture*. NY: Thomas Nelson and Sons, 1951.

Spicq, C., *Theological Lexicon of the New Testament* (3 vols.). Peabody, MA: Hendrickson, 1994.

Steinmueller, J. E. and Sullivan, K. (eds.), *Catholic Biblical Encyclopedia*. New York: Joseph Wagner, 1956.

Books

Achtemeier, P. J., Green, J. B., Thompson, M. M.,*Introducing the New Testament: Its Literature and Theology*. Grand Rapids: Eerdmans, 2001.

Barthélemy, D., *God and His Image: An Outline of Biblical Theology*. New York: Sheed & Ward, 1966.

Benoit, P., *Aspects of Biblical Inspiration*. Chicago: Priory Press, 1965.

Bertram, J. *People of the Gospel*. Oxford: Family Publications, 2006.

Blowers, P. M., ed., *The Bible in Greek Christian Antiquity*. Notre Dame, IN: University of Notre Dame Press, 1997.

Bonsirven, J., *Theology of the New Testament*. Westminster, MD: Newman Press, 1963.

Bouyer, L., *The Meaning of Sacred Scripture*. Notre Dame, IN: University of Notre Dame Press, 1958.

Bouyer, L., *The Word, Church & Sacraments in Protestantism and Catholicism*. New York: Desclee, 1961.

Burtchaell, J. T., *Catholic Theories of Biblical Inspiration Since 1810*. New York: Cambridge, 1969.

Carson, D. A., and J. D. Woodbridge, eds., *Scripture and Truth*. Grand Rapids, MI: Zondervan, 1983.

Conn, H., ed., *Inerrancy and Hermeneutic: A Tradition, A Challenge, A Debate*. Grand Rapids, MI: Baker Books, 1988.

Congar, Y., *Tradition and Traditions: The Biblical, Historical and Theological Evidence for Catholic Teaching on Tradition.* Granville, OH: Basilica Press, 1998.

Corbon, J., *Path to Freedom: Christian Experience and the Bible.* New York: Sheed & Ward, 1969.

Danielou, J., *The Bible and the Liturgy.* Notre Dame, IN: University of Notre Dame Press, 1956.

Danielou, J., *From Shadows to Reality: Studies in the Biblical Typology of the Fathers.* London: Burns & Oates, 1960.

Deiss, L., *God's Word and God's People.* Collegeville, MN: Liturgical Press, 1976.

Egger, W., *How to Read the New Testament.* Peabody, MA: Hendrickson, 1996.

Farmer, W. R., and Farkasfalvy, D., *The Formation of the New Testament Canon.* New York: Paulist Press, 1983.

Farrow, D., *The Word of Truth and Disputes About Words.* Winona Lake, IN: Carpenter Books, 1987.

Finan, T. & Twomey, V. (eds.), *Scriptural Interpretation in the Fathers: Letter and Spirit.* Dublin: Four Courts Press, 1995.

Froelich, K. (ed.), *Biblical Interpretation in the Early Church.* Philadelphia: Fortress, 1984.

Geisler, N., ed., *Inerrancy.* Grand Rapids, MI: Zondervan, 1979.

Graham, H. G., *Where We Got the Bible: Our Debt to the Catholic Church.* Rockford, IL: Tan, 1977.

Haffner, P., *The Mystery of Reason*. Leominster: Gracewing, 2002.

Haffner, P., *The Mystery of Mary*. Leominster: Gracewing, 2004.

Hagerty, C., *The Authenticity of Sacred Scripture*. Houston, TX: Lumen Christi Press, 1969.

Hannah, J. D., ed., *Inerrancy and the Church*. Chicago: Moody Press, 1984.

Harrington, D. J., *Interpreting the New Testament*. Collegeville, MN: Liturgical Press, 1990.

Heidt, W. G., *A General Introduction to Sacred Scripture: Inspiration, Canonicity, Texts, Versions and Hermeneutics*. Collegeville, MN: Liturgical Press, 1970.

Hopkins, M., *God's Kingdom in the New Testament*. Chicago: Henry Regnery, 1964.

Johnson, L. T., *The Writings of the New Testament*. Philadelphia: Fortress, 1986.

Keller, W., *The Bible as History*. Bantam Books: 1983.

Levie, J., *The Bible, Word of God in Words of Men*. New York: P. J. Kennedy, 1961).

Lienhard, J. T., *The Bible, the Church, and Authority: The Canon of the Christian Bible in History and Theology*. Collegeville, MN: Liturgical Press, 1995.

Linnemann, E., *Historical Criticism of the Bible: Methodology or Ideology?* Grand Rapids, MI: Baker, 1990.

Lubac, H. de, *The Four Senses of Scripture*. Grand Rapids, MI: Eerdmans, 2000. 2 volumes.

Matera, F. J., *New Testament Ethics*. Louisville, KY: Westminster John Knox Press, 1996.

McDonald, H.D., *Theories of Revelation: An Historical Study 1700–1960*. Grand Rapids, MI: Baker Books, 1979.

Meyer, B. F., *Reality and Illusion in New Testament Scholarship*. Collegeville, MN: Liturgical Press, 1994.

Morton, H.V., *In the Steps of the Master*. Da Capo Press: 2002.

Morton, H.V., *In the Steps of St. Paul*. Da Capo Press: 2002.

Most, W., *Free From All Error: Authorship, Inerrancy, Historicity of Scripture, and Modern Scripture Scholars*. Libertyville, IL: Prow Books Franciscan Marytown Press, 1985.

Most, W., *The Thought of St. Paul*. Front Royal, VA: Christendom Press, 1994.

O'Neill, J.C., *The Bible's Authority*. Edinburgh: T & T Clark, 1991.

Orchard, Dom B., *Born to be King: The Epic of the Incarnation*. London: Ealing Abbey, 1993.

Prat, F., *Jesus Christ: His Life, His Teaching, and His Work*. Milwaukee: Bruce, 1950.

Prat, F., *The Theology of St. Paul* (2 vols.). Westminster, MD: Newman, 1950.

Ratzinger, J. Cardinal, *Biblical Interpretation in Crisis*. Rockford, IL: Rockford Institute, 1988.

Ray, S. K., *St. John's Gospel. A Bible Study Guide and Commentary*. San Francisco: Ignatius Press, 2002.

Schelckle, K. H., *Theology of the New Testament* (4 vols.). Collegeville, MN: Liturgical Press, 1971.

Shea, M. P., *By What Authority? An Evangelical Discovers Catholic Tradition*. Huntington, IN: Our Sunday Visitor, 1996.

Spicq, C., *Agape in the New Testament* (3 vols.). St. Louis: Herder, 1963.

Steinmueller, J. E., *The Sword of the Spirit*. Fort Worth, TX: Stella Maris Books, 1977.

Sungenis, R., ed., *Not By Scripture Alone: A Catholic Critique of the Protestant Doctrine of Sola Scripture*. Santa Barbara, CA: Queenship, 1998.

Varillon, Francois, *Announcing Christ Through Scripture to the Church*. Westminster, MD: Newman, 1963.

Walvoord, J. E., ed., *Inspiration and Interpretation*. Grand Rapids, MI: Eerdmans, 1957.

Wenham, J., *Christ and the Bible*. Downers Grove, IL: InterVarsity Press, 1993[3].

Whiteford, J., *Sola Scriptura: An Orthodox Analysis of the Cornerstone of Reformation Theology*. Ben Lomond, CA: Conciliar Press, 1995.

From GRACEWING

By the same author

Mystery of Creation

In practically the only recent book in English to give a global picture of the theology of creation, Paul Haffner explores God's masterpiece, the spiritual and material cosmos, from the angels to man and woman centred in Christ. Mystery of Creation touches many well–worn areas of interest in Christian faith and experience, including creation out of nothing, the beginning of the world, man and woman , and original sin.

Many topics of current concern are treated, like the world of spirits, the evolution of the universe and of life, the problem of evil, and the place of animals. Not only does the book take at new look at scientific, ecological and women's issues, it also shows how this universe is our home and yet is a prelude to the New Creation: the best is yet to come!

ISBN 978 0 85244 316 3

The Sacramental Mystery

The seven sacraments lie at the centre of Christian life and experience, for here God the Holy Trinity touches human lives and hearts. This book is one of the few at the present time to offer a global synthesis of the main themes in the sacramental mystery in which the human and divine, the material and the spiritual realms are intimately intertwined. Paul Haffner outlines how the sacraments are the chief means in the Church through which God's people are reconciled to the Father, through His Son, by the power of the Holy Spirit. The treatise illustrates classical issues like the conditions for the validity and the efficacy of the sacraments, as well as the minister, recipient and effects of these sacred mysteries; it deals with particular topics like the necessity of Baptism, the sacrificial character of the Eucharist, and the nature of Marriage. As he examines each sacrament in turn, the work also explores how new ecumenical questions affect Christian sacramental understanding.

'I warmly commend this work on the subject of sacramental theology.'

Archbishop Csaba Ternyák,
Secretary of the Vatican Congregation for the Clergy

ISBN 978 0 85244 476 4

The Mystery of Reason

The Mystery of Reason investigates the enterprise of human thought searching for God. People have always found stepping–stones to God's existence carved in the world and in the human condition. This book examines the classical proofs of God's existence, and affirms their continued validity. It shows that human thought can connect with God and with other aspects of religious experience. Moreover, it depicts how Christian faith is reasonable, and is neither blind nor naked. Without reason, belief would degenerate into fundamentalism; but without faith, human thought can remain stranded on the reef of its own self–sufficiency. The book closes by proposing that the human mind must be in partnership with the human heart in any quest for God.

'This fine work may be seen as a response to the Papal encyclical *Fides et Ratio*. It is an exploration of the relationship between faith and reason, and in so doing it makes use of a variety of approaches including philosophy, theology and contemplation. It is wholly faithful to the vision of the Church.'

Dr Pravin Thevathasan

ISBN 978 0 85244 538 9

The Mystery of Mary

The Blessed Virgin Mary stands at the heart of the Christian tradition. She holds a unique place in the Church's theology, doctrine and devotion, commensurate with her unique position in human history as the Mother of God. In this book, Paul Haffner offers a clear and structured overview of theology and doctrine concerning Mary, within an historical perspective. He outlines the basic scheme of what constitutes Mariology, set in the context of other forms of theological enquiry, and, working through the contribution of Holy Scripture – in the Old Testament forms of prefiguration and the New Testament witness – he proceeds to examine each of the fundamental doctrines that the Church teaches about Our Lady. From the Immaculate Conception to Mary's continuing Motherhood in the Church as Mediatrix of all graces, the reader will find here a sure and steady guide, faithful to tradition and offering a realist perspective, not reducing the concrete aspects of Mary's gifts and privileges to mere symbols on the one hand, and not confusing doctrine and devotionalism on the other.

The *Mystery of Mary*, with a foreword by Dom Duarte, Duke of Braganza, was published to celebrate the one hundred and fiftieth anniversary of the definition, by Pope Blessed Pius IX, of the dogma of the Immaculate Conception of Our Lady.

ISBN 978 0 85244 650 8

Mystery of the Church

Mystery of the Church presents a global picture of the main themes of current ecclesiology. First, it deals with the institution of the Church and her essential nature. Subsequently the four hallmarks of the Church are described. Her unity and holiness are guaranteed by the sanctity of Christ her Head despite the sinfulness of her members. The catholicity of the Church is also examined from the perspective of Eastern Christendom. The apostolicity of the Church leads to a description of the Petrine Office. The Church is seen as the instrument of salvation, and her relationship with the State and with science is investigated. Finally the Church is pictured as leading to the Kingdom of God.

ISBN 978 0 85244 133 6

www.ingramcontent.com/pod-product-compliance
Lightning Source LLC
Chambersburg PA
CBHW021220090426
42740CB00006B/309